A FORM OF INFINITE PLAY

JOURNAL 1969-2022

Other Books by Tom Weil

Fiction

A Clearing in the Jungle (1979)

A Balance of Power (1981)

Travel

(Published by Hippocrene Books)

Last at the Fair: A Book of Travel (1986)

America's Heartland: A Travel Guide to the Back Roads of Illinois, Indiana, Iowa and Missouri (1989)

America's South: A Travel Guide to the Eleven Southern States (1990)

The Cemetery Book: Graveyards, Catacombs and Other Travel Haunts Around the World (1992)

The Mississippi River: Nature, Culture and Travel Sites Along the "Mighty Mississippi" (1992)

America's Heartland: A Travel Guide to the Back Roads of Illinois, Indiana. Iowa, Missouri and Kansas (2d edition, 1992)

America's South: The Atlantic States (2d edition, 1993)

America's South: The Gulf and Mississippi States (2d edition, 1994)

Hippocrene U.S.A. Guide to Civil War Sites (1994)

A Play of Infinite Forms (2021)

A FORM OF INFINITE PLAY

JOURNAL 1969-2022

A Companion Volume to A Play of Infinite Forms

TOM WEIL

HIPPOCRENE BOOKS, INC.
New York

For Mimi, in my life for many a year
as Time's wingèd chariot gradually grew near

For information, address:
HIPPOCRENE BOOKS, INC.
171 Madison Avenue
New York. NY 10016
www.hippocrenebooks.com

ISBN 13: 978-0-7818-1446-1

Printed in the United States of America

In this playhouse of infinite forms I have had my play
... let this be my parting word.

—Rabindranath Tagore

ACKNOWLEDGMENTS

I continue to appreciate and to miss my late publisher and friend, George Blagowidow, founder, owner and principal of Hippocrene Books. George was unforgettable and he's not forgotten by me or, I believe, by many who knew him.

My thanks to George's successors—his daughter Natalie Blagowidow, Chairman of Hippocrene, and to Priti Chitnis Gress, Publisher and Editorial Director, for their interest and help in publishing this book and its companion volume, *A Play of Infinite Forms* (2021).

My thanks to Brian Davis for his patient, proficient and efficient advice to help upgrade my word-processing to a digital format from a very solid-state Royal portable typewriter operated with my previous digital four-finger and thumb drive, an attachment to my hands.

To my friends, acquaintances—and in some cases kind strangers—around the world who hosted, helped, or otherwise enhanced or facilitated my travels to some 150 countries over more than half a century, I express my thanks.

My thanks to readers of *A Play of Infinite Forms*, the companion volume to this book. Anyone who also chooses to read this volume after reading the earlier one for sure represents the triumph of hope over experience—greatly appreciated by me, my publisher, the distributor, book stores, paper and printing firms, and other beneficiaries of your continuing interest.

CONTENTS

AUTHOR'S NOTE

A FORM OF INFINITE PLAY is a companion volume to my 2021 travel reminiscence, A PLAY OF INFINITE FORMS. Although I didn't consult my Journal when writing that book, many of its ideas originated in the notebooks I've kept for more than half a century. When I read them for the first time after publication of A PLAY OF INFINITE FORMS I was surprised to find that a number of the concepts included in the book were anticipated by Journal entries recorded during the previous fifty years. Even without re-reading those earlier thoughts many nonetheless found their way into the book. Although this may suggest that you can't teach an old dog new tricks, the reappearance of so many beliefs and opinions from earlier times might also suggest that already embedded in a new dog—a younger person—are tricks which remain useful all through life.

As stated in the Introduction which follows, I want to make it clear at the outset that this book doesn't reproduce the Journal entries as originally written. In finally reading the Journal half a century after I began the undertaking it quickly became obvious that the material needed to be rewritten to clarify, condense and otherwise to make the entries fit for publication. It was also necessary to eliminate many repetitions or topics whose multiple elaborations are variations on the same themes and redundant. So revised, this book doesn't present the Journal selections included here in their original form but in curated and edited new versions based on—not reproductions of—the original entries.

Although the material in the Journal has been shortened and rewritten, in no case have I included any after-the-fact content or comments based on events or information known only following the time a Journal entry was written. I've been careful not to let hindsight presented as foresight endow the text with undeserved insights. Hopefully, my original spur-of-the moment perceptions, contemplations, comments and opinions as expressed in bygone times, without the added benefit of any later perspectives to enhance the text, will serve to offer at least a few thoughts worthy of a reader's time and attention and (for those who bought the book) dollars.

INTRODUCTION:
NIGHT FALLS ON A DIFFERENT WORLD

1. Beginning …

On an unknown day sometime in 1969 I started a Journal with an undated entry, the first of what eventually filled some 1700 hand-written college-ruled notebook pages over more than half a century. Being so conscious of time, it strikes me as strange that I failed to note the date of the Journal's first entry. Even back in 1969 when I was still a young man, with the concerns of old age and proximate mortality and final thoughts still far in the future, I was aware of the temporal conveyor belt which relentlessly carried me forward, ever forward, toward the end, which for me will be soon as I've nearly run out of time. For me the belt will before long come to a dead stop. The Journal served me as a pastime to preserve on paper past-time thoughts and other passing ephemera in an attempt to record from expired time some of the transient sensory impressions which over the years comprised my experiment in living. But perhaps the true purpose of the Journal pertained to my contemplation of what has really been, as for Everyman, my life-long experiment in dying.

I was no doubt prompted to begin the Journal back in 1969 because as of January 1 that year I began a new way of being by restructuring my life. This revision was meant to supplement my rather routine, mundane and comfortable home-based existence by adding (as explained in A PLAY OF INFINITE FORMS) frequent adventure travel to far corners of the earth. This thought-provoking (for me, but of no interest to anyone else) substantial change probably inspired me to contemplate various matters irrelevant to the rather routine and uneventful way I previously lived. Leading up to and then following such a major change operated to stimulate my thoughts. I hoped to capture in writing in the Journal some of those fleeting notions before they vanished from my consciousness. Once gone, they'd disappear as if never having appeared. The Journal seemed something of a remedy for the fact that everything was in flux, transient and at any time subject to disappearance and oblivion. Although one's existence often seems stable with day-to-day continuity, that illusion contradicts the reality that every evening night falls on a different world.

Starting the Journal thus arose from my situational element: the change represented by my willed transition from a settled fixed and regular comfortable domestic existence in a provincial suburb to expanding my horizons with wide-ranging and adventurous travels. The ceaseless pressure of passing time—that conveyor belt which runs on and on, not to its end but to yours—and my eventual non-being induced me to try to capture on the fly, as the days flew away, some of the evanescent events, impressions and thoughts from the play of infinite forms as I happened to experience them. Without recording those passing momentarily vivid but insubstantial sensory impressions my memory bank would remain rather empty, so in effect voiding my past of most of its residue of deposits. To avoid such losses I sought to preserve in the notebooks what seemed to me noteworthy observations, momentary and passing perishable ideas before they—and I—disappeared. Although I will soon vanish, some perceptions derived from my experiment in living will for a time remain in the form of my Journal—created as a form of infinite play.

My attempt to capture something of my fleeting experiment recalls Holden Caulfield's belief, in *The Catcher in the Rye*, that the best thing about the Museum of Natural History in New York City was that "everything always stayed right where it was"—nothing moved or was different. "The only thing that would be different was you." But "the Catcher" never really managed to catch and hold any of the passing mercurial moments, as even moribund stuffed animals—like living humanimals—decay away, as do notebook paper and pages of books which eventually crumble into dust, also like humanimals. But we mortals work with what we have—life-like but defunct mounted specimens of once living animals, creative works, college-ruled pages which over time by degrees graduate into the commencement of oblivion as the end begins.

Many things change so slowly they seem durable and present the illusion of immutable permanence. J. J. Thomson, the renowned English physicist appointed in 1884 as head of the famous Cavendish Laboratory in Cambridge, discovered when investigating cathode rays that they consisted of tiny negatively charged particles called "corpuscles," later renamed electrons. Thomson's findings suggested that the atom (from "atmos"—indivisible—in Greek) was in fact divisible, which in turn implied that matter was unstable. This revolutionary view overturned Newtonian physics based on the concept that the atom was the standard unit of matter. Later research on radioactivity by Ernest Rutherford at the Cavendish Lab confirmed that units smaller than an atom existed. Although often imperceptible, change in matter which superficially seems fixed mutates it. Stable as things may appear, night always falls on a different world as at every dusk what exists varies from how it was at the dawn of that day.

Although George W. Bush wasn't known for his poetic prose—or for his prose or poetry of any kind—it was none other than him who pronounced the evocative phrase which (with a change of tense) titles this Introduction. Maybe a speech writer put the words into the President's mouth, but in any case they exited from that source. Just after the 9/11 attacks Bush evoked in a few words the explosive change: "Night fell on a different world." But of course he could have said the same—although with less dramatic effect—on any day before and after the attack as nightfall always shadows a different world. By dusk nothing has remained the same as it was at dawn.

As twilight darkens the scene everything and everyone has become a day older since the previous evening. The law of entropy—a natural law which can't be repealed or amended—decrees that all which exists inexorably mutates toward disorder and eventually disappears. Evening after evening night falls on a different world, everything—over time—evening out into the identical permanent state of non-being.

2. Leavings of Believings

Entries on the leaves of the Journal's notebook leaves resulted from the leavings of passing time. Without the Journal to preserve for more than half a century those passing thoughts the mental detritus would have been permanently lost. Such a loss would be of no importance at all to anyone else, but it bothered me that my evanescent perceptions would, if not recorded, disappear as if they'd never occurred to me. The Journal allowed me to capture in writing some of the immaterial material which momentarily happened to come to me as random sensory impressions. As night fell day after day on an always different world I managed to salvage a few fragments of the play of forms I deemed noteworthy. Most of the impressions, however, were left un-noted and have disappeared forever.

From my younger years I believed that my un-willed and unexpected randomly created terrestrial existence would be degraded if I seldom or never noticed and noted some of the more curious or thought-provoking play of forms which happened to comprise my life. Absent such attention to those sensory impressions, my brief earthly experiment would lack even the very limited meaning I could wrest from an otherwise meaningless experience. Just as well never to have been born as to live oblivious to what chanced to happen during my brief tenure as a humanimal.

A certain paradox permeates the Journal. Although it obviously records my own passing observations, the entries are in fact not about me. Other than as the observer, I'm immaterial to the material. The Journal deals for the most part with the outside world. My interface with life, rather than my life, represents the perspective which typifies most of the entries. It was participation rather than contemplation which interested me. I sought to reflect upon and understand myself only to the extent that self-knowledge might help me better to comprehend and engage with the outside world. As Albert Camus noted in his notebooks, "Life is action—not reflection about one's-self. You determine your life by living it. To know yourself perfectly is to die." I escaped that sort of death (but not the inevitable one) by acting rather than simply reacting in an analytical mode about the "me" element.

Discussing Stendhal's *Journal* in *The Rules of Chaos* (1969), Stephen Vizinczey delineates the difference between internally focused writings and those oriented to external matters. Stendhal "talks about us even when he is concerned only with himself," while most other authors "write about themselves even when portraying others." There's really little or nothing of interest I can say about myself. When old-time St. Louis Cardinal pitcher Dizzy Dean was hit by a bean-ball, the paper headlined its report, "X-ray of Dean's head reveals nothing." Similarly, any inside view of my life would reveal very little, or perhaps nothing—at least nothing worth writing about. My Journal is not introspective but extrospective. Seldom do I discuss myself, for almost all the entries relate to the world beyond my own existence. The Journal offers one minute form of infinite play as lived and recorded by a very finite and transient humanimal. Like Stendhal, I preferred to talk not about myself but about other selves and other external matters.

Obviously, a journal contains various perceptions, attitudes, viewpoints, opinions and conclusions as perceived by a particular person, but I tried to generalize most of those notions rather than limiting them to my own moods, emotions, feelings or other purely subjective considerations. I found no difficulty in recognizing and accepting primacy of the not-me over my own quite subordinate and ultimately insignificant presence on the lonely planet. In the grand scheme of things I was nothing, and even within the context of human life as it exists on earth and the eight billion or so fellow humanimals I shared the planet with I was nearly nothing. I didn't much internalize what lay beyond my own very limited place among the cosmic play of infinite forms.

Because the outside world offered much more interesting material than my inner being, I wasn't particularly interested in exploring myself. To me it was apparent that my role in the play of forms which involved interface with the externals rather than any inward-looking perspective offered the most noteworthy content to include in the Journal. The entries thus largely pertain to the not-me as filtered through my consciousness. I was simply the agent or mechanism, a go-between to absorb sensory impressions and then reduce some of them to writing. I served as a prism but not the focus for what I processed. The Journal thus isn't about me but simply documents in a small way, as a form of infinite play, a few perceptions which chanced to come to the attention of one individual who experienced the specific play of infinite forms which happened to comprise his life.

Because the impressions and my reactions to them which form the basis of the Journal came to me mostly at random, the Journal's contents were formulated not as a construct to form a complete system intended to be internally consistent and logically coherent. Like my experiment in living, the Journal offers eclectic and varied material which by accretion gradually formed a montage or mosaic put together in an *ad hoc* way piece by piece based on the vagaries of varied experiences and observations rather than being designed in a rational and holistic coherent structure.

As the minutes, hours, days flew by I hoped to capture on the wing some of the believings which helped guide my experiment in living. Although not meant as a didactic document, my Journal will perhaps benefit some readers who might find helpful some of the guiding principles I found useful in shaping my experiment as best I could under the circumstances which happened to apply to my situation. However, I recognize that many readers who by chance happen upon my Journal may find little of interest, and that some will learn nothing of value from the hard-earned lessons which by degrees—not awarded for my academic studies but earned from experience—life taught me during my by now long earthly existence. I can also envision some astute readers much more observant and perceptive than was I shaking their head in wonderment that I was such a slow or even no learner as so many years passed before I came to understand what other earthlings much more quickly realized. Still today I sometimes wonder why it took me so long to comprehend some of life's most obvious lessons, and all too many others never will I discern.

Whatever a reader's reaction to the Journal, I'm aware that it contains little or nothing new for anyone except me. Any originality pertains only to my experiences, as for me—just as for what happens with every humanimal—all of my endless (until my end) sensory impressions were new, even if many seemed somewhat repetitious. Over time the gradual accumulation of real-world impressions operated to form a certain world-view. The selected (and rewritten) Journal entries represent only my own version—based on what by chance happened to me—of how one finite earthling briefly existed on the lonely planet in a specific place during a particular time. I make no claim that what I learned applies to anyone else. If, perchance, my unique experiment in living happens to resonate with or prove useful to other earth-dwellers now or in the future after my time, that's simply an unintended by-product of my efforts to record in the Journal a few elements of my own nearly ended journey through life.

Humanimals experience the great play of infinite forms in a vast variety of ways. Much depends on chance, luck and randomness, of which individual circumstances form a subset. Given the infinite play of forms and the infinite ways earth-dwellers happen to experience the world, it's clear to me why I found that extensive not-me much more interesting than the narrow and self-referential workings of my internal life. As an obscure and infinitesimally tiny component of the entirety, dwarfed by the cosmos as is everyone else here on the lonely planet, my unimportant and ultimately meaningless personal existence in and of itself didn't furnish much to merit keeping a journal, nor did my inner being. Only my encounter with the great terrestrial spectacle outside my own limited and fleeting form into which I was by chance incarnated interested me.

Viewed from a cosmic perspective, that spectacle presents quite an odd play of forms. Strangeness represents the defining characteristic of our curious brief interlude—as a species of terrestrial animals and, even briefer, as individual humanimals—here on the lonely planet, truly strangers in a strange land. If the past is a foreign country, as L.P. Hartley famously wrote in the opening lines of his novel, *The Go-Between* (1953), so too are the present, the future, the world, the cosmos and everything in it, for whatever happened or happens to exist is all quite strange and without any transcendental reason or purpose. The whole thing—the great play of cosmic forms—is truly odd when you think about it, which I did a lot. Within that vast entirety every quite finite individual life is also strange. Both the macro terrestrial experiment and each specific micro experiment in living are truly foreign lands.

The earthly play of infinite forms presents a tremendous and strange spectacle, an inconceivable performance if it didn't already exist in its familiar form. What sort of weird creative force would conceive and bring about such an odd place and play? Seen from a local terrestrial viewpoint some of the show seems to make some sense. But viewed from a cosmic perspective the entire production presents an absurdist play of forms, a weird congeries of senseless scenes and seens. On the earthly stage unfolds an endless mechanical and insensate play of infinite forms. The constant motion and commotion of the kinetic forms is not informative but only performative. It would be impossible to imagine or to invent a place more eldritch than the lonely planet, a mite in the cosmos suspended and spinning in space, teeming with life and shadowed by death.

The absurd didn't faze but operated to fascinate me. I attempted to capture in my Journal a few of the random elements offered up by the system which the capricious play of forms happened to bring to my attention. Like each mortal earthling, and everything else which happens to live, I was simply a momentary finite form existing between the prenatal and postmortem nothings, merely a transient guest hosted in a strange world. The past is a foreign country, and for earthlings so is the lonely planet they happen briefly to inhabit.

3. Vision Revisions

Because the Journal was written in an erratic, sporadic and spontaneous way as thoughts happened to occur to me and created without preliminary drafts or follow-up revisions, the original content is not suitable for publication, nor did I produce it for that purpose. Some readers may judge that even the rewritten curated material in these pages isn't fit for publication. I respect the opinion of every reader, especially those who like the book and even more those who actually bought it rather than borrowing the volume from a library. My thanks for your purchase and even for your conclusion about the merits—or demerits—of the material. Whatever you think, "You may be right," as H.L. Mencken rubber-stamped at the bottom of unsolicited critical letters he received from the public.

As noted above, in keeping the Journal I didn't have publication in mind. The purpose was simply to transition into a written format in an improvised way what from time to time happened to enter my mind before those thoughts exited my consciousness. When I finally reread the Journal, fifty years after starting it, it quickly became clear to me that the material would have to be condensed, clarified, rewritten and purged of excess verbiage and repeated reflections in order to make the text publishable. With those changes, the book is best described as "based on" or "adapted from" the Journal.

The revisions raised the question of how much entries recorded at a particular time could be changed to improve their clarity or diction or other elements without distorting the original meaning or intentionally or unintentionally benefiting from hindsight. My goal was to convert an essentially impulsive stream-, or extreme-, of-consciousness record into a less unwieldy format, a curated version which retained the integrity of the original material by improving but without distorting it.

The procedure I adopted conforms to how Emily Nemens described her editing of author interviews in "The Paris Review" volume *Writers at Work Around the World* (2019): "These are not verbatim transcripts, conversations as they happened—the words as they were spoken have been shaped, and reshaped, by the interviewer, the writer, and the editors at the magazine, all with the aim of having the documents herein presented in their best possible iteration." In my case—with the Journal written as a conversation with myself—I've served as writer, reader and editor, a trinity which has hopefully produced a blessed result for readers, even if not a Holy one. But if not so blessed, at least one reader—the writer—deems the Journal a worthwhile work deserving of resurrection for an audience wider than simply the person who produced the material.

My faith in the merit of the material represents a little understood element of the creative process unappreciated by consumers of the works a few of us so laboriously produce. An enormous self-confidence and faith in the intellectual and cultural value of a creation is necessary to motivate the chancers who attempt to give airy nothings "a local habitation and a name." If an author doesn't believe in the worth of his work it's difficult, if not impossible, to write the text. Starting with a blank piece of paper (as I did for years) or, more recently, an empty screen staring back at you, the writer is faced with creating out of nothing an artifact worth something. To deal with what already exists—as do critics, reviewers, academics, editors, and others outside the creative process—is much easier than producing a new work which hasn't yet assumed a form. Only an unshakable faith in the project will inspire a creative character who deals with word characters to suppose that it's worthwhile to proceed with the great and time-consuming effort to write right.

The sort of deep-seated and irrational but necessary conviction necessary to motive creative types who type isn't unique to them. A compelling belief in your undertaking represents a character trait as tenacious as the vice-like grip which possesses religious believers. Without such unshakable faith it's really impossible to carry out a creative project, just as non-believers find themselves unable to engage in religious rituals.

Those who venture to produce cultural innovations also resemble business entrepreneurs, as both artistic and commercial risk-takers struggle to bring into being what doesn't yet exist. A writer is an intellectual entrepreneur with great faith in his enterprise, an activist possessed with the drive and persistence to produce results on the bottom line and on all the lines above. Both religion and venture capital—whether intellectual or financial—represent a stubborn refusal to accept the world as it is. Those who create hope to add something which will offer some value—monetary, cultural or even spiritual, for religion attempts to create something out of nothing.

The stark fact that no work of art is necessary presents a challenge to those who undertake to produce such unneeded additions to the play of infinite forms. The world could have continued spinning on and on without the creations of Shakespeare, Vermeer or Snoopy. Although mankind greatly treasures those outstanding artificial constructs (especially Snoopy's wisdom), all imagined works are essentially supererogatory to the lonely planet. What never assumes a form remains unknown and isn't missed. Non-existence represents the norm, both for what temporarily comes into being and that which never does. It's untrue that every dog has its day: Snoopy could well never have existed.

In an attempt to emulate the clarity of of Snoopy's wisdom—but not its quality: that would be impossible—I've added some supplemental passages to my Journal passages to explain, interpret, or gloss the original entries in ways that may be helpful to readers. Those current additions obviously benefit from a latter-day perspective but—as made clear earlier—none of the basic material has been endowed with any *ex post facto* content unavailable at the time when I wrote each Journal item. (You will find these current-day passages set apart by a different serif typeface throughout the Journal.)

Looking back into time by reviewing more than 50 years of Journal entries, the exercise surprised me by revealing how consistent my views have been over that lengthy time period. It seems that over half a century I seldom changed my early-day opinions about and reactions to my experiences and experiment. This consistency both consoled and concerned me. The continuity comforted me because the consistency in the Journal—and how so many of its ideas surfaced in A PLAY OF INFINITE FORMS—suggests that the world-view I formulated rather early served me so well that I saw no need to change my guidelines much. Because I adopted in my younger years many opinions, attitudes and perspectives which worked for me I decided to retain them. Although I sought and enjoyed various new insights and learning experiences which led me to revise or add to my preexisting views, it was gratifying to find many of my long-held perceptions confirmed by experience. My progress through life was thus as much confirmation as education.

Such long-term consistency resembles how Arturo Toscanini viewed his intellectual continuity over the years. In a July 4, 1938 letter the famed conductor noted after re-reading some of his favorite books in which he'd previously entered notations: "I congratulate myself because I very often find in each book observations that I rarely if ever want to change...[such] that even in those far-off times I had the same impressions and made the same comments!" (*The Letters of Arturo Toscanini,* 2002, edited by Harvey Sachs.)

But my largely unchanged views also concerned me, as such consistency perhaps evidenced fixed opinions and a closed mind unwilling to consider new ideas. Although my views were in fact at times informed by and supplemented with later experiences and evidence, still and all maybe I somewhat suffered from an inability to change and to adopt new perspectives. As comfortable as I was with many of my early beliefs, most of which were keepers, I tried to remain receptive to revising my views as needed, even if undoing fixed ideas proved more difficult than installing new ones. All around the world when I observed different ways of being and noticed practices and procedures which contrasted with mine I adopted the Mencken attitude, "You may be right," and accepted the corollary that I might be wrong. Differences didn't operate as threats to my settled opinions but as inspirations to reconsider them.

I was a great believer in the virtues of displacement, not only moving about to pursue adventures with wide-ranging travels but also, when possible, altering my beliefs and opinions by replacing them with new and hopefully improved perspectives. In fact, one reason I traveled was that seeing the world afforded me the opportunity to observe different ways of how people carried out their experiments in living. What I saw all around the lonely planet not only brought me some new ideas for my own experiment but also illustrated how arbitrary and in some cases odd and questionable were some common practices in my own country and culture. To preserve some of what I found I kept detailed travel diaries on every foreign trip. Without the diaries I'd have been a here-today/gone-tomorrow Houdini-type traveler: now-you-see-it/now-you-don't, my viewed illusions momentarily noticed and then disappearing like a magician's trick, the few infinite play of forms I happened to experience quickly formless—insubstantial stuff as dreams are made on, all melted into air.

In addition to travel I found that eclectic reading also operated to expand my horizons, even if words can never replace hands-on, mind-on, feet-on-the-ground experience. Although books read in an easy chair can't compare with the hard knocks of adventure travel, nonetheless writings can offer a convenient way to learn about unfamiliar topics. But an over-reliance on print and an exaggerated belief in its relationship to reality can turn you into a paper tiger. As Confucius observed, "it is better to travel 10,000 miles than to read 10,000 books." And you can earn frequent- flyer miles with journeys, but not even frequent-pager perks with reading.

Displacement presents difficulties because a new format often requires you to abandon fixed practices, settled beliefs and long-established habits by thinking outside the box and leaving your comfort zone. Because the protective box and pleasantly familiar zone originate to a large degree from various random and persistent formative influences, the confining box and zone are difficult to escape. Hard-to-transcend influences include your particular family heritage; your upbringing; your education; your professional activities; your socioeconomic endowment; where and when you happened to become incarnated as a humanimal; your inherited circumstances, both physical and situational; your basic personality; your intrinsic beliefs and opinions; your particular life experiences; how you act and how you react to what happens to you; and many other factors which factor into your way of life. How each of those elements operate to shape your mentality, sentimentality and other personality traits really can't be delineated to separate out each operative influence. Commenting on the characteristics of the human mind, C.S. Lewis called attention to its "set of preconceptions and assumptions so numerous that I can never examine more than a minority of them—never become conscious of them all. How much of total reality can such an apparatus [the human mind] let through?"

Travel served to "let through" into my mind many new and life-changing experiences. Far-reaching trips to distant and exotic—to me, but not to the locals—corners of the earth offered a literal displacement of a kind which at times called into question some of my received ideas and habitual practices. This resulted in a hybrid mentality based both on settled views from earlier years and later perspectives which supplemented those formed previously. I found the world a far better teacher than books and academics who profess what professors learn from studies rather than from experiences.

Apart from the displacements of travel and reading I also tried to displace myself from the flow of sensory impressions and my era by fracturing time so that neither the restrictive grip of the vivid passing moment nor the world as it happened to exist for my generation distracted me from considering the past and the future. In *Time and the Art of Living* (1982) Robert Crudin discusses the importance of an expanded view of time. Although we live only in the present, awareness of the past and of the future endows us with broader and more holistic perceptions encompassing an entire life rather than simply focusing on and reacting to immediate passing random sensory impressions. Crudin notes that it's advisable for people "not only to value the present but to grow beyond it, for we are not only savoring and understanding present time more fully, but also surveying it, as if from a hypothetical mirror placed in past and future ... [to give their] perspective in the continuum."

So it was that from a young age I projected my thoughts forward to old age, which for me is now, in an effort to visualize with a theoretical retrospective perspective how my life would look from this late vantage point. At the same time, I always tried to perceive the temporary, even if seemingly fixed, sights I viewed around the world with a view to supplementing the present with the past, much as Goethe noted after his mid-1780s visits to Pompeii: "Many a calamity has happened in the world, but never one that has caused so much entertainment to posterity as this one." Ancient and gruesome death, all too real to the ancients, over time becomes for later generations simply an historical curiosity of passing interest, a Michelin guide starred attraction to visit, then check off your list. Too bad about the volcano and all that molten lava, but hey—stuff happens. Take a few photos of the ruins, enjoy a delicious Italian meal, then on to your next sights and delights. But a more nuanced awareness of the long-ago past as well as some speculations about the far future serve to expand your perspective on the fleeting here and now of the only existence you'll ever know—that of your own brief daily life and era.

Although confined by mere chance to a short specific terrestrial tenure created by a random insensate play of forms, contemplating yesteryears and morrowyears far beyond your immediate knowledge can serve to bring you some new perspectives and understandings on how to conduct your brief experiment in living. No such experiment enjoys the certainty of proof of concept, but widening your frame of reference might facilitate noticing some new details in the image contained in that frame. But even such fine-tuning meant to help a humanimal better cope with the creature's strange terrestrial experiment will never clarify such a baffling experience. An earthling can only hope to deal, best as he or she can, with the given nature of things—"the sun-horses of Time" and mankind as "a troubled guest on the dark earth," as Goethe put it.

I always valued any displacements which happened to bring me some useful alternate version of reality. Whether by trips or by reading, which presented in-place surrogate travels—pale copies of the real thing—or by contemplating past eras or those to come, occasionally new perspective enabled me to see the nature of things in a different way. Such welcome altered mind states, always based on the real world and actual experiences, arose—unlike formal learning—at random, so I never knew what or when might occur opportunities which would inspire me to revise my opinions.

I found such opportunities at unexpected times in unexpected places. It was enlightening to come across by chance such thought-provoking observations as the comments in *The Existential Pleasures of Engineering* (1994) by Samuel C. Florman that in some countries engineers "are leaders in both the public and the private sectors. A third of French engineers go into government, finance, marketing, banking, and insurance. In other leading nations, including Japan and Germany, engineers are found in positions of authority throughout the social order. The United States, in stark contrast, is dominated by lawyers and MBAs." This somewhat startling revelation set off in my mind a train of thought freighted with mindful cargo, the caboose leading me to re-imagine how the U.S. might function if engineers rather than wordy lawyers, bottom-line MBAs, and Wall Street money men ran the country. I welcomed stimulating thought experiments, even if somewhat unrealistic like this example (unlikely the U.S. will ever favor engineers over the traditional dominant lawyer and MBA types) which often led me to revise previously settled matters or to add new ones to my range of perceptions.

For me the most telling displacement episodes originated from what I experienced, not from reading or from theories, opinions, academic constructs, economic models, social "science" doctrines, subjective beliefs unsupported by evidence-based factors, from views derived from opinions, personal attitudes, self-interest, or from substances meant to bring me induced visions, and other such dubious sources and influences rather than from how things actually operate out in the real world.

Schopenhauer (always an impressive reference to quote as his very name suggests an author's gravitas and erudition) was a great advocate of hands-on, eyes-on, brain-on engagement with real life experiences rather than vicarious learning through books. In "Studies in Pessimism" he notes that "if the imagination is to yield any real product, it must have received a great deal of material from the external world." Schopenhauer argues that "instead of placing books and books alone in the hands of children, educate them with ideas directly from real life." (But of course the childless German philosopher was speaking not from experience but only proposing a theory.)

One of Schopenhauer's fellow Germans emphasized the same idea. A pervasive and persistent theme of Goethe focuses on the need for direct experience with life rather than through theories. Many passages in *Faust* are directed against and satirize academics. Experience rather than knowledge motivated Goethe. In Part One, Mephistopheles advises a freshman student on his course of study. Cautioning against "the fantasy of [independent] thought," the Devil facetiously notes that the student will expand his mind "Once you have learned that all is reducible/ To labels in a semantic crucible"—quite the opposite of what Goethe actually believed. It's in this dialogue that Goethe includes his famous formulation that "all theory is gray."

As one who has spent untold pleasurable hours reading some thousands of books as well as an incalculable number of other printed materials, I can testify that none matches the didactic power of my experiences out in the world. However, perhaps by way of paradox I'll refer to a few books to support my view of the superiority of experience.

In *Tales From the Life of Bruce Wannell* (2020, edited by Barnaby Rogerson and Rose Baring), a contribution by David Summers recalls meeting Wannell in the mid-1980s in Peshawar, northwest Pakistan, at a United Nations unit meeting. The "Adventurer, Linguist, Orientalist" (as the book's subtitle describes Wannell) was "very different from the normal NGO [non-governmental organization] head or field director. He had, like myself, what some people may say, gone native. It was easy to spot the academics who talk and plan due to their Ph.D.s but who have not sat with the man in the street or the refugee camps, who have few ties with the area in which they work. I used to attend similar meetings in Geneva, good people but remote from any refugee child or experience of front line war, killing, rape or poverty."

Having been to Peshawar I saw the conditions Summers mentions and can well appreciate his point, even if I was simply passing through and lacked "ties with the area." As Goethe observed, no "semantic crucible," like a U.N. talking-shop meeting, can describe or adequately deal with the real-life horrors and misery you encounter, although never directly experience, by adventurous travels out in the world.

In *The Open Society and Its Enemies* (1962), Karl R. Popper echoed the disdain experienced practical people hold for academics, describing (in criticizing Hegel) "that poisonous intellectual disease of our own time which I call *oracular philosophy* [italics are Popper's]." In contrast to theoretical ivory tower versions of the world, Michael Novak in *Business As A Calling: Work and the Examined Life* (1994) endorses the superiority of experiential "knowledge that comes by alert living, doing, striving" which enable "practical wisdom" and allows you to keep "in touch with reality." Those direct encounters with the world Novak contrasts with such lesser touch points as "the knowledge that comes from books and the professed wisdom of academic circles" where "realism is regarded as outmoded. There is only opinion."

In the very lair of high ivory tower Ivy League pretentiousness, W.H. Auden dared (in his June 1946 Harvard commencement Phi Beta Kappa Poet address) to offer as a useful command, "Thou shall not ... commit a social science." Unfortunately, Auden's advice hasn't been followed in Cambridge or on many other university campuses. All too many of the volumes at Harvard's Widener Library offer not a widener but a narrower.

The primacy of experience over opinions and beliefs unanchored in the real world gave me a skeptical view of professorial and professional "experts" (other than science or technology trained specialists such as engineers or medical practicioners) many people consider authoritative. In *Obliquity: Why Our Goals are Best Achieved Indirectly* (2011) John Kay addresses the problem of how to operate in "a world suffused with uncertainty." He noted that abstract models which "don't invite response or interaction with the world" are of little use, and that while the unrealistic certainty of experts brings them attention, the more modest and practical views of decision-makers offer far more effective formats.

The ineluctable reality that experience tops theory represents a main theme of Edward de Bono's more than 20 books, many of them on "lateral thinking," more commonly known as thinking outside the box. In *Teaching Thinking* (1976), de Bono compares thinking derived from the outside world—"the deliberate exploration of experience for a purpose"—with the glib semantic-based mind games typical in "an academic setting in an academic tower" by tenured types "never confronted by the vagueness of the real world." The professors grind away in Goethe's "semantic crucible."

The "Botton line"—so to say—can by summarized by the reference in Alain de Botton's *Status Anxiety* (2004) to Oxford academic Frederic Harrison's comments on the uselessness of culture for everyday life. Believe it or not: a professor criticizing his own profession! For some people (but not me) such professorial acumen might prove that miracles exist! But the Oxford don's statement suggests to me only that Oxford probably exists (I'm without a doubt a doubting Thomas). Overly-educated and acculturated wise-guys claiming to be wise men typically behave, says Harrison, with "small fault-finding. Love of selfish ease, and indecision in action. The man of culture is one of the poorest mortals alive. For simply pedantry and want of good sense no man is his equal. No assumption is too unreal, no end too unpractical for him."

To avoid guilt by association with such undesirable and unrealistic pedants I've tried to exclude from the Journal and from this Introduction evidence which might support any allegations or claims that I am a "man of culture."

4. Noteworthy Notions

Although people often use the designations "diary" and "journal" interchangeably, those two formats are quite different. Unlike a diary, which records specific events and activities with day-to-day continuity, a journal contains disjointed, discursive and sporadic entries, many of them random and generalized rather than based on actual happenings with descriptive details. Of course, in both types of writings a single presiding consciousness creates the material, but a journal—eclectic and without any structure, other than chronological—lacks the regularity and connective tissue which typifies a diary.

While a diary is factual, a journal tends to be fanciful; a diary naturalistic, a journal impressionistic; a diary specific, a journal general. That general format offers more selective content than what a diary contains as there's no need to include in a journal anything deemed not worth noting. By way of contrast, a diary often describes trivial daily events of little interest, not even for the writer. A journal focuses more on mindful matters, while diary entries often cover mindless day-to-day routines. Because a diary emphasizes what a person does, it's largely self-referential and deals with personal activities. On the other hand—a journal-writing hand—journal entries originate from the world at large rather than the world at small based on what a particular person does every day. A journal is thus externalized and generalized, while a diary remains internalized and limited by the specifics of the writer's often routine diurnal rounds.

Long-time British politician William Ewart Gladstone (four times prime minister between 1868 and 1894) was peerless both as a diary keeper and by remaining a commoner. Every day for almost seventy years (sixty-nine years, ten and one-half months) Gladstone recorded, usually without comment, his "often bleakly factual" account (as described by Roy Jenkins in *Gladstone*, 1995) of his daily activities. When trying to convince his youngest son to keep a diary, Gladstone explained that the purpose was to preserve "an account-book of the all-precious gift of time." But at times the gift box—even Prime Minister Gladstone's—remained empty of precious stones in the way of valuable content. Much daily trivia isn't worth recording.

Gladstone began his diary in July 1825 at age 15 and continued it to age 85 until the last daily entry on May 23, 1894, after which he included only a few sporadic passages. On September 1st that year he explained, "After breaking up the practice of seventy years, I now mean to proceed by leaps and bounds, making an occasional note." This change in format in part converted the diary into a journal.

In contrast to Gladstone's compulsive seven-decades-long diary entries, 1986 Physiology or Medicine Nobel Prize Winner Rita Levi-Montalcini states in her memoir *In Praise of Perfection* (1988), "Trusting in my memory, I never developed the habit—nor do I regret not having done so—of keeping any kind of record. Still less a diary, because I believe that, if memory has not taken an indelible imprint of a given event, then it could not and should not be brought back to life by mere written witness." No Gladstone-like "account-book" of daily event for her.

Levi-Montalcini claims that people keep a diary or a journal "from the blatant desire to exhibit it to third parties" and also to get the writer's descendants to read about your life, and "if one is especially vain, for its value to posterity." Her anti-diary diatribe seems to suggest that a Nobel Prize winner's superior intelligence includes a superhuman ability (no doubt one of her "perfection" traits she praised) to remember all significant details of one's life. But the rest of us ordinary mortals with fallible memories need an *aide-mémoire* to preserve a record of evanescent passing events or contemplations. This explains why I have not (yet) won the Nobel Prize: unlike Nobel laureate Rita L-M (Long-Memory), I needed both a diary and a journal to remember what happened and what I thought. In any case, it's hard to understand why her memoir doesn't represent the very self-oriented behavior she criticizes and disdains—a "blatant desire" to preserve and display her life story.

In conformance with my own view of the function of a journal and with some of the reasons why I initiated and maintained that kind of record over more than half a century, Thomas Mann notes in his February 11, 1934 diary entry (in *Thomas Mann Diaries 1918-1939*, published in English in 1982): "I love this process by which each passing day is captured, not only in its impressions but also, at least by suggestion, its intellectual direction and content as well, less than for the purpose of rereading and remembering than for taking stock, reviewing, maintaining awareness, achieving perspective."

Unlike Mann, I kept my Journal in part to remember otherwise soon forgotten thoughts, perceptions noteworthy and memorable for me even if for no one else. But like Mann, I also wanted to take stock of my on-going experiment in living, review my perspectives and attitudes on the experiment, and maintain awareness of what happened in my life, mostly at random, to comprise the content of my brief earthly existence. Keeping a journal serves to sharpen your senses and to focus your attention, as an outlet exists where you regularly record your fleeting impressions. You become more aware of your experiences and thoughts by knowing that you'll formulate some of them into a written account, a freeze-frame word image which often transcends the personal and converts specific individual impressions into more general ideas and observations. Mann's formula seems to follow this format.

I feel qualified to analyze and comment on the differences between a journal and a diary because I've maintained both kinds of documentation. In addition to the Journal, continued by now for more than half a century, for an even longer time I kept a series of detailed travel diaries to record my every move during my overseas adventures. I'm thus familiar with both types of "account-books of the all-precious gift of time." The travel diaries primarily detail what I did every day while away, but they also include some journal-like responses to and reflections on daily events. However, most of the time when I was on the road the fast and furious on-rushing impressions came at me so quickly and unpredictably I seldom had time to reflect on them to any great extent.

Adventure travel was like drinking from a fire hydrant torrent; home-based daily routines, like sipping from a faucet. The two contrasting formats—diary for the flood of impressions during travel and Journal for the at-home trickle—reflect the two quite different ways I pursued my experiment in living. The Journal derives from my settled stable suburban provincial life, far too routine, conventional and uneventful to merit a diary. I recognized that keeping a diary would produce little worth preserving. But at the same time and place (at home), I believed that a few of my occasional thoughts, beliefs and opinions were noteworthy, so I noted them. When away, however, a diary suited the situation as nearly every day brought me many experiences I deemed sufficiently unusual and interesting (to me at least) to remember by recording them.

All forms of creative work represent an effort to impose some sort of order on the otherwise amorphous and random nature of things. The word "sanskrit"—"ordered, arranged, correct"—describes the common characteristic of my home-based Journal and the travel diaries, for both formats comprise an attempt to transmute transient and elusive reality into a comprehensible although arbitrarily imposed construct, in no way authoritative or conclusive but simply one of many possible formulations. One of the most famous examples of an attempt to order the chaos of sensory impressions which flood into a humanimal's consciousness is James Joyce's ultra-detailed diary-like account—trivia made into literature—of one June Dublin day in the life of Leopold Bloom.

Sometimes the keeper of a life record isn't himself sure which term to attach to his notebook entries. In his travel account *My Dateless Diary* (1969), R.K. Narayan states in the forward that "The following pages arose out of a day-to-day journal kept when I first visited the United States of America." He calls his pages both a diary and a journal. For my part, I was quite conscious of the difference between the two modes and I tried not to confound the content appropriate to be recorded in each type.

Whatever format a writer chooses, the highest and best use of his or her creative talents depends on a synthesis between real-world experience and contemplating it. One without the other will deprive the material of substance, breadth and depth. A thoughtful response to passing events and impressions combines both interacting with life and pondering its random happenings, but seeking experiences for the sake of writing about them won't do the job. As Cesare Pavese wrote in May 1947 in *This Business of Living* (published in English 1961)—his so-called diaries 1935-50, a misnomer as they're actually journals—"The greatest benefit that a writer brings to poetry, to literature, is that part of his life which, while living it, seemed to him farthest removed from literature." No life is literature, and for sure no literature is life. Living to write subordinates the primacy of existence to mere descriptions of it. Of course, the preservative of words is necessary to record the otherwise often unremembered passing sensory impressions. Ideally a journal and a diary should contain reality-based entries contemplated with and complemented by a coherent mixture of material sourced from the external world and some reactions to and thoughts about the experiential inputs.

Reality converted into imaginative fiction (not simply invented in an abstract mind-game-type exercise) yields works such as Gabriel Garcia Márquez's *Chronicle of a Death Foretold* (1981), the tale based on actual events. In his memoir *Living to Tell the Tale* (2003), the author describes (in Chapter 7) how he couldn't "continue living in peace if I did not write the story of Cayetano," the corpse featured in the novel, his death foretold in the "chronicle's" first line. Although described as "magical realism," the novelist's works were based more on reality than on inventive hocus-pocus-type magic, much as the imaginary Yoknapatawpha County world of William Faulkner—a great influence on the Colombian writer—derived from real life and true events in the Oxford, Mississippi area.

Like a journal or a diary, a chronicle (*chronikos*: concerning time) attempts to preserve "an account-book of the all-precious gift of time," as Gladstone put it. In Mexico persists the delightful practice of appointing an official local *cronista* to record in cities, towns and villages their historical and recent noteworthy events and details relating to social and cultural matters. A municipal *cronista* justifiably occupies a high status in Mexican society. Some places name the street where the *cronista* lived after him or her. In recent years two writers who favor the chronicle format have won the Nobel Prize for Literature—Svetlana Alexievich of Belarus (2015) and Ohran Pamuk in Turkey (2006).

Apart from the diary, journal and chronicle categories, Max Frisch's similar writings "concerning time" combine entries pertaining both to daily events (diary content) and more general matters (journal material), as recorded in his *Tagebuch 1946-1949* and *Tagebuch 1966-1971*. His translator Geoffrey Skelton dealt with the ambiguity of the word "*Tagebuch*," which in German means either "journal" or diary," by using the title "sketchbook" to designate Frisch's combination of fact, fiction, autobiography, travel impressions, general observations, philosophical speculations, and other categories of entries.

Frisch's eclectic comments covering a wide range of formats and topics offer readers many varied and unexpected insights. After a January 1949 conversation with Bertold Brecht, Frisch comments how "there is that something that distinguishes, unmistakenly, the creative person from the expert—a kinship, the knowledge, born of experience, that in the beginning there is nothing. ... Experts, when they see a drawing for instance, take it from Dürer or Rembrandt or Picasso onward; the creative being, in whatever sphere he works, is aware of the empty paper behind."

Frisch's observation presents a crucial distinction between those who create and after-the-fact on-lookers who comment. Creative types are active; experts, reactive. Originators who face the emptiness of blank paper or screen deal with making something out of nothing, while commentators, with their supposed expertise, often use their purportedly authoritative analyses—after the work has been produced—to make nothing out of something. Many empty pages and screens have stared at me expectantly as I looked back at them trying to endow a *tabula rasa* with some meaningful words. As I learned over the years, a wide range of varied experiences helps to enable the process of converting thought to text. Lacking such an essential component, writers without worldly resources are limited to the inferior process of inventing rather than imagining their works.

Finally, an intermediate format which often combines characteristics of both a journal and a diary is the personal letter. These frequently contain news based on daily doings along with observations about what happened during the day. Many letters Swiss historian Jacob Burckhardt wrote between 1938 and 1897 include a synthesis of both elements. As editor and translator Alexander Dru suggests in *The Letters of Jacob Burckhardt* (1955), they are "in a form which lies half-way, as it were, between a Journal and the formal historical work circumstances prevented his writing." The result created a kind of amalgam of the daily with more meditative considerations as if in a combined journal and diary (a "jiary"?).

An example of Burckhardt's mixed format appears in his December 12, 1838, letter, which in part details some of the day's events. He notes "the first ice of winter," mentions lectures he's attending, refers to going to Beethoven and Mozart concerts, and with those descriptions of daily life he also interweaves some general observations, one of which inspires a quote from Goethe. Goethe, in turn, also included in some of his letters both diary-type references to current events and activities along with more philosophical journal-like observations, such as in his June 1, 1803 missive to Karl Friedrich Zelter, a Berlin musician, regarding Schiller's death. Goethe notes: "people try to derive some entertainment from every loss and misfortune, and the actors and others are pressing me hard to commemorate the deceased in some way on the stage."

In recent years, late in life, my letters—both those typed old-form on paper and emails—have served to supplement my Journal and travel diaries with ancillary conversation-like personal information, some of which might not appropriately fit into either of the two more formal formats. My epistolary process resembled that described by Annette Tapert, "collaborative writer" with show business and literary agent Irving Lazar in his *Swifty: My Life and Good Times* (1995). She writes: a "prolific letter writer, ...he had composed lengthy letters to friends and clients and saved all the carbon copies...Lazar had, in essence, typed an ongoing journal of his social life." Although my life—social or otherwise—was nowhere near as colorful or on a fast-track as swift as Swifty's, many of my letters, like Lazar's, included details meant less to inform recipients than to supplement my Journal entries with additional material, some of it diary-like, I wished to preserve. Those who received my correspondence thus unwittingly served as silent interlocutors, so to speak, in a written dialogue, some of which didn't really pertain to them. I was really writing to and for myself.

Although I enjoyed my reading and my writing, never did I confuse them with living. No written account—journal, diary, chronicle, letter, notebook, book—can ever capture the true-to-life nature of the original experiences which comprise a humanimal's experiment in living. Many hours did I devote to word-related activities, but never did I suppose that those surrogates represented the granular reality of the world in which people actually live. Writings derive from life but are not it. In fact, most earthlings carry out their lives without ever writing much of anything (and some people in under-developed lands can't write at all) or reading creative works. It's possible to exist quite comfortably in an a-literate way.

I don't admire but feel sorry for literary types possessed with the compulsion to reduce passing events to writing in order to endow them with some sort of special significance or to validate real-world happenings by putting them into words. Such was the sort of obsessive behavior described by Brian W. Aldriss at the beginning of his essay in *Living with a Writer* (2004, edited by Dale Selwak): "I always wrote. I have always written. I wrote irrespective of conditions. I write now. I write on a variety of subjects. Volume 47 of a holograph and illustrated journal is now being compiled in a hard-bound AS notebook." To anyone cursed with such a need "always" to write I'd say: "Get a life." Over the totality of my by now long years, most always I did not write, preferring instead to live.

For me, encountering the great play of terrestrial infinite forms offered a much more appealing way of being than reading or writing about them. Filtering worldly happenings through words distances you from direct contact with the colorful, exciting and stimulating earthly spectacle. While admirable for their energy, concentration, discipline and productivity, compulsive writers willing to sit for hours on end on their end exist in word realm like a thick mesh which veils those lettered fanatics from the outside world. For authors like John Updike and Isaac Asimov, who non-stop produced thousands of published pages, reality served as a literary device to provide a source of material to be processed and converted into printed pages, so sentencing such writers to exist mainly through sentences, paragraphs, chapters. Just as "always"-writing writers exist in a vicarious way, a derivative of life, so too do compulsive readers remain removed from the world. Rather than living to read and to write I wanted to live in order to live. I was always careful to subordinate word-related activities to ones dealing with direct participation in the play of forms. I never confused the two quite separate realms. My Journal—as well as my other writings: travel diaries, books, articles—all represent forms of an off-stage play performed away from the great play of infinite forms out in the world, the main production of much greater interest to me than the side-show.

In any case, writing and all creative works represent a losing battle to salvage from the detritus of passing time and lived experience a few remnants which might endure. But, in truth, they won't. Those scraps are simply forms of infinite play, a passing few among the millions of other forms all fated to vanish. The seemingly solid stolid stuffed specimens in the Museum of Natural History Holden Caulfield admired for their stability (as noted in section 1 of this Introduction) imperceptibly and ineluctably decay away day by day, for at every twilight dusk falls on an always different world.

Like young Holden, Nabokov's little Lolita—also seeking respite from the ceaseless cosmic flow—watches the odometer in Humbert's car mutate as "all the nines are changing into the next thousand." She laments, "I used to think that they'd stop and go back to nines, if only my mother agreed to put the car in reverse." But *nein* to the nines, as there's no going back: the turns never allow returns, for there's no reverse but only verse and other kinds of writings to record the fugitive moments, words which might for a time preserve what's come and gone before the words themselves fade away.

No true displacement of time is possible by retaining what no longer exists, as constant eternal forward motion in time and space moves the passing moments and miles on and on, life and the play of all the other forms always driving ahead as described in the opening scene of Robert Penn Warren's *All the King's Men* (1946), with a car speeding along "the highway and it is straight for miles, coming at you, with the black lines down the center coming at you and at you...coming at you with the whine of the tires."

It all keeps coming at you and at you, and night once again falls on a different world.

5. Reviews of Views

As mentioned in the first sentence of the Author's Note which begins this book, the Journal is a companion volume to my 2021 travel reminiscence, A PLAY OF INFINITE FORMS. The source material for both books spans the same half century, as in 1969 I began the Journal and at the same time restructured my life by adding to my settled home-based way of being the quite different dimension of frequent wide-ranging adventure travel. In reviewing the Journal recently to prepare this book for publication it struck me as strange that although I never consulted my notebook entries for A PLAY OF INFINITE FORMS, that book contains many of the ideas, opinions, views and even some almost identical passages I'd previously recorded in the Journal. Long before writing the travel reminiscence its themes and threads—though of course not yet all the travel experiences—already existed as entries in the Journal. It seems that my adventures around the world tended to reinforce and confirm much of what I already thought. Many of the main assumptions, beliefs, values, attitudes, opinions and perspectives I held before the trips survived contact with reality as those views remained intact after my travel adventures. Because both books are in that way similar, I consider them companion volumes. Some of the commonalities between the two books I detail in this section—a review of my views.

From early days it was always obvious to me that pure chance governs much of what happens to form each person's experiment in living. Luck, happenstance, coincidence, fate, serendipity, randomness greatly influence every humanimal's lot in life. Some of those creatures inexplicably enjoy good fortune, while others are fated to face misfortune. Each and every earthling exists as a plaything of random forces. Chance, not choice, controls the conditions of your initial circumstances—your genetic make-up and then when and where and into what context you happen to be thrown into existence. It's a lottery. From that chance beginning onward, life keeps coming at you and at you—like the highway does at the speeding car in *All the King's Men*—with unpredictable, uncontrollable and random influences, now keeping you smoothly on the road and now steering you off onto rough patches. And always it's all coming at you and at you. the car and the odometer rolling on and on to the next thousand.

I came to believe that from whatever perspective you view existence—cosmic, terrestrial, temporal, generic, situational, personal—randomness shapes how humanimals happen to live or don't, as some fail to survive as long as expected and few as long as they hope. They become road kill on the highway. And a countless number of potential mortals who might be born but don't happen to materialize never even assume the form of a humanimal. Which are the lucky ones—the ares or the nevers?

In a cosmic way the earth itself is an outlier, a weird product of chance which somehow produced what is probably a unique exception to the otherwise life-averse universe and beyond, a vast realm no doubt empty of life as we know it. The exact conditions necessary to create and sustain the great earthly spectacle, that strange play of infinite forms, came into existence by chance, a macro experiment in being by nature analogue in a way to each earthling's micro experiment in living, with neither of the two strange phenomenons activated for any purpose or with any meaning. As described by astronomer Donald Brownlee and paleontologist Peter Ward in *Rare Earth* (2000), the advent and evolution of life on earth depended on its conditions and the solar system being precisely appropriate to support such life. It was thus possible but not probable for me, for you, for all the other humanimals who happen to live now or did in the past and will in the future, for all the individual beasts, plants, insects, and other forms of life and also for the system's terrestrial existential experiment to come into being.

The random existence of those macro factors which put the show on the road is just for openers. Chance and luck also permeate the specifics which apply to each individual, starting with the random development that any particular humanimal even happens to exist. Once thrown into being, the creatures then face further random circumstances: place, era, family, genes, various situational factors, personality, disposition, character, intelligence and many other elements which influence an experiment in living depend on chance. In my own case, I happened to originate in a pleasant mid-America town and came of age during peaceful and prosperous times in a stable society with propitious economic and political conditions, a rare and exceptional combination of many favorable factors. It was all just luck. For none of those enabling benefits which contributed to the chance for me to enjoy a favorable experiment in living did my personal agency play a part.

In retrospect, when I contemplated my good luck, it seemed to me rather "WEIRD" that by chance conditions endowed me with so many advantageous elements. The acronym derives from Harvard professor Joseph Henrich's book, *The WEIRDest PEOPLE in the World: How the West Became Psychologically Peculiar and Particularly Prosperous* (2020). As only an Ivy League professor can in his somewhat weird academic way, Henrich tries to cram an entire theory into an acronym: "Western, Educated, Industrialized, Rich, and Democratic." (As an appropriate academic touch, the good professor even uses the Oxford comma.) Those five factors describe the favorable conditions which happened to prevail during much of my time and in my place, both of which were exceptional by their existence and by their quality and how they combined in a synergistic way to offer many favorable opportunities.

Such exceptional conditions are the exception, not the rule. Seldom in the course of human events do good times prevail, and it was only by mere chance that beneficial circumstances gave my generation an advantageous context in which to pursue our experiments. All through history in almost every era most societies have suffered from much less beneficial, settled and fortunate circumstances than the propitious conditions earthlings enjoyed in my time and place. And if conditions happen by chance to be good they most often don't get better but tend to turn bad. Regression to the mean—including mean and brutish influences and outcomes—brings about unfavorable changes. Whether on a cosmic, earthly, societal or individual scale, advantages remain ever vulnerable to deterioration or disappearance by the operation of luck or chance.

But the ultimate regression to the normal state of being is non-existence. This applies in a macro as well as a micro way. The unique and strange earthly play of infinite forms will one day reach its end, the globe then becoming like other heavenly bodies –just another lifeless rock spinning in space. All terrestrial life and everything else will vanish. The sphere which for years furnished the hospitable setting hosting earthlings and where they experienced their odd brief experiments in living will become empty as eternal night falls on a completely different world. "WEIRD" may describe some temporary localized conditions on earth, but "weird" offers a true description of the lonely planet and its temporarily living forms.

Non-existence of the entirety seems more comprehensible and less threatening than does one's own non-being, a state difficult for a humanimal to imagine. But existing represents only a very brief weird exception, a chance interlude between prenatal and postmortem nothingness. Damien Hurst entitled his "art work" shark floating in a tank of formaldehyde "The Physical Impossibility of Death in the Mind of Someone Living." But I'm living proof (at least for a brief while longer) that envisioning one's own death is by no means impossible. In fact, I've always viewed such an imaginative image—if not the event itself—as quite desirable. From an early age I saw dark at the end of the tunnel. As a young man I was acutely aware that before long I'd no longer be alive. This realization led me to try to arrange my life, best as I could considering my own circumstances, based on what I comprehended long ago: time ending for me.

One conclusion I derived from my acute awareness of my terrestrial tenure's brevity led me to favor a simple way of life largely free of consumption and of possessions, other than the few I deemed necessary. This conformed with Seneca's observation in "On the Shortness of Life" that "people are frugal in guarding their personal property, but as soon as it comes to squandering time they are most wasteful of the one thing in which it is right to be stingy." I tried not to spend either my time or my money in frivolous ways.

Although indifferent to possessions, it never occurred to me to criticize consumers based on any moral or idealistic objections to buying stuff. I didn't disdain chronic shoppers but was glad that the stuff-collectors found an activity they enjoyed. If people chose to participate as a (credit) card-carrying member of the consumer society, who was I to object? Finding a few pleasures among the all too many oppressive infinite forms represents a welcome relief to the disadvantages of by chance being incarnated as a humanimal on the lonely planet. Some earthlings may even be grateful to be alive to enjoy such temples of temptation as Walmart, Target, Costco, IKEA, shopping malls, discount stores and other retailers, all of which I admired for their efficiency and proficiency but seldom visited.

The only truly valid arguments against consumerism Admiral Hyman Rickover presented in his profound and prescient March 1959 speech, entitled "Illusions Cost Too Much," to the Yale Club and the Yale Law School Association of Washington, D.C. The admiral listed three reasons why our high civilian standards of living may prove "an actual liability in the contest with totalitarian powers." First, a lower standard of living increases resilience, self-sufficiency and an ability to survive under hardships. Second, America's affluent society depends on complex interconnected systems which could easily be disrupted if a few of the links were severed. Third, America is the first civilization in history based on consuming nonrenewable resources. Nations with a more "austere standard of life" derive an advantage from their simpler systems. Rickover noted that among the most vital tasks for the country were conservation of natural resources and improving education.

Based on the remarkably far-seeing views of the admiral, it's probable that in the long run under-developed countries with less complex, wasteful and vulnerable systems and more basic economies may survive longer and more intact than the United States, most likely doomed to decline to states much less cohesive and maybe become completely dis-united.

Although my home country and many of its citizens seemed to like to live beyond their means, I tried to follow the more sober principles as listed by Admiral Rickover: a moderate standard of living, simplicity, and recycling, a practice I adopted long before the latter-day environmental movement after my first visit to India over the winter of 1973-1974 where I saw rag-pickers pawing through mounds of garbage to salvage a few cans, glass containers and scraps to sell. After that I found myself unable to toss away into the trash what people half-way around the world struggled to pluck from the piles of oozing, stench-noxious garbage to earn a pitiful living.

Living simply without too many possessions or amenities represented an attractive way of being for me. For one thing, this freed me up to concentrate on the activities I preferred to pursue without being distracted by the need to deal with less rewarding matters. Stuff needs dusting, cleaning, repairs, maintenance, service, security, protection and other time-consuming and costly attention. Apart from eliminating the need to deal with possessions, a simple life made me in some ways less vulnerable to chance, luck and challenging random events, both societal and personal. My goal was to minimized the ways I might become a hostage to fortune and to maximize my freedom to live in my own way without unneeded burdensome complications. Although in many ways dependent on the complex interconnected systems mentioned by Admiral Rickover, I tried best as possible to limit such dependence by keeping my needs and wants at a basic level.

In *Discretionary Time: A New Measure of Freedom* (2008), Robert E. Goodin, et al disassociated wealth from richness by pointing out that people who can free up time for discretionary use enjoy more prosperity than compulsive acquirers focused on amassing more monetary wealth. The true value of wealth is not to buy things but to buy time. As Morgan Housel observes in *The Psychology of Money* (2020), "The ability to do what you want, when you want, with who[m] you want, for as long as you want" represents some of the main factors which improve the chance for a favorable experiment in living.

Among my most valuable possessions were intangibles I couldn't actually possess. One—which I continually lost—was time. Two others were relationships and experiences, which for me represented the highest and best use of my time. Although neither offered the durability of things—people died, experiences were evanescent—both greatly enriched my life, far more than would have stuff. My wealth consisted in my freedom to establish a way of being of my own choosing. This reflected Christopher Morley's aphorism—one of the two which greatly influenced and guided me—that "There is only one success—to be able to spend your life in your own way." That kind of spending—rather than buying possessions—brought me the best possible experiment in living, given my circumstances and how I decided to view the play of forms on the lonely planet. Helping me to formulate this attitude was my early-day realization, which contradicted Damien Hurst's shark tank title claim, not only of the possibility but of the inevitability of my death. Knowing and accepting that the end would come greatly enhanced the way I reached that finality.

That realization of my mortality long before my end, by now soon to occur, enabled me to view my far future early enough to make a difference. My forward-looking retrospective perspective gave me a chance to change before it was too late. I tried to imagine how my life would look when I reviewed it in old age. By attempting to live in my own way I hoped to reduce regrets which would vex me toward the end, which is now. I didn't want to look back on my life as a failed experiment, with remorse and discontent by not having taken advantage of my ability to try to engage with the world in a pro-active willed way (always subject to luck and chance) rather than a largely reactive or dependent way.

Some people learn Morley's lesson too late. In *Chasing Daylight: How My Forthcoming Death Transformed My Life* (2006) Eugene O'Kelly, United States chairman of the global accounting and consulting firm KPMG, told how in May 2006 he was diagnosed with terminal brain cancer and given three months to live. The account presents an accounting of his life and his bottom line closing of the books and the book. O'Kelly observes how so many of his colleagues at the firm focused on their careers at the expense of their personal lives, disregarding their families for the sake of professional success. But to reach this enlightening conclusion toward the end of his earthly existence was far too late for the soon-to-be late cancer gene afflicted Gene to benefit from his new-found wisdom. Better never than late would probably have been preferable for him. "Chasing daylight" to find illumination is futile when deferred to a time when night has already fallen on a changed world. If you wait until the end to contemplate the means to reach the end, no time remains to shape your experiment in living.

Just as I had no interest in consumerism and worldly goods, so I carried out my experiment with only moderate ambition. Unlike O'Kelly's colleagues at KPMG, I didn't seek success but only a modest role in the great play of forms. A walk-on part was enough for me. In contrast to most of my peers—soon, like me, to be disappears—I felt little motivation to achieve the accomplishments and recognition commonly valued by many of my contemporaries. To strive to gain wealth, fame, possessions, respect, status, praise, power, prestige or any such other tangible or reputational credits didn't interest me. That's not how I wanted to spend my time, effort or energy. I didn't eliminate all ambition but simply limited it. I sought to occupy a small, modest place in the world. For me, a little success went a long way. I believed that even a small reward was its own virtue.

Low expectations offered the further advantage that they represented a more realistic attitude than exaggerated aspirations. My limited modality conformed with my average skills and the unlikely chance that I could excel. Even overachievers sometimes advocate the same sort of modest way of life. The adored (by women) and much admired (by publishers, critics, scholars, readers, reviewers, dogs, cats, gerbils and other critters) Albert Camus recorded in his *Notebooks* approval of "Poe and the four conditions of happiness: 1) Outdoor life, 2) To be loved by someone, 3) Lack of all ambition, 4) Creativity." "*Toute ambition*"? All, Al? Surely we're allowed some teeny-weeny itsy-bitsy ambition. Even I, a humanimal endowed with few apparent abilities or the temperament or desire for high achievement, harbored some ambition.

My view that I lacked any special characteristic which might enable great success didn't arise based on false modesty but only on a realistic assessment of my capabilities. Wit Oscar Levant once said that underneath all the false tinsel of Hollywood lies the real tinsel. Similarly, below any perceived false modesty on my part is real modesty. I willingly realized and accepted that I was, at best, average. I wouldn't regress to the mean as I was already there. I was one of the millions in the middle of the bell-shaped curve who made it possible for a few highly intelligent and competent (and lucky) humanimals to occupy the extreme nearly flat far right end of the curve. At the same time I thankfully managed to avoid the low points at the far left.

Although I didn't delude myself with any illusions of superiority, I didn't suffer from an inferiority complex either. There was nothing complex about my self-knowledge. I simply accepted my limitations and tried to accord my hopes and ambitions with my fairly modest capabilities. I knew that I was quite unlikely to be a superstar, but at the same time I believed that I wouldn't end up simply as a black hole, even if I'd occupy one after my time. I realized that I was just another face in the crowd, quite a finite form as just one of the eight billion or so other humanimals I briefly shared the earth with. Very few of them, myself excluded, would somehow—thanks in part to ambition, ability, personality, energy, grit, perseverance and other such personal factors, but most of all by luck and chance—rise above the billions and become stellar characters with leading roles in the play of infinite forms. The rest of us were bit players, supernumeraries—the only "super" characteristic we could claim.

A pretentious attitude to suppose you can excel indulged in by someone like me of average ability seemed to me a frail basis on which to shape a life. To pursue over-achievement represents a quest for possible but not probable accomplishments, a lottery only won by few. Success offers only potential, a will-o'-the-wisp proposition fraught with chance and luck which often motivates compulsive and often life-distorting behavior. For chancers there lurks ahead on the far horizon, years ahead, the often fatal attraction of possibly winning the lottery, a *fata morgana* phantom which may never materialize into reality. It's out there, you can see it but only as a chimera which doesn't yet exist, and might never. Meanwhile, you've spent a lot of your limited time, effort and energy to try to convert potential into reality.

How a humanimal views the sources of its success tells a lot about the creature's understanding of its life experiment. Many and perhaps even most accomplished performers believe that their own efforts represent the main elements of achieving favorable results. In the spirit of H.L. Mencken, I admit that those exceptional earthlings "may be right." Speaking with authority only from my own experience, it's clear to me that much of what brought me good fortune resulted from chance and luck rather than from my own skill and agency. Random and uncontrollable factors played the leading roles in the play of infinite forms which formed my life. My lesser contribution consisted of trying to expose myself to good luck, but lots of luck to any earthling who depends on activating that capricious influence.

Ambitious types who suppose that superior success originates from personal efforts view the experiment in a way different from those of us who recognize the primacy of luck and chance as the determining factors. We believe we're children of chance, not masters of our own fate. The degree to which a person supposes that he largely controls his experiment, rather than recognizing how little he actually shapes his life, represent two quite opposite existential considerations about the way things work here on the lonely planet. Acknowledging the influence of randomness and "the rules of chaos" (as discussed below) worked for me, but I recognize that such a view might be inappropriate for other earthlings.

By something of a paradox, I viewed myself as fortunate that luck and chance never operated to elevate me into prominence. Such good fortune, which left me with modest accomplishments, both eliminated the possibility of losing a favored status by a run of bad luck and gave me free time to allocate as I saw fit. I considered over-achievement as a curse in disguise. Without the burdens that often come with great success I could continue to live in my own way, and in any case most of the benefits of success didn't interest me.

I was content to remain on the sidelines, present but not featured, rather than to occupy a superior higher place looking down on the masses below. But I did seek to accomplish enough to give me some identity, a place in the world, and ways to maintain some functional connections with the community as well as to establish relationships which would allow me to enjoy some human connections and participate in everyday life. I was neither a do-nothing lay-about nor a mover and shaker but operated in between those two extremes.

My limited aspirations enabled me to strike a balance between spending my life in my own way and being involved with the world in other ways. The cautionary comments of Alan W. Watts in *The Wisdom of Security* (1951) helped to guide me: "the more we become involved in [life], the more we are trapped, limited and frustrated." It's advisable, he observes, to avoid being stuck in sticky situations "like flies caught in honey," which may be sweet but also confining. I always kept in mind the primacy for me of Morley's formula, that true success is to live in your own way. As noted previously, that's one of the two aphorisms which served as a major guiding principle for me. The other fundamental formula—one which evidences that even academics can occasionally stumble upon useful worldly wisdom—which guided me originated with Jacob Bronowski: "The world can only be grasped by action, not by contemplation."

Those two succinct formulations told me much of what I needed to try to curate my life in the best possible way, given my circumstances. Based in part on Bronowski's principle, I realized that only a direct engagement with the world would yield a satisfactory life experience. Reading, thinking, mental constructs, theories, contemplation, invented notions, models and other such abstractions can be enjoyable and often stimulating, but they won't enable you to create a life in full. Relying on those sorts of passive activities bring you only a life in empty.

One way I relegated sterile analysis and theory to a subordinate role involved focusing on the "what" rather than the "why." After Jack Burden wonders why he's one of the men working for such an unsavory character as "King" Willie Stark in *All the King's Men*, the Boss replies, "There ain't any explanation. Not of anything. All you can do it point at the nature of things." This echoes the Spanish phrase, "*no hay porque*"—"There's no because." I rarely pursued an analysis of why anything exists or why something happened. I preferred instead to accept the reality that most things inexplicably happen—by chance, luck, fate—to assume an earthly form or to occur. One example is the earth itself and everything in it. What exists or what happens—not why—is what I concentrated on.

Willie Stark's stark truth explains human affairs better than contemplating unanswerable "why's," an exercise which doesn't make you wise. At best we can only gain an occasional glimpse into the opaque dark corners where chance, luck and fate operate to influence much of our lives. Such random glimmers provide fleeting flashings of light like the flickering fireflies Cuban society women in colonial times sewed into their hair and silk gowns worn at grand balls. Other than those evanescent blinking little glows of illumination which give momentary enlightenment, almost all else remains shadowed in the twilight, as do we mortals from dusk to dusk and dust to dust, as night falls again and again on a ceaselessly changing different world.

6. Unruly Rules

Now near the end, a few reflections on chance and luck serve to mirror some of the most influential images in how I viewed my experiment in living. Such factors (as mentioned in section 5) as my disinterest in consumerism and moderate ambition, along with various other considerations, served to shape how I addressed the challenge of trying to live in my own way. As explained above, the primary principle which guided me stemmed from my belief in the role of luck, chance, happenstance, coincidence, serendipity, fate and other such capricious and random influences which operate as controlling influences on an experiment in living. Such a belief I based not on abstract thinking or theoretical concepts but on what actually happened to me. As time went by, I recognized how little control my own efforts exerted on how my experiment evolved.

My views on luck and chance were not inspired but were articulated and confirmed by a book I happened to come across in my late years long after it was published in 1969 (by coincidence the same year I started my Journal, which was eventually to contain some of the same notions as in the book). Passages in *The Rules of Chaos* by Stephen Vizinczey (died August 2021) described my beliefs—reached independently years earlier—so well that I could have written his book myself. Such a resonant chance discovery occasions both grin and chagrin—the one because it's gratifying to come across someone who shares and so eloquently expresses my own views, the other because it's vexing to find out that another author so articulately expressed my thoughts and in ways better than can I.

The fate of this book presenting an adaptation of my Journal will most likely be the same as for the Vizinczey volume, by now obscure, largely forgotten and no doubt little read. Just as for him, long after my time perhaps a few lucky readers will chance to happen upon my book, eventually to be out of print, out of sight and forgotten. If perchance the Journal happens to inspire readers in the far future to communicate with the author, don't bother: your mail will be delivered to the dead letter office.

Chaos presents an extended meditation on how chance, luck, uncertainty and unpredictability operate as the ultimate factors which influence every humanimal's experiment in living. The author notes "that success is good luck and failure is misfortune." He explains the book's title by observing that "life is chaos not because there are no laws, but because there are innumerable laws and they are constantly in haphazard collision." A chaos of rules—as Vizinczey might have phrased it, but didn't—entangles every element of the play of infinite forms. Conditions are "continually changing as the situation expands with the recurrence and recombination of events. This haphazard interrelating is what we call chance." It's what's I call "a play of infinite forms"—a continuous whirligig of random whatevers, with no answers to why whatever happens or exists actually occurs or has assumed an earthly form.

After time yields the content which becomes the past the outcomes somehow seem rational and maybe even in a way inevitable, but in fact that which takes place or occupies a place as a form is almost entirely contingent. Although "in the past everything makes sense, everything appears logical ... when we consider an event in the light of other possibilities which did *not* materialize, when we think of some of the circumstances that could have produced quite contrary results ... we begin to sense how chancy the past was when it happened." Everything is in motion, constantly mutating. All the kinetic and random moving parts which activate the chance-driven play of infinite forms arise from the rules of chaos. Life keeps coming at you and at you, and night always falls on a different world.

Chaos rules, chance reigns, luck presides. There's no telling when, how and why (for sure, not why) luck—good or bad—operates. Some people have all the luck, others little or none. Whatever fatalistic force operates to distribute luck allocates it unevenly in capricious ways. Many humanimals who enjoy favorable outcomes seem to believe that those successes resulted from personal agency based on skill, intelligence, merit, persistence, hard work and other such self-referential characteristics. While those factors may play a part, in reality every earthing is primarily a child of chance.

The most astute and realistic winners realize that luck is the controlling factor, as described by John Cohen in *Chance, Skill, and Luck* (1960): "I suggest that all our decisions and predictions are guided or governed, implicitly if not explicitly, by what we imagine what luck and unluck might bring and not merely by cold-blooded 'objective' calculation." This view recognizes not only the influential role of luck but also that in the end not logic and rationality but intuition and instinct represent the main factors for almost all important decisions.

I carried out my experiment in living with the realization that no matter how well I analyzed, contemplated and calculated matters the results would depend primarily on such determining elements as luck and chance. Given that viewpoint, formal analysis based on mathematics, statistics, models, equations, abstract constructs and other theoretical sources—all as advocated by Warren Weaver in *Lady Luck: The Theory of Probability* (1963)—seemed to me of little value (apart from the fact that I didn't understand much of what he said), as two of luck's main characteristics are its improbability and its unpredictability. As such, luck resists most attempts to coax it to favor you or to prevent it from disfavoring you. Luck simply happens, and all too frequently Lady Luck behaves in an unlady-like way.

Although I respected and to a certain extent even feared the randomness of luck, at he same time I was interested in thoughts on *How to Attract Good Luck* (1952), as A.H.Z. Carr titled his book. His observations both confirmed some of my luck-seeking practices and introduced me to a few new ways to try to attract good luck. As Carr points out, the increasing complexities of the modern world (even 71 years ago when the book was published) have accentuated the influence of luck: "as a result of the expansion of the world's population and ever-faster means of communication and travel, the power of chance in our lives has been growing."

Discussing how to "expose ourselves" to luck, Carr notes that most good luck comes to us through other people and especially strangers. He advocates "unexpected friendliness" by reaching out to people. Such outreach, along with other elements useful to attract luck, originate from a zest for life which involves taking "an explorer's interest in the world we live in." In short, if you expose yourself to Lady Luck by becoming an active character participating in the play of infinite forms it will be easier for Her to find you. In *The Luck Factor* (2003), Richard Wiseman (by chance lucky enough to enjoy a marketable name as a sage) endorses the kind of outreach advocated by Carr. The "wise man" observes that extroverts eager to experiment are more likely to attract luck than are wall-flowers.

It seems that luck, like a humanimal, just comes and goes with no explanation possible for why each such creature or why good fortune exist. The terms of engagement which define an earthling's experiment in living feature chance and luck as primary factors in outcomes.

Failure to recognize and attempt to cope best as possible with that reality will produce less lucky results. But the rules of chaos make even the most diligent efforts to attract good luck ineffective. Even a "wise man" like the author of *The Luck Factor* can't explain the elusive and capricious operation of chance. Nor can chance or luck explain why a certain humanimal arbitrarily named "Richard Wiseman" happened to be incarnated into being on the lonely planet. Stuff happens and "There ain't any explanation," as wise guy Willie Stark said.

So vast and varied are the cosmic and even, in a more limited way, the terrestrial play of infinite forms, few of the specific elements which influence what happens and what exists can ever be known. Science explains some things, but not the reasons why the particular scientific principles which prevail on earth happened to have come into existence. Are the rules which govern science inevitable and invariable or could they have been otherwise in a parallel but quite different universe? For sure, on an individual scale any life might have been different based on how chance happened to operate on an earthling. As Leonard Mlodinow writes in *The Drunkard's Walk* (2008), not a biography of me but a commentary on "How Randomness Rules Our Lives": "in all except the simplest real-life endeavors unforeseeable or unpredictable forces cannot be avoided, and moreover those random forces and our reactions to them account for much of what constitutes our particular path in life."

Some people reach only late in life the belief that luck governs much of one's particular experiment in living. Those late-comers finally realize that luck rather than merit, effort or other such personal factor represents the main influence on outcomes. But like Eugene O'Kelly, who finally transformed his life only months before he died, failure to recognize the importance of luck until late in life will prevent you from trying to change your experiment in beneficial ways early enough to make a difference. In *Luck: What it means and Why it Matters* (2012), one-time cricket star Ed Smith confesses at the outset, "I am the least likely person to be writing a book about luck. For most of my life, I haven't believed in it at all." But Smith then came to realize that luck was "the most important idea I'd ever confronted," as no matter how hard you try to succeed luck is the main determining factor.

Arthur Miller's little-known and luckless 1944 play, *The Man Who Had All the Luck*, which closed after only four performances on Broadway, presents the story of David Beeves, a car mechanic in a small town who happens to enjoy a series of lucky happenings. But as his good luck continues, Beeves becomes ever more introspective and concludes that he doesn't deserve all his good fortune. His unlucky state of mind unsettles him, leaving the once favored character unable to enjoy the benefits chance happened to bring him. This version of regression to the mean—good luck followed by bad—perhaps suggests that Lady Luck is eventually succeeded by Miss-Fortune, a proposition which may be one of the main inevitable inconvenient unruly rules of chaos. The Lady and the Miss play leading (and sometimes misleading) roles in the play of infinite forms.

7. ... to End

An artful exit strategy applies to books as well as to venture capital investments and to a life. My Journal details some thoughts on how I pursued my experiment in living, as I saw that quite odd brief interlude between two nothings. Publication of a description in the form of my Journal detailing how I dealt with my unwilling chance presence on the lonely planet as a stranger in a strange land represents an effort to present some concluding observations as my earthly existence draws to a close.

My somewhat frequent references to mortality might suggest that I suffer from a life-threatening condition. For now—at my age a crucial modifier—only a few minor inconveniences afflict me, such as (for example) "*sinistra centrum piedi pendente naegel*," better known in plain rather than doctored English as a hangnail/center toe/left foot. But—like you and all humanimals—I do suffer from one terminal condition: I'm alive. Fetal is fatal: if it bleeds, it leaves; if it lives, it dies. The day I disappear night will really fall on a different world—but different only for me, not for a world indifferent to whether I exist or not. In any case, I won't know the difference as I'll be shrouded by the darkness of eternal nothing, not just the passing night.

Hopefully, those who survive me and also future generations not yet actors in the play of infinite forms will find something of value in this valedictory statement. But in no way is my Journal meant to serve as a *vade mecum*. My purpose is not didactic but only to describe how one soon to disappear humanimal coped during his brief existence with life on the lonely planet. My Journal meditations served me as a primer for life and a preparation for death; maybe this book will in the same way inform readers about such existential matters, but that's not my purpose.

Most readers, if there are any, will come across these pages, probably by chance, after my time. By then truly a ghost writer, I will be speaking to you from the grave. My fleeting form which once participated in the infinite play will have vanished and I'll be the late author, one whose experiment in living has become an experiment in non-being. That phase will no doubt be rather less challenging and more chance- and luck-free than my present tenuous state as a still living humanimal.

Just as I evoked and in a way momentarily revived many "lates" by quoting in this Introduction some passages from various defunct authors, so I hope that you'll spare a thought as you read these lines by their (soon to be) late author. That ex-humanimal will at the time you come across these words be comfortably installed safe and sound underground without a sound, forever immune to the ructions and cacophony of the world, the play of chance and luck, and the rules of chaos. Meanwhile, you remain sentient and a hostage to fortune. Unlike you (as least for now), no longer can I think outside the box I occupy or do anything at all outside my container. As a still living humanimal, with all the advantages and disadvantages of that state, you continue to retain a role in the play of forms. Which of the two states—mine or yours—is preferable? By now your opinion on the matter is the only one which counts as I don't count any more—or read, write, think, travel or anything. I'm now (postmortem) down for the count, senseless and not counted in any census or part of any consensus or dissents but just a discarded carcass. The play of infinite forms plays on without me.

As noted at the beginning of this book, A FORM OF INFINITE PLAY is a companion volume to my 2021 travel reminiscence, A PLAY OF INFINITE FORMS. Although I didn't consult the Journal to write the earlier book, both works include many of the same ideas and in that way a number of sinews and ligatures connect the texts of the two books. This Introduction serves to summarize some of the main beliefs and principles which appear in both books. Those ideas, common to the two volumes, formed my world-view which set the rules I used to deal with the rule of chaos.

I considered designating this companion volume to A PLAY OF INFINITE FORMS with the variant title AN INFINITE PLAY OF FORMS, as both the forms and their play are infinite. But I chose A FORM OF INFINITE PLAY to suggest how one particular individual happened to format his brief and soon to end passing experiment in living. Like each and every life, mine consisted of a form of play in the on-going terrestrial spectacle which plays on and on without us. The Journal presents a few fragmentary samples of how my specific form and its part within the infinite play of forms happened to develop.

As I hope the Journal reveals, my general procedure for the experiment entailed acting in the play as a character Roy Heath in his 1964 book called *The Reasonable Adventurer*. It's perhaps something of an anomaly to learn about how to live an adventurous life from writings rather than roamings out in the world. As Bronowski said, you can understand the world only by action, not by contemplation. Nonetheless, I found Heath's list of the six attributes of a "reasonable adventurer" quite useful: "intellectuality, close friendships, independence in value judgments, tolerance of ambiguity, breadth of interests, and sense of humor." Apart from omitting "close attention to Snoopy's profound wisdom," those six characteristics represent the ones I most aspired to adopt.

Although I tried to assume the attitude of a reasonable adventurer, as suggested by many of the Journal entries I was somewhat too rational, cautious and conservative to fully function in an adventurous mode. Wide-ranging adventure travel indeed brought me some of the benefits of an active worldly life, but at the same time my mentality remained too cerebral, logical and contemplative to allow me to profit completely from Heath's "the sanctity of the unexpected." In many ways I preferred the more likely—even if always subject to luck and chance—supposed certainty of the expected.

Looking back, I feel that my sense of adventure and pursuit of activism in conformance with Bronowski's aphorism were too tempered by caution. At times "if-ism" caused me to contemplate various courses of action with "if this, then that; if that, then this." This somewhat tentative attitude recalled the episode involving the Spartans whose ancient Lakonià homeland inspired the term "laconic." To Philip II of Macedon's threat, "For if I bring my army into your land, I will destroy your farms, slay your people and raze your city," the Spartans replied with the laconic response: "If."

My experiment in living was both graced and marred by my rationality. But of the two traits—too much thought or more impulsive behavior—the rational rather than the spontaneous suited me better and most often led to satisfactory results, so I saw no need to give up my tentative "if" format. My weighing of pros and cons in the nature of a cost-benefit analysis represented not analysis paralysis but decision precision. I analyzed not to dissect situations and theorize about them but to activate action. This thought process entailed an attempt to consider as many factors as possible relating to a situation or a decision before proceeding to shape how I would respond. Of course, certainty never comes calling. Incomplete, contradictory and ambiguous factors complicate most decisions as chaos rules more than do rules. I tried to avoid reacting in a spontaneous and unmeditated way to what chance happened to confront me with, a protocol usually unavailable during helter-skelter on-the-fly adventure travel, which is no doubt one reason why I chose to pursue such an activity. In the end, when a choice must or should be made, subjective trace elements like instinct, intuition and gut feelings take over. At that point I tried not to let the courage of my convictions suffer from the discouragement of my doubts.

Recognizing the influence of the rules of chaos enabled me better to cope with the iffy nature of existence. L-if-e inevitably includes "if." Similarly, ti-me—both life-giving and toxic—includes "me," just as I'm always in the middle of "dy-i-ng." Inherent in those words is the truth that an experiment in living represents an extremely tenuous, problematical and if-suffused state. Life on the lonely planet is a casino where the spin of the roulette wheel mimics the spin of the earth.

My sometimes too provisional and tentative mentality permeated not only how I acted but also what I thought. At this advanced st/age and page (one of my last, but not lasting) my experiment concludes with no proof of concept or proof of much of anything else. A question mark punctuates the strange and puzzling experience of being by chance incarnated as a humanimal to exist briefly on the truly odd lonely planet, spinning on and on in a mechanical and insensate cosmos. A "who knows?" or "maybe this" or "perhaps that" characterized my tenuous attitudes, much as how in the late nineteenth century the prominent Feilding family, a clan which included the Earldom of Denbigh title, suppressed their dubious claim of kinship with the Imperial House of Hapsburg by calling themselves "Perhapsburgs." So it was that I thought of myself as a "maybeing"—a Doubting Thomas certain only of uncertainty, with just about everything for me a "perhaps."

My far-ranging travels allowed me to supplement my conservative mind-set with a more spirited attitude by helping me to un-set my otherwise cautious behavior. It was precisely for that reason that in my early thirties, when I began this Journal, I decided to add to my experiment occasional journeys to exotic far lands. This enabled me to enliven my settled, routine and comfortable provincial suburban home life with a dash of—and to—some iffy experiences beyond my comfort zone. I sought a discomfort zone which would bring me some "rational adventurer" experiences, all the while maintaining my ties and roots back on my native turf where I was rather unadventurous. Some of my trips (described in A PLAY OF INFINITE FORMS) took me to places so unsettled, dangerous and challenging that in some ways I became an unreasonable adventurer, with chances and risks beyond the realm of reasonable behavior.

My travels operated to get me out into the big wide world, a practice which can help to attract luck. This reflected Goethe's remedy for "if-ism" which advocated activating engagement with the world to get the ball (or the suitcase) rolling and set in motion the wheel of chance so as to facilitate the operation of luck. This activism would bring about chance random events and other capricious influences which might (but might not) enhance your experiment in living. "The moment one definitively commits oneself," Goethe wrote, "then providence moves too. All sorts of things occur to help one that would never otherwise have occurred. A whole stream of events issues from the decision." Whether you'll sink or swim in the stream is unknowable in advance. All you can do is jump in, and leave the rest to the tides of chance and the tugs of luck.

I reasoned out how to act as a reasonable adventurer mainly by referring to my experience and also by reading as wide-ranging, but less informative, as my wide-ranging travels. To establish my operative principles I remained largely immune to the opinions and views of such characters as politicians, professionals and "experts" in non-science fields, social "scientists," advisers, wealth managers, economists, fortune tellers, astrologers, academics, commentators and other supposedly authoritative figures. Such figures didn't figure in my reasoning. I endorsed Charles Kane's attitude in "Citizen Kane," when he responded to a collection truck driver's comment that there was nothing to pick up at the *New York Inquirer* building by scolding the man, "You're getting paid for opinions or for hauling?" No gracious *gracias* or "you may be right" from thankless Charlie, whose comment was probably right.

A few outside opinions I sought from trusted, well-informed and astute friends I greatly treasured, but almost all other professed beliefs I disdained. Because there was so much of the noisome substance around I equipped myself with what Ernest Hemingway called a bullshit detector. *Calling Bullshit: The Art of Skepticism in a Data-Driven World* (2020) by Carl Bergstrom and Jevin West offers a primer on assessing doubtful claims based on false data. Of course, many opinions are based on no data at all. But in a random world saturated with chance and luck, both good and bad, and in which the rules of chaos rule and the only certainty is uncertainty, humanimals crave guidance and some rules to help find their way through the chaos. Lots of luck finding such help from advisers and "experts."I never did.

So great is the demand for guidance there's always a large supply of the mostly useless stuff, a bull market in bullshit. Reducing the noxious excretions would be both mentally and environmentally beneficial, but that's about as likely as limiting the methane burps cattle produce. Bullshit receptivity—the propensity to find supposedly productive advice in useless statements—attracts many people looking for answers. Bullshit became a kind of accepted academic concept (for whatever that's worth) after Princeton University Press published in 2005 Princeton University philosophy professor Harry G. Frankfurt's *On Bullshit*, so making P.U. a leading center of the bullshit movement. Frankfurt distinguishes that malodorous category of misinformation from other types. It was gratifying for me to learn that at least one academic recognized and wrote about bullshit rather than just professing it, as so many of his colleagues do.

Many of my Journal entries represent the self-discovered bullshit-free beliefs and principles which enabled me to function without seeking or relying on outside opinions. In that way the Journal contains my rules to help mitigate the rules of chaos. Looking back now as a senior senior citizen, I can see that most of my views stood the test of time as over the years they worked well to guide my way. Revisiting the Journal toward the end of my life to prepare it for publication contradicted Marcus Aurelius's belief that "you are not likely to read your notebooks or your deeds of ancient Rome and Greece or your extracts from their writings, which you laid up against old age." My enterprise in adapting the Journal for publication has for a time served as a welcome companion in my old age by bringing me a pleasing retrospective perspective on my now largely concluded experiment. As noted by yet another early-day sage, the seventeenth century Jesuit Baltsar Gracian, "It is dangerous to undertake something when you doubt its wisdom. It would be safer not to act at all. " I didn't doubt the wisdom of the project but was concerned if enough time remained for me to complete the job.

I never envisioned that one day I would prepare the Journal for publication. For more than 50 years the notebooks reposed unread in my files. I viewed the Journal as a private dialogue with myself, a kind of interior monologue, an "inspoken" rather than an outspoken document. Presenting the material (as adapted from the Journal) to the public doesn't change the nature of the entries, which were meant not for dissemination but only to preserve in writing for my own purposes memories of some fleeting fragments of my experiment. I somehow felt that it would be rather useless to let it all go to waste and disappear when I did.

Although readers who access my Journal are in effect eavesdropping on a private conversation, some observers believe that anyone who writes a journal or a diary secretly hopes that it will be published someday, and they may be right. In *A Book of One's Own* (1984), Thomas Mallon maintains that "no one ever kept a diary for just himself." But that view seems to belie the title of his book, as once you start writing a journal or diary for other readers the book no longer remains "a book of one's own." In fact, I did maintain the Journal for just myself. Now, publishing the material, it doesn't remain a book of my own, although some readers may wish that it had.

After having produced a few million published words, I now conclude my final writings as I draft this Introduction after completing work on the Journal. I've lived my life and had my say. The bottom line below represents not only the end of my writing but also the approaching end of my earthly existence. When an experiment is over, the investigator shuts down all the moving parts and dismantles the set-up. Why should it be different for an experiment in living? Once completed, no longer does the experimenter need a body. Still a home-body for my short remaining time, one day soon I'll be just a disused defunct body, the late "what's-his-name?" as I lie inert on the floor of my long-time former home where once I lived. Late? That will hardly describe my postmortem state when I won't only be late but an eternal no-show, never again to participate in the on-going play of infinite forms.

Although I can't know how much time remains for me, whatever measure I use—day, week, month, year—each passing unit represents a very large proportion of what's left. The world I came to know—came to involuntarily, unwillingly cast into existence as is every hum-animal—is for me beginning to end. Before long my consciousness will be severed from the outside world. I will then, finally and eternally, be an insensate ex-animal like the stuffed animal specimens at the Museum of Natural History. But there is really no natural format or reason for anything—only strange visions and odd unnatural mutating random forms as the play of infinite forms keeps playing. The world, the universe, the cosmos—it's all too vertiginous to absorb or to comprehend. I never did. After my time night will continue to fall on a different world, but no longer will I be a hostage to time, chance, luck and the rules of chaos. For me the darkness will be perpetual.

Kenkō, the fourteenth century Kyoto Japanese monk, begins his *Essays in Idleness*, "what strange folly, to beguile the tedious hours like this all day before my ink stone, jotting down at random idle thoughts that cross my mind." So it was that for more than half a century I similarly entered thoughts idle and otherwise into my Journal, using a pen rather than an ink stone. In a way, that habit indeed seems a "strange folly." But somehow I suddenly began the Journal and now the folly nears its end, as does my earthly existence. Kenkō notes that "In all things, the beginning and the end are the most engaging." Now, here at the end, I'm disengaging.

In *Dandelion Wine* (1957), Ray Bradbury's fictionalized account of a Midwestern teenage boy in the summer of 1928, the author says that the "wine metaphor" represents his store of images from which he tried to open "the memories out and see what they had to offer." At the end of the first brief section, "Summer 1928 began." At summer's end, days and pages later, the season and the book come to a close as "the town winked out its lights, sleepily, here, there, as the courthouse clock struck ten, ten-thirty, eleven, and drowsy midnight." Time was running out as night fell on a different world, and finally the boy "sleeping, put an end to summer, 1928."

The delights and lights of my experiment in living will soon wink out. I now end this Introduction, here become Conclusion. To finish in the most artful way I can, I adopt the ending solution of Oxford scholar Robert Burton, who in "The Conclusion of the Author to the Reader" in the last lines of *The Anatomy of Melancholy* (perhaps better titled "The Melancholy of Anatomy") writes: "From my Study in Christ Church, Oxon. December 5, 1620," and to the reader he bids "Farewell & be kind."

From my suburban house in the heart of America's heartland,
Labor Day, September 5, 2022
Farewell & be kind.

JOURNAL 1969–2022

~PART ONE~
EARLY YEARS

I. Beginning Entries: 1969–October 1971

The Journal I began on an unknown day in 1969, rather like spontaneous combustion. The urge to start recording my passing thoughts suddenly came over me. Before then my life was a blank as far as preserving any of my transient sensory impressions because they simply passed through my mind momentarily and then disappeared. My new—and, as I soon learned, compulsive—habit no doubt originated in part because as of the beginning of that year I'd restructured my way of being by abandoning my professional life to embark on a new format which would include far-ranging foreign adventure travel. My thought-provoking change and the time it freed up both played a part in inspiring me to begin a journal.

At the time in my early thirties, I also realized that unless I made an effort to capture on the fly a few of the evanescent thoughts which from time to time happened to come to my attention they would vanish without a trace, a fate which unsettled me. I felt it would be useless to go through the process of existing briefly as a terrestrial humanimal here on the lonely planet without capturing any of the quickly passing impressions or ideas I noticed. Most lives slip away day-to-day like that, momentary awareness lost and irretrievable. The Journal allowed me to avoid that destruction of life experiences and served to preserve a few fragments of what comprised my experiment in living. I didn't want to carry out that experiment without a little something to show for it. My Journal, my travel diaries and my other writings serve as that "something."

In the early years rather few entries preserved my random observations which in later years became longer and more frequent, adding to the amount, if not the quality, of the material. It seems that as I got older, but perhaps not wiser, I became more verbose, as if age intensified my urge to convert thought to page. However, I've spared readers excess verbiage by condensing the original entries, eliminating repetitious ones, and omitting many passages by selecting and rewriting only the material I thought worthy of inclusion.

In returning to the entries more than half a century after beginning the Journal to prepare the material for publication it struck me as strange that someone so conscious of time failed to note the day when I began the enterprise. I later remedied that kind of omission and began recording the month and, soon after, then the specific day of each entry. The dateless sporadic opening items included topics and attitudes which continued to feature over the years in later Journal entries, such as: word-play; an "expert"-averse skeptical mentality; paradox; mini-philosophical observations; thoughts on mortality; the influence of randomness and luck; time consciousness; an eccentric way of looking at things; inverting commonly-held opinions and received wisdom. Here's how it all began:

1969

"Overlook" vs. "oversee": similar, but opposite. A more limp leg means less leg limp. A cheap product can be expensive if it fails to function properly. The maddening (for learners of the language) prepositional endings in English: "closing up" and "closing down," "burning up and burning down" and all too many others [as detailed later in the Journal with entries as those in October 2005, January 2010, and March 2022]. "Project your feelings"—could that mean to "screen them"? To a restaurant cashier who replaces another at the cash register: "A changing of the guard?" She replies, "No, a guarding of the change."

The problem (or terror) of life: that it is cumulative.

Those most removed from life are the most philosophical about it. Everyone else just lives it.

I pass a sidewalk artist scratching out chalk drawings; on the way back later I see that rain has washed them all away.

A neon sign at a flop-house hotel near Times Square flashing "TRANSIENTS": so are we all.

Do the workers who change the days and dates on *The New York Times* every day perceive time's incessant rhythm more vividly than do other people?

A photograph really doesn't hold the past: it reminds us that the past can't be held.

Could a person's behavior be considered normal and customary in one society but insane in another culture?

The only universal constant in the world: for traffic everywhere green signals go and red means stop.

In modern life the over-developed means of communication have led to a decrease in understanding.

In 1968 there were on average 322,000,000 daily phone conversations. "Since 1959, while population has increased 13 percent, telephones have increased over 50 percent and long distance messages have more than doubled." One of the most beneficial developments in the modern world is improved communication, and one of the most pernicious is over-communication.

Life lessons which bring regrets are useful, as regrets serve as lessons.

Being alone in a big city is not all bad, as it means you're free to follow your own agenda.

Death is not only a taking but also a deliverance.

Death is useful as it brings to life an orderly structure—a beginning and an end. Without death the benefits of closure—desirable in other matters—wouldn't be available.

Both the past and the future are in different ways absolutes. Nothing can change what's already occurred, and what might occur remains absolutely unknowable.

Echo is a sound shadow.

Why do people avoid taking the top newspaper stacked in a rack? Buyers often pull out a copy below the top. Is this because the papers below are somehow deemed more pristine than the top copy which passing readers may have glanced at and somehow degraded?

One of the most meaningful and satisfying phrases in conversation is "Do you remember when ...?" The words indicate that with the listener you have some common memories and enjoy continuity of the relationship.

View of a face through a transparent disc shows the image perfectly proportioned, but as the angle shifts the face becomes distorted: cheap glasses. Is this a metaphor for how perceptions blur as our sensory perceptions perceive the constantly changing kinetic outside world?

Enjoying the ability to choose can at times cause anxiety, but it would be foolish to give up the freedom of choice in order to eliminate the possible anxiety.

A person's freedom and independence is disturbing to many less fortunate people, as the ability to shape one's life implies possibilities and benefits unavailable to others.

Recall Wren's profusion of drawings for projects which could have but never did develop in place and time. Such contingency also applies to how the world developed as from its original conditions when everything remained only potential and possibility. For the most part random forces influenced what happened to evolve into the world we know.

Pain and suffering of others brings two reactions in those who observe the problems: their effect on the sufferer and a realization that the same sort of ailments could also afflict the observer.

In a billion years or so, give or take a few million, after the current version of human life on earth is long extinct, there evolves a new form of sentient life. Would an alternate format for sensory organs create the ability of the new-model beings to perceive and organize terrestrial phenomena in ways different from how we now experience existence? If so, that would for better or worse create an alternate and perhaps more comprehensible reality of life on earth.

In my thirties I came to the realization that the dogmas, beliefs, professed wisdom, received doctrines, supposedly authoritative pronouncements for the most part represented only opinions, not truths. As such, many commonly-held beliefs failed to provide any valid lessons for life. At one point in the early Journal, I entered at three different places the following quotations which reflected my disdain for purported authoritative sources:

Tolstoy—"What do I care whether Christ is risen! Is he risen? Well, God be with Him! What I care about is to find out what I must do, how I must live!"

Thomas Hardy in *The Old Woman*—When Rhoda Nunn leaves her husband Phillotson and quotes John Stuart Mill, he replies, "What do I care about J. S. Mill. I only want to live a quiet life."

Henry (as the Frenchman spelled his name) de Montherlant in Pity for Women—"What do I care about Goethe ..."

Abstract views and philosophical generalizations often suffer from failure to offer guidance on how to live. Sooner or later you have to consider proscriptive rather than merely descriptive formulations. Although writers of the absurd accurately describe the nature of things, awareness of absurdity doesn't suffice to guide you how best to cope with with it.

Many and perhaps even most decisions which seem wrong, because their disadvantages are obvious, may in fact be better that what another choice may have brought.

Although I never brooded in a melancholy mode about the challenge of creating a satisfactory experiment in living, I did try to recognize the many rather gloomy realities which pertained to conditions here on the lonely planet. The Journal contains frequent entries relating to my attempts to settle on how to live during what I viewed as a very brief interlude in a quite strange, baffling and perplexing context. The following four existential contemplations illustrate my early-day thoughts on ways to cope with how to proceed with my terrestrial experiment.

Death isn't the worst misfortune as life needn't be preserved at all costs. Many compromises, discomforts and inconveniences are necessary to remain alive. Existence has no absolute value; what you do with it represents the meaningful element. The quality of life ranks almost equally with the fact of life—"almost," as being thrown unwillingly into existence is a necessary precedent for what follows. Being born, however, is just for openers—table stakes which guarantee nothing. A man can't create his life and become the son of his acts (as Don Quixote said) if he hasn't first been incarnated to father his acts. But mere existence, in and of itself, isn't necessarily an absolute benefit and doesn't always produce a satisfactory outcome. But what does? Such is the question whose answer I'm exploring.

The idea of seeking happiness seems in a way strange. If found, happiness will eventually come to an end, leaving you to regret its disappearance, a regret perhaps even more unpleasant than never having found happiness to begin with.

The objective and the subjective defines how all people exist. Everyone is alike but each person experiences the world from his or her own individual subjective perspective. For Quixote a windmill seems an adversary; for Sancho Panza it's a windmill. What exists in the outside word represents reality and the nature of things: the moon is the moon. But the perceived and received sensory impressions often mean different things to different people. Does one say in Japanese, "Now it's time to go to bed" where you sleep not on a bed but on a tatami mat? In Japan you'd probably say, "I'm going to sleep." How you respond to raw sensory impressions indicates if you accept and relate to the outside world as given or if you process the impressions to try to reconfigure what comes to you in order better to pursue your experiment in living. I'm attempting to think about the nature of things, not just to take them for granted.

The death of a person close to us is more significant than our own. Loss of an intimate prods us into questioning our own existence and trying to make some sense out of it. Our own death merely extinguishes us with no further consequences, so there's nothing further to be worried about. Were it not for the death of others we observe, little else in life—if anything at all—would provoke us to become introspective and contemplate how to carry out our own life. In that way, mortality serves a valuable purpose.

You give it away, but it's still yours; you guard it carefully but others get it; it belongs to you but other people use it; there's only one but many possess it. What other paradoxes apply to one's signature?

Our willingness to adopt alternative ways of life is based on the extent to which we refuse to take the pre-existing conditions for granted.

Imagine someone who seemingly takes photos but without film in the camera. Why? Perhaps such carefully composed views helps the would-be photographer to organize what he sees, even without the benefit of recording the scenes on film.

Wet wheels of a moving baby carriage leave two tracks which quickly disappear: image of the baby's life ahead.

1971

By now the home-based Journal advanced to 1971 with no entries in 1970 as I spent the entire year in Europe, including some months at the Sorbonne in Paris, followed by studies at the University of Vienna. The following entry no doubt originated during my stay in Paris.

In the Luxembourg Gardens in Paris a child climbs up a few steps only to have his mother pull him back to where he began: image of the child's life ahead.

To a Swedish girl I met I said, "Your affair with a married man isn't a new story," to which she replied, "It is for me."

A toilet paper roll plays "Whistle While You Work" as you unwind it.

A person who dies violently by trauma or by performing a daring dangerous feat is killed by life, not by time. He dies—perhaps just as well—before something inside him eventually bursts, snaps, cracks, stops, fragments, clogs, closes or opens, deteriorates or otherwise fails. Whether by external accident or internal failure, same result in the end—just a different and more desirable way of getting there if your demise is sudden and quick.

Both conceiving a child and conceiving and creating a work of art produce public evidence of what began as a private personal act.

A writer is asking someone he doesn't know, the reader, to give the author some of the stranger's limited time and energy. The writer's challenge is to offer in return something of value to the anonymous reader.

Writing, and all art, is an attempt to make rational the irrational, which then becomes ordered, controlled and arranged into a comprehensible format—but only an arbitrary construct which scarcely compensates for or explains the confusions out in the world.

Sports provide the clarity of a binary outcome. Once a winner is declared, no ambiguity remains—a certainty which contrasts with most of the rest of life.

English speakers seldom realize how difficult their native language is. What seems so simple and natural those who learn English from their early years tortures foreign students with such inexplicable oddities as how to pronounce "police" and "lice," "plague" and "ague."

Imagine a person so fastidious that he hesitates and agonizes over which sardine in a can to choose to consume.

Coleridge's idea that man's fall from grace offers an explanation for the otherwise inexplicable phenomenon of human existence as it is seems much too grandiose. Although the Fall from Edenic conditions into a world of sin and sorrow might explain something about the terrestrial situation, more specific and telling are the series of individual falls faced by everyone thrown into existence as they progress through life and on to the end. From the purity of childhood on to youth and then into adulthood and continuing on through the years, a humananimal faces a gradual decline from the creature's prelapsarian innocence to a realization of how things really are. This kind of downward path through life stages seems more useful to explain human nature and the prevailing conditions than does the myth of humanity's fall from grace.

The Creator—whatever that force was or is—happened to create a world in which dwell reasoning, feeling, thinking animals unable to comprehend their world. That all-powerful force which engendered the strange terrestrial system might have chosen any number of more user-friendly formats which would allow humans to understand their situation. Maybe such a better system exists elsewhere, but for sure not here.

In his *Notebook V*, Albert Camus wrote, "God himself, if He exists, can't change the past." But maybe He, She or It can annul it. In Lewis Carroll's *Sylvie and Bruno* a magic watch is able to wipe out an hour and restart it. It seems likely that what the presiding creative force happened to produce as a cosmos represents a failed experiment, one fated eventually to disappear. This will offer the opportunity for another attempt at creating a better world, a development which won't change the past but would in effect eliminate it by bringing about a new version of reality.

Love in a way resembles death, as both serve to get you out of yourself.

The more the "I" dominates your perspective, the greater the loss when the I-ndividual vanishes from view. Transcending one's self represents a more realistic and desirable way of looking at things, as the world beyond your own individual being is much more interesting and enriching. If you don't transcend your own very limited life and get beyond yourself, death will do the job without your having experienced much of life.

Searching for some fixed points in life, each person rapidly spins through time and at the same time everything around us is in motion. But eventually each humanimal will find stability as eternal stasis will deliver to every such creature a fixed position in time immune to chance. Meanwhile, the cosmos will continue on in its usual kinetic insensate way.

Even the unfortunates who live in poverty and misery with their existence marred by hopelessness, ugliness, oppression don't view death as a deliverance. The possible terrors and mysteries of non-existence far exceed any difficulties which afflict the living.

Although we take for granted who our friends and contemporaries are, it's quite odd that we all happen to live at the same time, and in some cases at the same place. It may seem quite natural that the particular individuals we know represent the inevitable cast of characters in our life. But in fact only mere chance determined just who would be alive when we are and would feature in our equally arbitrary time and place of existence.

The advantage of starting to write at an older age: you no longer look at the world as if words can actually represent it. The disadvantage: less time for you to produce your writings.

As you gradually grow old for a long time you believe that you're younger than you really are. But toward the end you start to feel older than your actual age.

In a book about the Quartier Saint-Germain in Paris I bought there years ago appears the name Franz Punkenofer-Tuba, an "*artiste paintre.*" Such a name is truly more fanciful and suggestive than any used for a fictional character. I wonder if the France Franz faced problems getting his name properly entered on official documents.

For most happenings and situations it's useless to address the "why" of the matter. The only worthwhile factors are the "what" (what the conditions actually are) and the "how" (how to proceed, given the prevailing condition).

During the year 1970 when I was in Europe I made no entries in the Journal. Not long after I resumed the Journal when back home I started to include the month of the entries. I later also added the date of each entry, but in the book have included only the month and year, not the day.

APRIL 1971

Like a child, a writer sees things in a different way.

Writing a book is like walking a dog. The animal sniffs at different possibilities, scratches around to prepare the ground, spins his tail (tale), does his business and then, when finished, moves on to the next plot. Such is the procedure of a writing animal.

Style no more makes the book than clothes the man. Hitler wearing a Brooks Brothers suit remains a well-tailored brown-shirted monster. A terrible text clothed in an elegant style doesn't drape the contents with a garment which improves the material.

Some writers specify that a particular work or works are those "by which I wish to be remembered." But writing is a way to live, not a way to be remembered. In most cases no author's writings will be remembered. Of the millions of aspirants who hope to enjoy some postmortem fame through their words almost none of the scribblers manage to achieve such immortality. But perhaps they enjoyed the premortem pleasures of a creative life.

One reason people write is because they are unable to live that which they choose to write about.

I write to learn, not to teach.

An arranged estrangement is a strange arrangement.

A suitor makes a flinging pass in hopes of a passing fling.

JUNE 1971

A writer is someone who notices too much by absorbing a large number of sensory impressions which he's unable to contain, and so divests them by putting the excess into his writings.

The archaic era: clueless. The pre-scientific era of religion: other-worldly and too remote from man. The scientific age: too worldly and limited only to verifiable natural phenomena. The age of humanism: too focused on each individual. Conclusion: no general closed doctrine or general description to define civilization, society and the culture is entirely satisfactory.

In France, those who control Paris and just a few of the country's institutions based there control the country. The pluralistic federal system in the United States where authority is more decentralized and less rigid and dirigist from the center is seemingly more prone to social disorder. Under which system—the centralized or the more permissive—is revolution more likely?

Schopenhauer raises the interesting question of who the word "person"—from "persona," a mask—designates: an individual as perceived by others or someone hidden as if wearing a mask. Freud's emphasis on the ego behind the mask seems to assume that one can understand and explain a person's true personality, while Jung views an individual more as an enigmatic masked character who behind the facade is a mercurial ever-changing figure not subject to a fixed identity or analysis. I have no opinion, as I leave it to others to pronounce on such indeterminate matters.

JULY 1971

Someone told me the following story: "I once met a man in Africa who said he knew a place where the lion and the lamb co-existed near one another, and where the birds never flew away at the sight or scent of a human, and where crocodiles or alligators presented no threat to people. When I asked where this idyllic paradise might be, the man said that it was the Basel zoo where he was an animal keeper. He was in Africa on vacation."

A label on a can of succotash boasts that the corn and the lima beans were "carefully mixed in the right proportions to create a perfect blend of flavors." This is probably the closest we can come in this flawed world to perfection. Everything else falls short.

By now the only originality in art is the process of creation itself, which is new to the creator. An author's works may offer him some new insights, but not the world.

In life the stakes are so low why do we play the game, which in the end we are sure to lose?

One difference in how Americans and Europeans view history relates to the uses of the past. In America places like Mystic Seaport, Monticello, Williamsburg are seen as historical curiosities as if fossilized relics. In Europe history seems more a living presence present in contemporary life. In Rome people still live in the Marcellus Amphitheater in Rome, and in Cairo's main cemetery residents occupy some of the tombs and mausoleums.

Many machines are both labor and time saving. But what do people do with their left-over energy and time? A lot of what's saved is spent in frivolous activities.

Beethoven deaf, Borges blind—but why not the reverse? Humans suffer enough random unfortunate problems without fate introducing even more perverse misfortunes.

Which is preferable: writers who think or thinkers who write? Or neither?

Forms are structured but arbitrary; content is flexible but unstable. Neither satisfies the human longing for order—something firm, fixed and meaningful in a cosmos churning with change. Putting passing events into a form—such as religion, political or social theories, models, philosophical systems, or similar artificial constructs—to attempt to structure and make sense of the flow simply confines the random heterogeneous phenomena to invalid categories. Forms may offer a kind of arbitrary structure but one which doesn't fully reflect reality. Formless random and evanescent passing sensory impressions, too amorphous and fleeting to enable earthlings to format reality into comprehensible categories, doom humans to a permanent state of being baffled by their strange and inexplicable existence in a remote corner of the cosmos.

The quantity of pleasant solitude you can enjoy is in part limited by the number, frequency and type of claims on you from people entitled to make such demands.

Moderate expectations are more likely to result in satisfactory outcomes than exaggerated hopes. One example is the test of a good marriage. If, before the ceremony, you realistically envision the prospective spouse as he or she in fact turns out to be after a few years of marriage, then the relationship has been successful and you're not disappointed.

Suicide is in most cases ridiculous because it means that you've taken life seriously enough to destroy it. With patience nature will in any case do the job for you.

It's difficult to get used to the idea that mortality means the world will continue on without me. But it will. It's difficult to imagine that the world existed before me. But it did.

A life is not lived in paragraphs or chapters, and so recording an account of existence in that orderly literary way simply represents a bookish attempt to bring some structure to what otherwise is a random chaotic clutter of sensory impressions. The real purpose of writing a book is not to benefit the outside world but to help the author order and understand, in so far as possible, his own life.

Sealing the envelope containing a letter creates a strong sense of closure. Mailing it brings finality.

The modern age is one in which bullshit has become acceptable, respectable and its content deemed significant. Even the mere odor has its admirers.

Anything as common and ubiquitous as engendering a child violates the principle that the more scarce the supply the greater its value.

The world and all in it, including the humans who perceive the place, seems an insubstantial shadow play, to which mankind adds a miasma of beliefs, doctrines and practices in a useless attempt to understand the strange planet.

OCTOBER 1971

To produce a creative work implies that the world lacks something which might be beneficial. But both nature and mankind have run rampant, creating a chaos of worldly content which continues to mutate and to proliferate. Since more than enough of everything (except maybe common sense) already exists there's really no need to create anything else. The ambient plenitude suffices. The only justification for new written works is to satisfy an author's wish to organize some of his chaotic sensory impressions into something of a comprehensible, but arbitrary, imposed format.

Imagine the case of a German Jew who fled his native land in the 1930s to settle in another country, where he feels deracinated. After the war he returns to live in Germany, explaining that he lacks roots in the new land to which he emigrated. Which is preferable: returning to your roots in toxic soil or remaining in an untainted place where you have no roots? The choice represents choosing between the rational and the emotional.

Without time, life would be dull and lacking in urgency and drama. With time, life is exhilarating but too urgent and dramatic.

It was both a curse and a blessing for Camus to be born a Frenchman. A curse because he thought it was worth the time, effort and energy to attack religion. Why bother? No realistic or logical person takes religious doctrines seriously. But being a Frenchman also blessed Camus, as his formation in the best French rational tradition enabled him to address in a logical way the irrationality of the world and its human life.

People speak of a writer's freedom. Precisely the opposite is true. His incubus is that he's always on the job, observing and absorbing and trying to make some sense of the chaos of sensory impressions which happen to reach him. It's that compulsion to comprehend which compels people to write.

The world's great writers have depleted nearly all that can be usefully said, which is precisely why they're great.

Both fiction and non-fiction are the same in that each seeks to present a convincing narrative. But the former requires a willing suspension of disbelief, while the latter depends on persuasion based not on belief but on evidence.

Had Christ not been born, from what event would religious believers who adopted Christianity date the years? Same question for Muslims, who date their era from Mohammad.

Some thinkers (among them Pascal and Coleridge) say that only Original Sin and the Fall of Man can explain the human situation. If so, it's a paradox that such a truly damaging and irredeemable flaw of creation comes with the great benefit of making life comprehensible. The paradox is easily resolved by refusing to believe in the explanation.

At a recent meal a spider-like mushroom was entangled in the pasta strands web.

Your friends and acquaintances who don't know one another and who will never meet exist together only in the nexus between them all in your mind. You know everyone but each has no knowledge of the others. As the only link between them you represent the organizing consciousness of a category which is meaningless to anyone but yourself.

From the outside world we take nourishment in the form of food, liquids and oxygen. all of which become part of us. Into the world we deposit bodily waste products, children and our corpse. Would that be considered a fair exchange?

All creative people are somewhat eccentric, ideally a functional and productive sort oi eccentricity. Only the reaction to the creations from the outside world can assess how much the oddity of creators has managed to produce practical and useful works.

A sense of justice is too seldom accompanied by a sense of its limits.

II. Home Thoughts Between Far Travels: April 1972-April 1974

A Journal entry for April 1972 reads "back from my trip. Same walls, books, objects around me—as if I were never away." As I was away from November 1971 to April 1972 there were no Journal entries during that period. During those five months I took the first of my three five-month-long trips. The first one took me all through South America; the second over the winter of 1972 to spring 1973 to North Africa and the Middle East; the third in late 1973 to April 1974 to the Far East. While I was away, the Journal back at home remained empty of new entries. With the three long trips covering most of the countries in each region I initiated and began to carry out my plan to see as much of the world as possible. Many later journeys to far lands continued to help fulfill my goal, but none of those subsequent travel adventures lasted more than a month or so. Although I made no Journal entries during the intervals away from home, I kept detailed travel diaries recording almost everything I saw and what happened each day. My experiences on the trips influenced what later appeared in the Journal, creating a synergistic relationship between my worldly adventures and my later home thoughts inspired my adventures. The outside world, rather than internalized self-oriented considerations, nourished many of the entries which appear in the Journal.

APRIL 1972

A trio of English language subtleties (three of all too many): (1) "I'm tired of walking" versus"I'm tired from walking." (2) The difference between "tasty" and "tasteful." (3) The difference between "self-service" and "self-serving."

In under-developed societies water jugs represent primitive attempts to control the future, for the vessels hold what otherwise would flow away and pass into the past. Storage of water to provide on-demand piped access to it deals with present availability, not a future one. Always-on electricity currently available eliminates the need for its storage in batteries. In some ways advanced countries live more in the "now" than do less-developed lands.

If any object, concept or conceit can be turned into "art," then either everything is potentially art or nothing is.

The difference between being sensitive and being sentimental: sensitivity applies to a generalized feeling, while sentimentality relates to a particular person or specific situation.

In Italy people speaking on the phone often gesticulate or change their facial expressions in response to the conversation. What's the purpose of gestures unseen by the person being spoken to?

Gaucho Marx: a Jewish Argentine cowboy.

The animalistic passions which possess people in the acts of giving life and in taking it manifest the same basic human drives—power, control, energy, ecstasy.

"Make-up" applies both to art and to cosmetics, both of which are a falsification.

A medieval-type dialogue: "What do you do, my good man?" "I'm a jailer: after tying people up I confine them in the wooden frame." "I see—stocks and bonds."

MAY 1972
It's a minor but satisfying passing pleasure when you see a bird on the branch of a tree you've planted. When the bird takes wing the moment has passed, so reminding you of the evanescence of every lived experience. But I never needed to be reminded of that.

Exploring the curious Easter Island erections involves resurrection, while archaeological studies and excavations elsewhere are mere digs.

Each individual feels his defeats, disappointments and failures as one-of-a-kind happenings unique to him, but many commonly afflict all humans at one time or another.

A man goes on a hunger strike to protest against thousands of demonstrators on hunger strikes. Will he starve before his adversaries do?

The ideal strip-tease club: no cover, no minimum.

AUGUST 1972
Listening to a broadcast of Orson Welles's "The War of the Worlds" recalls what the electronic generation is missing: imagination, a faculty which has atrophied. With so much presented in the form of an image, little is left to the imagination. The audible but invisible broadcast of the "War" was more terrifying than if shown on TV or in a movie. Unfettered from prepared images, the mind of a radio listener conjures up scenes more vivid and frightening than the visions pictured by film or video.

SEPTEMBER 1972
The publicity of the press generates the press of publicity.

A farm scene: one farmer bales hay, another hails a bay.

As time goes by, happenstance congeals into circumstance; chance becomes factual; luck turns into reality.

A housewife who watches soap operas is subject to dishpan head.

Even a corny statement or joke evokes a kernel of truth.

Images of transience: (1) Mirror-shiny knife blades momentarily reflect slices of your face as you pass by the utensils. (2) Wind-blown leaves on trees casting moving shadows pattern a stream as it flows by below. (3) Across a white shirt hanging outside to dry play changing luminosities which seem to crease the cloth. (4) A breeze like an invisible hand passes over a dog's coat and ruffs the hairs. (5) From a tilted wing of a single-engine plane high in the sky the fading dusky early evening light glints as the setting sun fades away.

NOVEMBER 1972

Comparisons: A bad dream which returns is like an allergy. As empty as a losing candidate's post-election headquarters.

JULY 1973

What would a study analyzing humor as presented in *Punch*, *The New Yorker* and *Mad Magazine*, and *Le Canard Enchâiné* reveal about the national character of the English, the Americans, the French? What would comparing the appearance, operation, food service, hospitality, uniforms, room decor and other characteristic of hotels in London, New York and Paris reveal about those cities and national character?

AUGUST 1973

A textbook entitled "English Grammar and Spelling Made Easy": the pages are blank.

Passions possess us but, for a rational person, so do doubts about indulging our passions.

As you grow older choices seem to become more limited, but in fact the range of options retain the same variety and possibilities as when you were younger. What's different in old age is that the future in which a choice can make an impact, for better or worse, is foreshortened by the limited time which remains.

Being thrown unwillingly into existence is the ultimate invasion of privacy.

As Proust shows, you must retreat from the world to describe it, must shun reality to create an alternate version of it in writing, you must absent yourself from society to gain the presence of mind to write about the social scene, you become dead to the outside world to bring a story and its characters to life, you withdraw to draw portraits and vignettes in words. So you can't live and at the same time write and shouldn't live to write: you have to first live and then write.

It's fun to conceive a child, but it may not be much fun to raise the creature. Probably better to get a dog, as that kind of companion is more likely to bring you some fun. And the animal doesn't outgrow its clothes.

Everyone ages at the same speed but each at his own rate.

III. Entries While Writing: May 1974–December 1993

After my three five-month-long trips in the early 1970s to South America, the Middle East and the Far East I stayed more regularly in the Middle West, my natural habitat. I continued to travel, but somewhat less frequently and for shorter trips than those three earlier adventures or my year-long stay in Europe in 1970. Over the next 20 years I began, developed and concluded (until publishing A PLAY OF INFINITE FORMS in 2021) my professional writing career, which produced two novels, eight travel books, and some 170 travel articles for newspapers from coast to coast, from *The New York Times* to the *Los Angeles Times* and in such other papers as the *Chicago Tribune*, the *Kansas City Star*, the *Des Moines Register*, the *Memphis Commercial Appeal*, the *Atlanta Journal* and for 13 years a regular travel column in the Sunday *St. Louis Post-Dispatch*. Work on what became a few million published words produced in a relatively short period exerted on the Journal an effect similar to my trips, as during my writing years I wrote little in the notebooks. I put most of my thoughts into the books and articles rather than the Journal. But once liberated from the time-consuming and intense concentration necessary to produce the published works, in January 1994, which begins in section IV below, I turned to the Journal and recorded more frequent and longer entries. Even after putting aside my writing for publication, it seems that I still wanted to preserve some of my experiences and thoughts in a format which would retain the otherwise fleeting and mostly soon forgotten sensory impressions which happened to reach me.

MAY 1974

A money-spinner scam in an under-developed country: a vendor who sells expired lottery tickets to illiterates.

Two hints to enable you to understand a country: (1) Analyze a society based on its signs, both their style and content. They display a culture's values, problems, needs, wants, aesthetics. (2) Note the characteristics of what the locals put up—buildings, architecture, infrastructure—and what they put up with.

Fortunate is the writer who confines in his brain characters who can be paroled when he needs them for life sentences.

SEPTEMBER 1974

I have learned rather little from creative works about life, but from life I've learned something about creative works.

Fiction: evocative; non-fiction: provocative.

One indicator of the good society: people's aspirations are realistic and possibly achievable, and may result in useful and productive outcomes.

1975 (no month noted)
A woman so reclusive she makes Garbo look like an exhibitionist.

"Pants" designates a single garment, so why is the word not simply "pant" rather than seemingly plural with the "s"?

DECEMBER 1975
The hardest part of becoming a writer isn't the writing itself but to maintain the belief, or the pretense, necessary to persist. To begin and then continue to write in the face of the outside world's complete indifference requires tremendous will-power, which all too easily degrades into won't-power. No creative work is necessary other than to its creator, and sometimes not even then.

After the last entry just above, over the following four and one-half years the Journal contains less than a page of comments. I tried to explain the unusually long gap in the next Journal entry, the first after the December 1975 one above, the one just below dated July 27, 1980.

1980
Long time between notes. Why no flow of ideas? Perhaps being a published—and still publishing—author means that now in speaking to the world I needn't continue to speak to myself. My intensive and almost continuous writing along with my fairly frequent travels leaves little time for stray thoughts appropriate to record in the Journal.

At what point in the history of the world did it change so that more people had died than the ones currently alive?

Some English language twists and turns: (1) A well-worn garment versus one well worn. (2) To over-rule versus to rule over. (3) House work versus home work. (4) Farewell versus welfare. (5) She is well turned out, and turned out well. (6) To say "I'm stressed" means to be anxious or pressured; to be "distressed" is not to become free of stress but to be upset, afflicted, under stress or strain.

AUGUST 1981
Humans have imagined a vast range of beliefs, religions, nostrums, constructs, value systems, social practices, taboos, and other such often arbitrary formats, each meant to comfort, console, control or otherwise impose some order or to bring some meaning to mankind. Those artificial doctrines help keep poor earthlings, seeking some sort of structure, from falling into the abyss of meaningless, even though the imposed systems themselves for the most part lack meaning.

A paradox: both husband and wife are physicians.

A doctor recommends that a male patient give up sex to preserve his health, to which the patient replies that he'd prefer to die happy.

One's success in life depends not on how the outside world judges the way you live but only how each person evaluates for himself how things turned out for him. An honest and objective judgment based on your aspirations, standards, interests and values, and including consideration of your particular circumstances and conditions, form the proper basis for your self-assessment.

It's an oddity that adding an "e" to "Jo" turns the feminine version of the name into the masculine one. Are there any other examples of converting a female name to male by adding an "e"?

Other long gaps in the Journal now reduced it to just a few entries over the next decade or so. After just one notation in December 1981, nothing until three items in August 1982, then less than a page in 1983 (June), one entry in August 1986, in 1988 two in April and one in June, one in all of 1989 (August), three in 1990 (March, June and August), then one in 1991 (October), one in 1992 (August), one in 1993 (April). I essentially abandoned the Journal during those years.

The reason for my neglect of the Journal in the 1980s and early 1990s was not hard to determine. Those were the years (including the late 1970s) during which I produced some 170 newspaper travel articles and ten books, which rolled off the presses at a regular and rapid rate: two adventure novels (1979 and 1981); a book of travel essays (1986); travel guides to the Midwest (1989) and the Southern states (1990); in 1992 two books, one on cemeteries around the world and one on the Mississippi River; three expanded second editions of the Midwest and the South travel guides (1992, 1993, 1994); and in 1994 a guidebook to Civil War sites.

All those published works both depleted my time and served to satisfy my interest in producing written accounts of my thoughts, travels and interests as well as capturing in print some of the fleeting sensory impressions which had come to me. This in turn eliminated the motivation for me to enter comments in the Journal and also depleted what I might include in it. Only after I retired from my writing life did the Journal again assume a major and regular role in my attempt to capture on paper my passing thoughts.

AUGUST 1986

Some 17 years ago I began entering random thoughts and impressions into this notebook. The nearly complete absence of entries in recent years no doubt reflects my unexpected success in managing to address a wider public rather than confining my material to a single reader—myself. By publication, my internal perceptions and ideas have become externalized. Getting published, widely and regularly, surprised me. I took a chance, and somehow it happened to work out. This is my first Journal entry in months, years even.

APRIL 1988

Belief that creation of the universe, with its apparent structure and regularities, brought order out of chaos contradicts the reality that with the Big Bang explosive disorder produced continued chaos. A human longing for order activates creative efforts. Art brings new artificial perspectives on the natural world, in that way reordering how people see reality. This deconstructs and reorders how the world is perceived by fragmenting and reassembling previous perceptions of it. But, paradoxically, by proposing alternate realities, art makes what exists less settled and more chaotic.

Writing is one of the few fields in which you're constantly being judged by your inferiors: editors, publishers, reviewers, book store buyers, academics, some of whom have never written a book and a few of whom wouldn't know how.

MARCH 1990

One of many oddities in English: "I dig you" means "I like/understand you." "I make digs at you" means "I criticize/ridicule you."

AUGUST 18, 1991

Yesterday I completed the last details on the manuscript [*The Mississippi River*]. And so—after miles of travel and years of effort—maybe the time has come when I should put down my pen [literally, as I wrote by pen on paper] and end my authorial labors. It will be quite a change for me to revert to the time, some 13 years ago, when I had no major writing projects at hand. But after nine books and some 170 newspaper articles perhaps I'll enjoy a writing-free way of life—and maybe my readers will as well.

OCTOBER 11, 1991

Today I entered a few additional lines into *The Mississippi River* manuscript. These perhaps represent the very last of my book writings, in which case my writing career now nears its end. *The New York Times* called today to commission an article—I can hardly believe that I'm being asked by the *Times* to continue to contribute to the paper's travel section—so my pen may remain slightly active, but I believe that most of my work has been done.

This proved to be incorrect, as in 1994 I published a book on the Civil War, my last one for 27 years until my travel reminiscence, A PLAY OF INFINITE FORMS, appeared in 2021.

AUGUST 10, 1992

Entries few and far between now for the Journal, but here's one: X does Y a favor by taking him in to live with X for a while. When Y tells someone, "X took me in" he means that as a compliment, but the listener took it to mean, "X deceived me." What a language! I'm glad I never had to learn English as a foreign tongue, truly a tongue-twister.

~PART TWO~
MIDDLE YEARS

IV. Post-Writing Writings: January 1994–December 1999

After my tenth and last (until 2021) book was published in late 1994, I finally did retire from writing. Other than contributing a chapter to a biography and to a memoir, I published nothing until I decided late in life to write a travel reminiscence, A PLAY OF INFINITE FORMS. I then turned to this companion volume to prepare my more than 50-year-long Journal for publication, surely my last book. After my retirement from writing in 1994 I continued my private writings in the Journal. As from 1994 the entries became more frequent and longer, many of them like mini-essays on specific topics. The Journal thus evolved from mostly a kind of grab-bag repository of briefly expressed random stray thoughts into a series of more substantive extended entries on a wide range of subjects. The 24 years from 1969 to 1993 contains only a very small part of the entirety, while the more than 95 percent of the total during the 28 years from 1994 to 2022 comprises by far the main content of the Journal.

Below appears the first 1994 entry, marking the advent of (more or less) the second half—by time but not by quantity—of the Journal, begun 24 years before and by now continued on, as from 1994, for another 28 years.

JANUARY 1994

Very infrequent entries these last years. Perhaps I no longer had any thoughts worth recording. Maybe I never did: some people might say none of my thoughts merited preservation in written form.

Often people ask themselves, "Where did the years go?" Never have I posed that question, for I know just where they went. In general they went where I told them to go. For me time didn't slip stealthily away day by day without me being unaware of their content. I know where the years went because I guided them, best as I could, to bring me my desired kinds of experiences. The past for me doesn't represent time vanished or lost but simply time elapsed, days and years which for the most part delivered what I'd hoped they'd bring me. As always and for everyone, the time went by quickly but not so fast that I couldn't see where the days, weeks and months were taking me.

AUGUST 1994

The writing life demands deliberation; retirement from it brings liberation.

Both reading and travel offer useful antidotes to solipsism. As for writing, perhaps it's essentially nothing more than an exercise in solipsism.

On a recent trip to Romania a member of the group said that he traveled as a "filler," as good a reason for travel as any. In truth, whatever we do in life is only a filler, meant to fill in the time from our beginning to our end, after which we end up as landfill. Mortality is both unique and common. No one is singled out for what everyone must experience. Even larger-than-life figures end up smaller than life.

On December 15, 1964 Lyndon Johnson wrote to Jacqueline Kennedy: "Time goes by too swiftly, my dear Jackie. But the day never goes by without some tremor of a memory or some edge of a feeling that reminds me of all you and I went through together." This surprising rather poetic comment, untypical for an a-cultural character like LBJ, echoes Vladimir Nabokov's "blessed shiver" which inspired him to capture in writing such evanescent "ethereal" impressions as sunsets and their celestial formations. It's that pesky, insistent edge of feeling "tremor" or "shiver" which impels some of us to write.

Every journey imposes limitations of time which evoke the more general brevity of the time available for one's allocated earthly span. The heightened sense of urgency on a trip should also apply to one's often more languid and routine familiar home-based life. But dilatory and frivolous behavior characterizes how people in their ordinary daily existence often spend their time, as if it's unlimited.

While some adventurers hopes to become a Field Marshall with a commanding presence over his exploits, many stay-at-home arm-chair warriors without arms at hand prefer to fight other consumers for bargains at stores like Marshall Field.

The strange and improbable terrestrial setting here on the lonely planet originated either by chance or from sort sort of design. Either way, the world is a baffling and incomprehensible place.

Although most of my friends quickly change the subject whenever I refer to mortality—they seem in denial about it—I've found it quite helpful to contemplate my end as this serves the practical purpose of inspiring me to make the best use of my remaining time. An awareness of death is a great organizer.

SEPTEMBER 1994

A change of scene which produces a change of seen may not have any effect on the viewer. To alter our perspective on the world depends less on seeing new views than on revising our existing ones.

OCTOBER 1994

Life always hangs by a thread; scissors lurk everywhere. A tiny change, external or internal, can operate suddenly to cut off our ties to the world and our ability to experience sensory impressions.

DECEMBER 1994

It's a trite analogy to compare a life to a journey, but in my case much of my experiment in living did consist of journeys.

MARCH 1995

By now I've depleted most of my terrestrial time. Even if I survive another 10 or 20 years, the remaining portion will be much less than what's already passed. Because an extended life expectancy at my age would no doubt bring me ailments and disabilities, death ahead of a lifeless life might be preferable to continued longevity.

The seconds, minutes, hours, days, weeks, months, years, decades pass away, just as do people. But time never dies.

If an elderly mortal can honestly say that he would have done little or nothing differently, does that claim reflect a lack of imagination or a truly satisfactory life?

APRIL 1995

The oft-ignored time value of time is as important as the time value of money. Unlike compound interest, which accrues income, time compounded destroys life.

DECEMBER 1995

A lawyer as trustee who breaches the terms of a trust is a reprobate attorney.

JULY 1997

Almost a year since my last entry [August 3, 1996]. It seems that my noteworthy insights are now out of sight.

It's embarrassing to be dead. You can no longer think clearly, can't say anything, no more ice cream, travel, reading or anything, no way to act or react. You just lie there motionless in the moribund thoughtless state time forced on you. But non-being represents your normal and inescapable condition.

AUGUST 1997

So familiar is the settled format of your past and the forms in the world around you, what exists in past and present time seems normal, natural and even in a way inevitable. But in fact all those familiar and established phenomena were for the most part contingent and random.

NOVEMBER 1997

The expiration of my passport after 10 years inspires me to recall many of the places I visited with that now lapsed document: Ethiopia, Yemen, Bulgaria, Romania, Poland, the Baltics, Vietnam, Cambodia, Laos, China, Tibet. I wonder if I'll expire before my new passport does.

A writer's books may survive, some to be marked-down on the sale table, but the author himself can never be remaindered.

DECEMBER 1997

It was 24 years ago this month when I moved into my cozy little secluded suburban house on a dead-end lane. To this comfortable little corner of the world I returned after my many far journeys. Here books, old furniture, travel mementos and other familiar objects along with many memories and even the chronic dust and blemishes comforted me. Transient everywhere else, here I'm at home—at least until at my dead-end house my transient earthly existence ends. A humanimal is essentially nothing but an inessential passing form.

JANUARY 1998

It's a mistake to be self-satisfied, but quite desirable to be satisfied.

APRIL 1998

A week ago today was my last day in Havana, and now once again I'm back in my own familiar little corner of the world. The transition between the greatly contrasting here and there, juxtaposing within a brief time-frame two radically different places, requires a few days and a mental reset to adjust to the extreme change of scene.

AUGUST 1998

Although time's actual duration remains ever the same, for older people the days do seem to pass at a faster pace. No sooner do I finish a meal than the next one is due; just after I awake I once again soon prepare for bed; daily routines seem to follow in quick repetitions. As my life winds down everything appears to speed up.

OCTOBER 1998

Among the many challenges the English language presents to those who try to learn it: "I decided to stand her up" (somewhat the same as "to put her down"); "I can't stand her"; "We always stand for prayers"; "He's a stand-out athlete"; "I've decided to stand down"; "It's a stand-off"; "Take a stand on the issue"; "We need to find a stand-in for the part"; "I stand on my principles"; "It's time to take a stand for freedom." And why "understand"—to under-stand rather than to grasp the meaning of something? A better way to describe comprehension would be "overstand," which implies you get the point well.

NOVEMBER 1998

Yesterday [November 8] I returned from Hawaii, so some 9000 miles of (round-trip) travel separate this entry from the previous one. In the Journal the time intervals between entries but not the distance I traveled or my experiences when away are apparent. What happened during my trip or, for that matter, what occurs anywhere at any time—the granular reality of everyday life—can never really be captured on a page.

The disadvantage of the solitary life is that it leaves you with too much time to think; the advantage of solitude is that it leaves you with enough time to think.

JANUARY 1999

Yesterday 1998 expired—before I did. So now I live on into a new year. Years ago as a young man I hoped to survive until the turn of the century and millennium, now a mere year away. At my age that's a long time. Only another 364 days and I'll realize my long-time ambition.

"Close" designates two quite unrelated meanings depending on how the word is pronounced. When written, only the context determines whether "close" refers to shutting or to proximity. "Read" presents the same sort of ambiguity.

FEBRUARY 1999

Freedom and independence conflict with emotional, professional and societal commitments. How to balance those two competing factors—to live in your own way while including other people in your life—represents a challenge for those who hope to produce a satisfactory experiment in living.

MARCH 1999

Although nightmares sometimes unsettle us, we don't suffer from daymares. This is because the nocturnal visions arrive unsummoned from sensory deposits deeply embedded in our subconscious, while our waking images can be willed and in that way limited to pleasant scenarios called daydreams.

Daydreams allow us to fantasize favorable and desirable alternative realities. Perhaps nightmares function to suggest alternate scenarios as a reminder that most of what happened could have developed in different ways.

Two words which could be added to the English language (or slanguage): "Flagriculture": a country plants its banner in foreign soil to root the newcomers' presence there. "Winterlude": a vacation taken during the winter months.

Vermeer's painting represent a synthesis of the eternal and the immediate. His works depict scenes which evoke a moment in time while at the same time picturing a timeless view as if an archetype of all moments in time. Almost no other painter has so skillfully combined those two opposite dimensions of time. Similarly, a writer like Shakespeare presents specific believable characters who also represent general types. The definition of a great work of art is one which includes both a realistic in-depth image of what exists and an evocation of its essence.

MAY 1999

Five days ago I returned from a month-long trip to India and the Himalaya country, including Rajasthan, Darjeeling, Bhutan, Sikkim and other nearby areas. The adventure exposed me to many strange and wondrous scenes and practices. I saw that people in the region still seriously put faith in astrology, which influences what believers think and how they behave. But such an odd "Mysterious East" belief system as astrology is in some ways no different from various strange doctrines and beliefs which pass for truth in my own country.

Three characteristics which typify most of the figures viewed as creative geniuses: simplicity, versatility, productivity.

JULY 1999

Friday [July 1] marks the beginning of the last half-year of the twentieth century and of the millennium. Years ago I hoped to survive to see the transition into the new age. Only very few babies born now at the end of the twentieth century will remain alive long enough to continue on into the twenty-second century.

The on-going chain of life links generations and eras. It seems like a lot of energy and effort to keep continuing the process on and on, generation after generation for no reason or ultimate meaning. Breaking the chain would serve to eliminate many problems, sorrows, concerns. Hopefully, the scrap metal wouldn't be recycled.

That was my last entry until three days before the century and the millennium changed. Perhaps I held my breath, my thoughts and my pen to conserve energy in the hope I'd survive to the end of the year. I made it and by now, so far, have continued on for more than two decades into the third millennium—probably my second and last, unless I go on for another thousand years, in which case I should probably develop a few new hobbies to keep busy during my extended terrestrial tenure.

DECEMBER 1999

Now mid-day on this December 31, the last day of the last week of the last month of the last year of the last century and millennium. For nature that mouthful of time description means nothing, but mankind has endowed these 24 hours with a construct which imposes on them a kind of order. Some tribes, clans, sects and groups in remote and isolated areas live outside time as measured in the outside world. If I manage to survive for another half-day I will finally experience the momentous moment of the triple transition (year, century, millennium) significant to the tribe I by chance happen to belong to.

V. Twenty-First Century Entries: January 2000-December 2009

JANUARY 2000

How those millennia fly by! Yesterday afternoon I watched the celebrations all around the world as the earth spun while the hours moved across the globe. For a time one part of the lonely planet remained in the old era, back in the 1990s and the second millennium while other regions had already entered the 2000s. Earthlings celebrated the transition with balloons, fireworks, noise, dancing, parades, energetic and loud rituals everywhere as if giving a shout-out to the universe that something big was happening here on earth. But it all fell on deaf ears, as only here on mankind's homeland did this new era mean anything. Elsewhere, nothing.

My early January comments regarding the new year, century and millennium seems to have exhausted thoughts suitable for the Journal, as two-thirds of 2000 elapsed before I returned to the notebook. Then, suddenly and rather mysteriously, in August I wrote non-stop every day from the 3rd to the 31st.

AUGUST 2000

I'm able to walk the streets of many foreign cities, even the biggest, without a map, as those places are familiar to me from previous visits. Many of the sights, vistas, twists and turns, byways and other views—for me, reviews—I know well. Obscure corners no longer remain hidden from me, as long ago I discovered those off-the-beaten-track areas, for me on-the-beaten-track. Miles and years have enabled me to write this entry, which I record with gratitude for my good fortune in getting to know so much of the world—and having survived the experience.

Now that I've managed to survive to see the twenty-first century and the third millennium, they seem no different at all from the preceding periods designated with different numbers. This suggests how arbitrary many human constructs are.

When I asked a young man about 30, "At what age do you think old age begins?" he replied, "When you start asking when old age begins."

Each day is like an organic cell: just as the cell contains the components for life, each day holds the contents of life. Taken all in all, the cells and the days form the entirety of both the body and of the corpus of one's existence.

Many changes occur so slowly it seems as if nothing is changing at all. Day by day no one looks, feels or acts older, at least not until some sort of physical ailment suddenly intrudes, at which time time takes a quantum leap from health to disease, discomfort and disability. The grand Grand Canyon landscape (or grandscape) took millennia for time and nature to carve. Such slow but inevitably vast changes sometimes operate in an imperceptible way, as if nothing ever changes. In other cases, things happen suddenly. Either way, nothing holds steady very long.

Existence is a wasting asset—if, that is, being alive can be considered an asset. I wonder if my suddenly compulsive daily writing in the Journal somehow represents a rhythm in conformance with the passage of the days. As time keeps moving, I keep writing. My usual only occasional entries functioned as snapshots, while the daily ones now resemble a moving picture of time's passage.

The present is at the same time both intensely vivid and utterly evanescent. In contrast to the dynamic kinetic present fraught with chance and uncertainty, the past offers the considerable advantage that your set place in history keeps you out of harm's way. Nothing can happen to you in the past. As for the future, we hope that it promises unexpected benefits, but what's to come also represents threats because, like the present, future happenings bristle with uncertainty and possible misfortune. Living too much in the past or anticipating what the future might bring may tend to degrade your present-day experiences. Living without any consciousness of the past or future will also diminish your on-going day-to-day existence.

Time is both a friend an an enemy: it's constructive and destructive. With time, everything eventually becomes nothing; without time, nothing can become anything.

Designations of a few time units—the day and the year—with their obvious cycles are clearly de-marked periods. Other temporal measures—such as seconds, hours, minutes, weeks, decades—represent artificial units imposed on duration by mankind in an effort to order a disorderly cosmos.

Are months in our sub-lunar realm here on the lonely planet only an imposed arbitrary time-unit, or do the phases of the moon justify considering the January to December delineations as valid natural time periods?

Time is a void. How you fill it is what matters. To be endowed with the privilege of deciding for one's self how to use time represents a rare and very valuable but fleeting advantage.

The days roll off time's assembly line, which never breaks down or can be shut down. Its permanent and maintenance-free daily production and destruction rolls on and on forever.

Humans consume time, which offers an unending supply of days—the unit of consumption—as long as the user remains alive. Postmortem, time no longer exists for the decedent, as even a timely death is timeless.

As relentlessly corrosive as time is for the living, the dead enjoy the great advantage of escaping it forever. When mankind becomes extinct, would time continue to exist even if no human consciousness at all was aware of the on-going persistence of temporal change?

Although earthly time develops at the same pace every place and for everyone, earthlings experience duration in relative ways based on various factors. These include youth or old age, status, situation, wealth or poverty, health or recovery from illness, earning power potential, educational curriculum, vacation time, the dynamics of an exciting life or the boredom of a routine existence, and other variations and subjective factors. In that way, perceptions of time—friend to some people, foe to others—are not absolute, even if its nature is.

As should by now be obvious, I enjoy thinking about the baffling characteristic of time, an activity which inspires me to ponder many puzzles, paradoxes, problems, perceptions which I contemplate, in part, to occupy my time.

Time operates on the human body as does air on a balloon. At the beginning an infant grows and fills out, then continues to puff up. The form holds its shape for a time, then gradually starts to shrink until what contains a life finally shrivels and collapses. Graphed to show how the elapse of time affects the body, the chart would show a bell-shaped curve, off the chart at the end.

Each day resembles music in that it proceeds as if note-by-note to denote over time an entire composition, but—unlike music—the life which time composes in the end decomposes.

Each of a person's later-in-life zero years—60, 70, 80, 90, 100—signifies both a decade and decay.

In some places the weekend begins on Friday; in others, on Saturday. Some areas may not have a weekend at all. Primitive tribes in remote areas perhaps make no distinction between so-called weekdays and weekends—an arbitrary imposed designation. That tribal state-of-nature practice accords more closely with the natural order, which doesn't offer any markers to indicate which days should comprise a weekend.

Although every baby born on the same day gets the same daily allotment of time, each child's terrestrial time span differs. Chance and luck determine the length of a life. But who is luckier—a humanimal limited to a very short existence or an earthling given very long life?

One of the few constants in life is the regular and relentless arrival of days. They always appear on schedule—never late, never on strike, no vacations or long weekends or holidays, no break-downs or seize-ups or outages, no defects or rejects, never short of parts or fuel, always the same perfect production and progression. The advent of each new day is a certainty; how it will be filled, by its possessor and as shaped by chance, always remains subject to great uncertainty.

The regularity of my entries this month suggests to me that the count-up from day 1 to day 30 or 31 (or 28 or 29) should be replaced by a count-down to show the remaining rather than the elapsed days. This change to tally depletion rather than accretion would let you know how much time is left in the month, more useful information than knowledge of how many days have already passed. Such a forward-looking measure would also be useful to indicate a person's probable remaining time, based on his or her life expectancy. If set at, say, 80, then someone age 50 would be designated as 30, meaning that three decades represents the imputed span to the end. This sort of count-down might encourage people, as they aged, to make better use of their highlighted dwindling years.

The last day of the month, almost all of which included daily inkings into the Journal. But no matter how much I record and whatever I think or do or whatever happens, time keep moving on and on and by now the month has slipped away into the fixity of the past. Although time continues on, it brings to humanimals a here-today/gone-tomorrow sensation.

SEPTEMBER 2000

Although the past seems fixed and immutable, it's possible to destroy history by removing all the physical evidence time produced. The atom bomb in Hiroshima almost completely destroyed tangible leavings of the city's past and also killed many people with knowledge of their era. With the cityscape and many citizens gone, both Hiroshima and much of what time brought to the city disappeared.

We live life retail, moment by moment, experience by experience, sensory impression by impression, but can understand its patterns and themes, if at all, only wholesale.

2001

Some 60 percent of the total time had elapsed between when I started the Journal in 1969 and the end of 2000, but by then the notebooks contained less than 10 percent of their eventual contents. The more than 90 percent which remained to be written between 2001 and the present time evidences that the Journal is primarily a document composed late in life by someone with by then long experience of an experiment in living. Perhaps the longer the experiment the more it furnished food for thought, which I tried to digest in the form of Journal entries I chewed over in my mind.

When I reread and edited the Journal, starting over the Covid-confined winter of 2020, I was both surprised and concerned at how little my views had changed over the years. I'd incorrectly supposed that my opinions and conclusions would evolve and change based on all my travels, reading, experiences and other such influences. But somehow none of them managed to make much of a change in how I viewed the world. It seemed that I wasn't so much of a slow-learner as a no-learner. Over more than half a century of the Journal, the consistency of its ideas evidence something of a lack of development in my thinking. Apparently my early-day mind-set remained quite set, an absence of flexibility which bothered me. I wondered why the travels and all the rest over the long years had somehow for the most part failed to affect my views. I attributed this consistency to my belief that the way I saw the world accurately represented reality, as I knew it, and in that way served as useful and workable principles to carry out my experiment in living. Since my perceptions, ideas and opinions seemed to work well, I found no need to change them.

JANUARY 2001

And now [January 2] a new year. The traditional Christmas events recalled earlier holidays: music, year-ending rush, rampant consumerism, the usual festive seasonal rituals, the same sort of gatherings, similar motions, emotions and commotions, the presence and exchange of presents with familiar people, all the rest. At my age it's all a re-repeat. By now I've absorbed most of the worldly play of infinite forms which will soon comprise my entire terrestrial existence. Much of what I continue to experience represents simply a variation on themes already familiar to me.

It's both exhilarating and worrisome how from beginning to end a life passes through so many random twists and turns, convolutions and mutations. A wrong or a right turn here or there, going right or left, this way or that, one fork or the other, and all would have turned out differently. No matter how vigilant, careful and cautious you might be, making your way through the strange and baffling amazing maze presents real challenges. All too easily you can lose your way.

A deceased friend of mine used to say, "The days are long but the years are short." He was half-right, as looking back it seems that every time measure was all short—days, years, an entire lifetime.

The disjunction between the required investments—emotional, temporal, financial, conversational, behavioral, and much else—and the brief pleasure attained with sex seems greatly disproportionate. The substantial front-end costs and energy expended scarcely justify the fleeting feeling of the benefit.

"Plaire aux femmes, ça coûte cher," say the French (well, about half of them anyway): pleasing women costs a lot. Lord Chesterfield (1694-1773), who fathered an illegitimate son, supposedly (the phrase doesn't appear in Chesterfield's writings) expressed the same opinion—"the pleasure is momentary, the position ridiculous, and the expense damnable"— but nonetheless, in spite of the unfavorable cost-benefit analysis, the good Lord rose to the occasion to produce and engender a little squirt.

Where lies the balance between bravado and a sense of adventure on the one hand and a more hands-off and cautious attitude on the other? Timid behavior results in many missed opportunities, but hesitation to commit to a course of action also prevents many mistakes, some of them irremediable, and offers the possibility of encountering better options. But whatever your approach, in the end luck and chance represent the deciding factors for how things happen to work out.

FEBRUARY 2001

What seems so fixed and familiar can at any moment become unfixed and even strange. It seems strange to me that never again will I see a friend who just died in his sixties and for whom 36 years ago at his wedding I served as an attendant. One way to prevent this kind of loss is never to have any friends. More advisable is to enjoy as many close relationships as possible while always engaging with those who people your life on the basis that they could at any moment disappear.

A mere week ago my late friend was not yet late, but no longer can he be better late than never getting together with me, as now he's past all earthly delays and will be late forever.

The illusion of the familiar tends to make us believe that what we know so well—house, possessions, neighborhood, friends, the nearby cityscape, routines, habits, much else—represents stable, on-going and changeless surroundings. But as my late friend's recent sudden death evidences, nothing stays the same. The ominous portent of his demise shatters the illusion of permanence and compels you to realize that each humanimal exists as if standing on solid ice which gradually begins to break, opening gaps in the fragile and insubstantial temporary support as slowly the ice melts away, leaving you standing an an ever-shrinking platform where you begin to lose your footing until, finally, the once-firm foothold dissolves into the waters.

Losing a good friend is like removing a piece of a once complete and symmetrical mosaic. As passing events lift out each tessera, the pattern slowly develops gaps and becomes less recognizable. The newly distorted design disturbs the viewer's equanimity, as he realizes that a pleasing design can at any time lose some of its symmetry. Which will be the next piece in my picture to be removed? Perhaps me, in which case I won't know the difference.

MARCH 2001

My just-completed trip to Antarctica inspires me to reflect on how creative yet raw nature is. Mother Nature produces a fantastic fantasia of terrestrial forms, some delightful but many oppressive and even threatening. For nature the earthly setting serves as a playing field where experiments with chemical and physical elements constantly seethe and churn, bringing ceaseless change. Nature's playful antics serve no purpose, even if at times the spectacle happens to entertain humanimals, no less a toy to nature than is anything else. In the far distant future the forbidding Antarctic ice cap will be doffed to give way to the equally forbidding rock continent beneath, a mutation brought about by playful but insensate meaningless natural forces.

APRIL 2001

The imbalance between exaggerated expectations and realistic aspirations leads to many disappointments and much unhappiness. A satisfactory experiment in living requires conforming hopes with reasonable possibilities. For this you need to assess your strengths and weaknesses, your circumstances, capabilities, values and willingness to exert yourself and then judge if those elements will be sufficiently effective to make it somewhat likely you can accomplish your intended goals.

The challenge with a close personal relationship is to invest as much time, energy and emotional commitment as necessary to maintain the connection without at the same time diminishing to an unacceptable level your own privacy, solitude, freedom and independence. To establish and continue such a desirable balance represents not only a challenge but also a near impossibility. Something or someone has to give.

By chance rather than by choice I inherited a temperament which gave me a mentality characterized by rational, analytical, logical, cerebral, calm, cool, collected, careful, cautious, contemplative, common sense-based traits. This both eliminated and activated various benefits and disadvantages. On balance, I believe that I benefited rather than suffered from my extremely thought-full and hopefully thoughtful endowed mental format.

AUGUST 2001

It's sobering to realize that in just a few years I will have lived (if I survive) longer than the interval between the Civil War and when I was born. This perspective changes my view on time-spans. A mere two long-lived generations ago, as from my birth, occurred the immediate pre-Revolutionary War era in U.S. history. What will conditions be two generations hence after my time?

Of course, in less than a month conditions in the U.S. would greatly change following the 9/11 attacks, of which Americans were in a blissfully oblivious way unaware at the time I wrote the above entry. In less than a month, night fell on a very different world.

My great familiarity with my house and its contents as well as my near neighborhood and the nearby village I walk to a few times a week comfort me and endow my daily life with a pleasing regularity. The stability and regularity in my home-based habitat contrasts with the dynamic ever-changing various experiences I enjoyed during my frequent and far-ranging trips. But wherever I roamed far from home I was consoled by the knowledge that I belonged somewhere, integrated into my familiar setting which I could always return to and where I could enjoy and appreciate its many comforts and conveniences

Then suddenly out of the blue came the 9/11 shock. Shortly after the attacks I wrote in the Journal a short entry, part of which appears below, and also a long letter to a friend in Europe commenting on the effects the terrorism might bring about. In my analysis I was both right and wrong. I incorrectly predicted a recession and maybe even a depression, and damage to the traditional American can-do spirit. But I foresaw that there would be "more controls, less security, less freedom, and the imposition of many restrictions." I faulted Americans for believing that "it can't happen here," but of course it did, for "we are just as vulnerable to the problems of political, social and economic life as is any other country. Maybe the Americans have now learned that lesson."

I further observed that in the future physical attacks presented less of a threat than enemy intrusions "on the computer/internet/electronic networks" which, by now, control many operations (airplanes, electricity, information, manufacturing) in modern-day society. The vulnerability of the U.S. (and other advanced societies) to disruption of information technology systems, I wrote, seems to be very high, and my guess is that eventually an enemy will try to corrupt and even destroy some of these systems. This will cause chaos and a breakdown of everyday life. When communication systems, electricity distribution and factories stop operating, how will Americans—those sheltered, innocent, likable, friendly people—react? I believe that this question is even more relevant now, as disruption of critical systems and infrastructure is not only highly likely but has already occurred.

SEPTEMBER 2001

Little more than a week ago today Americans slept soundly, and when they awoke they saw images of the World Trade Center as it collapsed, along with many of the country's assumptions and foundational beliefs. High-flyers almost always lose altitude and crash. When the skyscraper lost its footing and, brought back to earth, crumbled into a land-scraper so too did part of the structure of how the nation perceives the way the world works.

OCTOBER 2001

Since returning home 10 days ago from the Pacific Northwest and Sun Valley I've appreciated even more than usual the haven of my cozy little house. I think that the 9/11 attacks have re-emphasized to me the value of a hideaway from the turmoils of the outside world on a quiet and obscure provincial suburban dead-end lane here in the middle of the continent.

Even here at home in the remote Middle West, far from international borders, the great wide world intrudes in the form of bombers flying overhead on their way from a military air base in Western Missouri to Afghanistan to bomb America's enemies in that distant land. There's really no way to escape from signs of humanimals' bellicose behavior, worldly violence and the often unkind nature of mankind.

One way to assess if you've enjoyed a satisfactory life is to contemplate how willing you'd be to revert to an earlier age to gain the prospect of an existence more satisfactory than your actual outcome. For someone who's content with how things turned out, giving up your actual life experiences to return to earlier years would most likely be a bad trade as starting over probably wouldn't improve how your terrestrial existence happened to work out. In any case, why bother to relive any of it? You have only one life, and for fortunate folks once is enough while for less favored people once is probably too much.

Capital is monetized time, a statement which depends for its validity on a rather rare intricate web of political, geopolitical, societal and economic conditions and circumstances. The alchemy which transmutes time into capital presupposes a belief in the future, a view which implies a settled society with rules, laws, security, fairness and functional political and other institutions. Such efficient, effective and necessary components of the open society (as Karl Popper called it) inspires confidence in the future, which motivates people to pursue education, risk-taking, investing and productivity. Those kinds of conditions allow you to operate with the confidence that actions now will offer you a reasonable chance in the future to benefit from time-nourished investments not only of capital but also of energy and effort. Lack of belief in the future—typical of many under-developed and unsettled countries—demotivates activities based on producing wealth over time. In such uncertain places, time offers little value as its passage yields far too little to make any attempts to create wealth worthwhile. For the "time value of money" principle to justify its worth, time must lead to valuable results which their creators can retain and benefit from.

DECEMBER 2001

Dusk falls; the year ends. I have now seen the millennium+1.

JANUARY 2002

The cold light of a winter day opens a new year. I saw in 2002 at an elegant black-tie seven course sit-down dinner for 22 last night. I chatted with people from afar drawn here for work or for personal reasons, their lives turned topsy-turvy and now distanced from where they began. Conversing with those locals from other locales emphasized how deeply rooted my fourth generation existence is here.

I never left my native habitat except to study and to travel, and I always returned home. This long-time presence here in my hometown brought me much comfort and many advantages as well as, no doubt, some drawbacks, such as perhaps an over-attachment to the familiar, a disinclination to try new formats, a nostalgia swathed in the security of my very small local world, unimaginative routines and habits, clinging to the familiar rather than seeking new experiments for my experiment in living, and lack of an adventurous spirit for my everyday way of life. But because my well-rooted home life suited me and functioned well I was never tempted to change my situation.

MARCH 2002

A true sign of getting old is when museum historical displays illustrate events you lived through or include exhibit objects you were familiar with and perhaps used in your younger days.

Back from nearly six grueling weeks of travel in India. Animal life—cows, elephants, people, dogs, many other creatures—swarm through the streets or in the countryside. Noise everywhere. No privacy or solitude, except in one's hotel room. A Technicolor country, with colorful scenes everywhere at all times. A great and exhausting travel experience, one I enjoyed and which also makes me glad to be back home.

Since returning from India (my third visit there) I've stayed close to and savored my home. The ultra-stimulating but difficult trip made me appreciate even more than before the comforts and conveniences of my house and regular way of life. No more bottled water, and I can eat anything anywhere. Here I enjoy privacy, silence, peace, greenery, uncluttered and cow- and dung-free streets, uncrowded stores, efficient services. There we faced pollution, incessant activity, ceaseless noise, masses of humanity, garbage-littered cities, poverty, disease—a glorious and memorable contrast with conditions at home. Sheltered and demanding Americans with unrealistically high expectations of how things should work and low exposure to how things actually do work in much of the world would benefit from travel in a country such as India, where most visitors experience a culture shock which usually sparks a new way of looking at life.

A month ago today [March 24th] I was in remote Hyderabad, which by now already also seems remote in time. From the trip to India remain some remnants meant to preserve a few memories of the adventure: my detailed travel diaries; a few souvenirs and minor mementos; books I bought along the way and have now read; not much else. In truth, nothing can recapture the ceaseless and perhaps too stimulating flow of sensory impressions which inundated my consciousness every day in that spectacular, kinetic, exotic, extraordinary and demanding country.

APRIL 2002

Deciding late in life on the highest and best use of your rapidly depleting time presents a challenge which really can't be met because you can't know when, where and how your life will come to an end. Perhaps the only realistic policy is to assume that your last day may be any day now.

JULY 2002

By now I've traveled to so many places, read so many books, seen so many museums, attended so many performances, encountered so many people along the way, enjoyed so many experiences, written so many words both published and, as in this Journal, unpublished, that it took me many years to accomplish everything, and I had to grow old to fill my life with it all. For me that was a fair exchange.

Back from a month in Ireland and England. As much as I enjoy every trip, I also equally enjoy returning home and being here. When away I often long to be home, and when on my native turf I think about possible trips. Those two somewhat contradictory characteristics indicate either something of a split personality or a well-integrated one.

OCTOBER 2002

I went to an open house now for sale (not far from my present residence) where I originated and spent my early years. My visit to the place where my life began inspired some reflections on it. In the small room at the top of the stairs where I was installed after being brought home from the hospital I formed my first memory (my parents talking), and steps away is the bedroom where I was engendered long ago one early November night (or was it a day-time activity, a "nooner"?). From that moment of conception until now an inconceivable (unlike me) play of chance happenings unfolded to form the content of my earthly existence. As from that seminal early November event, what followed was highly improbable and completely contingent, but now I know how it all happened to turn out. The gift of time gave me present knowledge of the evolution of my nearly concluded experiment in living, which time in its fullness will soon take from me.

After returning from Reno, where I gave an after-dinner talk to some 700 guests in honor of a close friend inaugurated that evening as chairman of an international trade association, and then two weeks in Sun Valley, I renounced another trip opportunity in favor of staying home to savor the Midwestern autumn. No telling how many more of these delightful seasonal changes I'll be able to enjoy before I suffer my own change into the eternal winter of oblivion.

The generally favorable transition for me of the once contingent and uncertain future into favorable experiences and a satisfactory past depended almost as much as what didn't happen as what occurred. The absence of negative developments enabled many positive ones. Avoiding problems permits you to avoid being forced to address them.

I engaged in my experiment in living as both a self-starter and a self-stopper. I was at the same time active and also passive, as I usually refrained from action until I could assess with a cost-benefit analysis possible courses of action. This caution prevented a lot of problems, even if my frequent hesitations left me less adventurous than I sometimes wished.

NOVEMBER 2002

Very vivid vignettes and visions during sleep. No need to detail them as recording dreams is boring and a waste of time—no one knows why they occur, why their particular scenarios happen to surface, or what they mean. I will note only that some of the dreams seem rather realistic and coherent, as if I exist (or once existed) in some sort of parallel universe.

DECEMBER 2002

Because no fixed schedule or obligations constrain me—other than the routine chores and maintenance imposed to enable a humanimal to continue to exist—I face each day as a tabula rasa on which I can write the agenda. Many people would feel uncomfortable with no set or predetermined structure, forcing them to face a blank slate every morning, but I appreciate and enjoy the open book I can fill with content of my choosing, especially now when the book will soon close.

JANUARY 2003

Another new year. Language designates a terrestrial end-point in words such as "finisterre" and "land's-end." For year-end I would say that yesterday 2002 reached a "finis tempus."

Humans designate time units to order the temporal flow into comprehensible divisions. For a similar reason earthlings address the chaotic and unpredictable terrestrial conditions by trying to identify and manage them with arbitrary imposed names and practices. These include rituals, habits, social conventions, belief systems, laws, routines, religions and other such procedures and constructs meant to respond to the unruly conditions and randomness which prevails on the lonely planet.

Whatever happens to come into being—both a person and in general—exists as a chance creation. Each individual, mankind, the world, the universe, the cosmos all represent exceptions, rarities of a capricious nature which toys with its playthings to form improbable combinations of what happens to emerge temporarily from innumerable random elements.

Although humans should find it comforting to revert to the norm of non-being, the means to reach that status—death—greatly unsettles living beings. Mortality may be frightening, but there's nothing to fear in being dead, the condition which allows a person to conform to the norm. Moreover, for many earthlings non-existence would no doubt be more desirable than remaining alive. It seems logical that the most luckless, abject, impoverished, miserable, diseased, uneducated, hopeless mortals would view death as a welcome release from their bad karma. And yet even those unfortunate souls with nothing to lose but their lives cling to existence for dear life.

MARCH 2003

The answer to "When are we?" is sometimes as telling as the responses to "Who" or 'Where" or "What" are we? Two days ago [March 1st] when in Johannesburg I visited the Soweto area. Now back home, far from South Africa, I feel both an extreme geographical displacement and also a temporal one. As if a lagging indicator, my sense of time now remains stranded back in Africa where only 48 hours ago I was literally "here today, gone tomorrow." By my current confused perception of time I remain in Johannesburg, "there today and still there tomorrow."

APRIL 2003

As life plays out over time the play of infinite forms which define your daily existence gradually becomes limited to regular routines, rituals, habits which seem to offer on-going familiarity and a sense of regularity. But beneath that illusionary superficial image lurk luck, chance and other random capricious forces which can at any time upset an apparently well-ordered and regular life.

MAY 2003

Early on-set of difficulties, problems, adversities may help people overcome such challenges later in life. Dealing with setbacks, defeats, disappointments and misfortunes when young forces you to cope with the kinds of situations common when you're an adult. Successful over-protected, sheltered and privileged young people suffer from a false view of reality. Over the years I've observed that many of the popular and respected over-achievers in my high school class became under-achievers and ineffectual in later life. Those who managed to resolve difficulties when young did better later on.

The good fortune of being able to do nothing offers a rare and truly treasured benefit, but should be used only sparingly and not become a habit. To spend your life doing nothing represents an unfortunate kind of good fortune.

A book I recently read on daring wildcatters who took wild risks in oil country prompted me to ask myself, Who gets ahead in life? Although scientific data guided the well explorations, in the end chance dictated which of the venturers did well. Of the thousands of chancers who sought oil, only very few struck it rich. The book discusses only those fortunate few; almost all the failed aspirants are forgotten. For all human endeavors in the terrestrial play of infinite forms luck, chance and fate favor only very few of the players, while most are also-rans and some never-begans. Whether in the arts, business, politics, science, sports and all the rest many aspire, perspire, conspire to excel, but most never succeed. Fortune favor the prepared mind, so it's said—but of course many things are said about all sorts of matters. In truth, even the most diligent, cultivated, knowledgeable, capable and prepared mind often fails to enable favorable results. The wildcatter's exploratory drill bit serves as an image to evoke the capricious nature of success. Fortunes are made or missed depending on the luck of the draw, or the bite of the drill. A whirling drill bit spinning into the earth to seek pay-dirt operates as a wheel of fortune or misfortune, depending on luck. Whirl is king.

JUNE 2003

The lucky few unable to conceive of a life better than the one they actually lived either enjoyed an unusually satisfactory existence or suffer from a lack of imagination.

My age cohort by chance happened to live during the most favorable conditions of the twentieth century. Because we were the second smallest number of babies born in any year that century we faced less competition. We were too young for military service in World War II and in

Korea, too old for later American bellicose adventures. We benefited during our active years from mostly benign social and political conditions and enjoyed favorable economic developments, as in our time the country grew and prospered. Science and technology brought many beneficial changes and advances, while in other ways things remained stable and settled. My age group by chance existed in the best of times. If you happen to be incarnated as a humanimal and thrown into existence, the era in which you're extant—a purely random matter—will to a significant extent affect your life chances.

As noted above, in August 2000 I couldn't stop writing: Journal entries every day from the 3rd to the 31st. Between the two June 2003 entries just above and the single August 2004 notation just below, and after it, I didn't start writing again until a year later in August 2005. Just why these long lapses empty of noteworthy thoughts occurred I don't know, but for some two years both my mind and the Journal notebooks remained blank.

AUGUST 2004

While I was away my neighbor, who had also become a good friend, died. During my trip I was unaware that she no longer existed, so although dead she remained alive for me. But facts exist even if you're unaware of them, so my illusion that she still lived was based not on an erroneous perception but only on a lack of information.

AUGUST 2005

Because I've recorded almost nothing in the Journal over the last two years, it seems in a way as if I haven't really lived during that long interlude. The bygone days have all blurred together. Because I've captured none of my passing thoughts on paper, all my sensory impressions and my reactions to them passed by unrecorded and by now are unremembered and have disappeared.

SEPTEMBER 2005

Some years ago a lifelong friend of a generation senior to mine asked me to attend his funeral, a request I promised to honor providing that I'd then be in town and that the occasion of his death would be at a time convenient for me. He graciously complied, and I attended the memorial service. My friend had for 87 years enjoyed an unusually successful life of a very high quality of a kind unknown to most mortals. In that way the decedent had a lot more to lose than those of us with more modest accomplishments and fewer successes. Which sort of life, and then its death, is more desirable—high achievement, all of which you lose, or a less successful existence which, when it ends, deprives you of much less?

OCTOBER 2005

Last month's Labor Day exemplifies the many traditional repetitious rituals, birthdays, celebrations, Sundays, holy days, holidays, special days, opening and closing days and all the other arbitrary time markers mankind imposes to bring some order to the otherwise undifferentiated passage of time. The artificial designations represent only human constructs which have no relationship to the natural order of things.

Having by now, after an inexplicable two-year hiatus, resumed my Journal makes me aware of how little of my experiment in living survives in a form I can recall. What I left unrecorded has for the most part disappeared. The negatives—what doesn't happen, what you never experience, what you don't remember—far exceed the actual content of your life as you know and recall it.

A successful life is one in which you reduce your regrets—in so far as possible given your particular circumstances— to as few as possible.

Even an acute sense of curiosity becomes dulled later in life, as after you reach that stage many experiences have become repetitious and lack novelty. By old age you've absorbed so many sensory impressions they lose their power to amuse, inform, interest, inspire or titillate you. You're not so much world-weary as simply somewhat detoxed from the often inconvenient addiction to curiosity.

English language eccentricities no doubt greatly challenge students trying to learn that complicated communication system, a challenge I thankfully never had to face. Taken literally, the expressions "What's going on? and "What's up?" don't offer much in the way of a clue to their meaning. Something going "on" suggests that you're putting an item upon a place, while the "up" form implies that you're referring to something above. Like its related German language, English uses a number of prepositional phrases, many of which don't on their face reveal their meaning. The poor students tasked with learning the language have to put up with many such off-putting and outlandish confusions which make it hard to know what's going on.

Each living thing, thrown by chance into existence as a plaything of nature, becomes an unwilling participant in a fantasia of infinite forms created as a meaningless experiment. Many dangers threaten humanimals—pathogens, violence, accidents, physical and mental deterioration, disease, natural disasters, radical social and economic and political turmoil, revolutions, systemic collapse, cataclysmic natural events and all too much else, a witches' brew of churning change in a cauldron boiling with chance, luck and fate. All the horrors and hazards of the fiendish terrestrial experiment make the lonely planet a dangerous place. What sort of force or source ever conceived of and created such a world and its creatures? Even if an earthling manages to survive many years the poor creature faces an inevitable outcome which is an out-go. Is there any point to all this?

A theoretical retrospective thought experiment, trying to envision when young how you'd evaluate your life near the end, will help you reach that late stage in a way satisfactory to you.

On the train from the airport into Rome last month a young American woman sitting across from me said she was visiting the city for the first time—from San Francisco to San Pietro. Although I treasured my long familiarity with the city based on many visits to friends there, at the same time I in a way envied the newcomer her opportunity to see Rome in a new way with a fresh perspective. So long ago did my first visit take place I can't remember my impressions of Rome at first sight.

People refer to Rome as The Eternal City as many administrative, bureaucratic and official matters there take an eternity to complete.

A great city —of which few exist—offers an inexhaustible number of attractions and distractions and is exhausting to visit. Dr. Johnson said that if you're tired of London you're tired of life. After a long day of activity I've often been tired in London, but never of it.

Independent and solitary souls should never become too comfortable with their own company as before long you'll start boring yourself.

Both travel and reading enlarge one's world, but in greatly different ways. Through travel you engage with the outside world in an active, participatory way, while books offer passive and derivative views based on but not in the world.

Those who abandon established conventional practices and beliefs in an effort to improve their format should take care that the refit doesn't make them a misfit.

It's risky to remove even ugly, peeling and unappealing wallpaper as this may reveal something less attractive underneath. Similarly, it may not be advisable to look underneath or to analyze too realistically the superficial practices, beliefs and values of ordinary every-day suburban provincial life. Seeing what underlies what in some ways is an inauthentic way of being may greatly disillusion you.

Toward the end Churchill said, "I'm tired of it all." It's sobering to realize that even a great man like Churchill finally wearies of life. Those of us with lesser lives may well be even more susceptible to becoming tired of it all.

If the unexamined life is not worth living, neither is the over-examined life. In my Journal, begun more than 35 years ago, I've tried to avoid introspective self-oriented analytical matters. With my recorded observations I preferred not to disassociate myself from the outside world but to engage with and respond to it. Focusing on subjective internalized matters would have been of no interest to me, as the worldly spectacular play of infinite forms offers much more interesting food for thought and for action.

It's a rare and much valued privilege to be able to spend an entire day without listening or talking to someone else. To avoid verbal interactions offers a luxury unavailable to most mortals, a captive audience forced into dialogues with others. Other people are constantly telling you what to do, how to think, how to behave, what to buy, where to go, what's in and what's out. My Journal serves as a refuge from all the clatter and as a silent substitute for spoken forms of communication, as the entries represent an unspoken dialogue with myself.

Because we get used to what exists—both in a personal and in a more general terrestrial way—it's somewhat difficult to envision alternate formats. But what's familiar to us, including our very being, is really only provisional, came about only through random influences, and can at any time change by similarly capricious forces.

The contrast between how some people behave in professional activities as compared with how they deal with other matters can be striking. In their job they act in rational, reasonable, methodical and unemotional ways, while in such other common pursuits as affairs of the heart, religion, handling money, eating and drinking, and indulging in addictions humans operate in emotional, impulsive, irrational and illogical ways. This evidences something of a split personality, divided between pay-day matters and pay-spend activities.

Over-thinking often leads to under-performing.

Art is a message to the future from the creator that he or she was once alive, but it's a message which most often fails to get through.

The only creative act for most people involves procreating. Engendering a child serves as a surrogate for creating a work of art, as perhaps does a creative work in substituting for a child. Producing offspring and works of art both involve such characteristics as private activity, contingency, continuation, individualization, a unique product of a non-essential nature. For those mortals unable to leave their mark on a canvas, a printed page, a sheet of music a child can offer an adequate surrogate. For people uninterested in producing a child, a creative work yields a diaper- and college tuition-free form to add to the play of infinite forms. A pet dog also serves a similar function.

To enjoy two completely different modes of being—such as my stable, settled conventional home life and my far-flung kinetic adventure travels—evidences not a split personality but a doubled one. I looked forward to and enjoyed both ways of being. When at home I thought of being away, and when out in the world I envisioned my cozy comfortable home setting and often longed to return to that little corner of the globe. In that way I had the best of two of the sub-worlds in the larger world which is the lonely planet—not the best place to pursue an experiment in living but the only one available to humanimals.

For most people the dawn of a new day brings a set-piece with the schedule and activities for the most part mandatory and prearranged: feed the dog and the children (in that order), prepare the kids for school and yourself for work and the dog for nothing, then on to the office/factory/shop/wherever for your revenue-producing interlude, then perhaps some errands after work on the way home to face once again the canine-child needs and demands, then dinner with the spouse and maybe some TV, surfing the web, computer games or other mindless entertainments or escapes before sleep, and then repeating the same cycle the next day. Fortunate is the fellow who can live without these seemingly endless on-going day-in and day-out routines.

The frequency and length of the Journal entries gradually increased. Mini-essay-type writings expanded the contents in 2006 to 43 pages, more than in any previous year. By this point—as from 1969 when I started the Journal—my recorded views had established a fairly coherent world view, a perspective which served as a functional framework for me to carry out my experiment in living. Although my imposed format represented only an arbitrary and artificial construct, it helped me to deal with what I saw as an unruly and chaotic seething play of infinite forms suffused with chance and luck. My construct may not entirely have represented reality but it served well enough to depict my reality, one which worked well for me.

JANUARY 2006

Nature operates in both rather regular, orderly and somewhat predictable ways and, more commonly, with much disorder. Both organic and artificial bodies—like organizations, institutions, economic and political systems, governments, societies and civilizations—seem to continue on with a certain degree of regularity, but in fact neither homeostasis for the human body nor permanency for whatever else exists represents the natural state of things. Somewhere in his writings Miguel de Unamuno says that "insecuridad y confución" characterize life in Spain. The same could be said about life on the lonely planet, but apparently Spaniards are twice cursed.

Evolution adapted the human brain to the task of collecting and analyzing sensory impressions to enable mankind to cope with the challenge of existing on the lonely planet. Nature happened to endow the terrestrial setting with science-friendly forms and other resources earthlings can use to help them survive and to enhance their experiments in living. Those available elements include chemistry, biology, physics, medicine, botany, geology, minerals, petroleum, oxygen, carbon and all the rest of the endowed environment. At he same time, humanimals employ many of those resources for destructive and pernicious purposes, such as for warfare, crime, oppression, terror, intimidation and other beastly behaviors, more animal than human. Was it on balance a good trade-off to create the resources for man to produce both constructive and destructive innovations and practices?

As natural as the human smile and laugh may seem, that facial characteristic represents something of an oddity. No other animal possesses the ability to express itself in that way. Although smiling and laughing are usually not consciously willed but only rather automatically reactive, people no doubt enjoy the ability of being able to exhibit pleasure, well-being, a non-threatening attitude, friendliness, amusement and other such positive signs. For my part, I'm grateful for the smile and laughter as without them no one could respond to my jokes properly.

Observed without its known welcome and friendly significance, a smile seems like a facial twist. Stretching the lips to reveal teeth may mimic the practice of some other animals which bare their fangs. Since people normally don't bite other humanimals, showing teeth by that species denotes the opposite: not threat but a benign rather than a biting display. Another distinguishing factor is that humanimals don't accompany the baring of teeth with growls and snarls. In that way, if in few others, humans don't behave in the same aggressive animalistic way as do lesser aggressor animal kingdom species. Another such telling sign unique to humans is the frown, a slight silent distortion of facial features which can speak volumes.

Truly blessed is the life which enjoys the time and the leisure to contemplate such trifles as the human laugh, smile and frown. Few people possess the opportunity to consider such matters. Most earthlings are engaged in productive activities and smile, laugh or frown without giving a thought to those common reflexes.

The vast majority of humankind holds mundane or unpleasant jobs, work which serves to make a living but not to make a life. The bottom of the hierarchy includes rag-pickers and the rickshaw pullers in India. At the next level toil garbage truck drivers-handlers, sewer workers, septic tank cleaners, asbestos clean-up crews, enema technicians, and similar hands-on laborers dealing in noxious touch-points. Subway personnel, miners, tunneling crews, safe deposit box attendants and other underground laborers spend their working lives confined to subterranean dark holes of a kind where they will spend eternity. Morticians, coroners and grave diggers can perhaps be classified with the garbage collectors. Slaughterhouse employees, kitchen staff on cruise ships, ditch diggers, dish washers, lead smelter workers, manure handlers and other such types probably don't much look forward to going to work, nor do museum and security guards, supermarket check-out cashiers, call center operators. But even many people with higher status and better paying jobs suffer from unsatisfactory or oppressive work conditions. Meeting rigidly enforced sales quotas, performing plumbing services, working in a toxic chemical factory, supervising an animal shelter, drone-like civil service jobs all represent toil unlikely to inspire enthusiastic participation. It's the sad fate of most human beings to roll out of bed at an early hour to face yet another day of drudgery. Meanwhile, some of the fortunate few while away their days contemplating all sorts of useless ideas, such as a few (or many?) of the thoughts entered into this Journal. (Note: in the list of unpleasant jobs above I've omitted one of the most undesirable: editing my books.)

Religion serves as a labor-saving device. Instead of thinking for yourself you can simply adopt a ready-made preexisting set of rules, rituals and doctrines which bring you a complete belief system. This comforting and consoling supposed certainty offers an off-the-shelf package which eliminates the need to contemplate the matters religions purport to resolve. Non-believers face the challenge of reaching on their own their self-customized conclusions about such existential puzzlements.

At times I refuse to answer the phone. Admittedly, this is a strange response to being wanted: a call obviously means that someone wishes to reach out, give you some attention, talk to you. To activate the connection the calling party has to think of you, access a phone and then dial, all just to contact you. Nonetheless, sometimes I ignore the summons. At times the ringing seems too insistent and intrusive, and the noise represents an unsought demand to interrupt what I'm doing in order to respond. Not even curiosity impels me to answer. My discipline in avoiding the annoying ring-ring-ring of the bell should qualify me for the No-Bell Prize.

MARCH 2006

At a gathering following a funeral last weekend most of the purported mourners I encountered talked only about themselves: Not a thought spared for the deceased. Some dead just don't get no respect.

Strange change regarding the variance in how English pronounces "child" and "children."

JUNE 2006

My 23-day-long trip to London, Amsterdam, The Hague accounts for the more than month-long gap in Journal entries. It remains to be seen if I'll now resume my previous recent momentum for the Journal or if it will lie fallow for a while.

The natural state—or, more precisely, non-state—of everything which exists is non-existence. Whatever happens to come into being violates the natural order of things. For an eternity both before and after being, oblivion is the norm. A momentary random appearance in the realm of the living represents an exception to the nothingness which is in fact the nature of things.

A seemingly arbitrary law of nature decrees that humanimals must lose one-third of their life in sleep. The nightly demand seems to be an odd imposition on the benighted creatures. Perhaps an overload of incessant stimuli from the outside world during waking hours requires withdrawal to refresh the receptor brain-mind. Or maybe sleep functions as some sort of precursor to prepare humans for the time when they'll never awake.

As a thought experiment—which probably created an increased need for me to sleep—I contemplated the effects of a different arrangement for the nightly withdrawal. If people required no sleep at all, that would no doubt substantially change how society, culture and civilization function. But if sleep depleted, say, two-thirds rather than just one-third of our lives, that would create a major disincentive to pursue many activities as the time available to enjoy or benefit from long-tail endeavors would be greatly shortened. Examples include extended and difficult educational programs, highly specialized and technical professions, world-class sports, entrepreneurial undertakings and similar time-consuming and challenging undertakings. At what point would an additional sleep requirement—10 hours? 12? 14? or perhaps more—start to diminish people's willingness to exert themselves to achieve successes?

A few of my poems have been published privately (not by me) in limited circulation special edition booklets. In that I normally think in prose rather than in poetry, it's rare for a poem to happen to enter my mind and demand an exit into written form. The poem below is the first of the six I've included in the Journal. Others appear in entries for April and October 2021 and January, February and May 2022.

Fleet Sweet Days

Some sweet day
When the years have flown
And I'm alone again at last,
On that sweet day I'm sure to say:

"My sweet day was any day that I could be with you.
Of all the days in all the years that so quickly passed,
Those sweet but fleeting days with you
Didn't last, alas."

If you live long enough, life stories tend to become rather repetitious. Those accounts typically include details relating to personal trivia, activities of little interest to the listener, vacations and travels (mostly to mundane destinations), health problems, marital problems, business problems, money problems, job problems, child problems and similar concerns. Often the only bright spot consists of rave reviews for the family canine, always a favorite and a favored topic of discussion. I can often tell the stories before I listen to them. One function of a parent, a spouse or a close friend is to serve as a captive audience to listen patiently to whatever you have to say. But sometimes it's preferable not to listen. One woman I know told her children that she wasn't the complaint department, an attitude they complained to her about.

Repetition (as discussed in the last entry) applies also to life in general for senior citizens. It's in fact something of a relief at my age to opt out of many activities of the kind avidly pursued in my earlier years. By now I'm content to ignore many of what comprises the terrestrial "play of infinite forms," as Tagore called the strange and chaotic happenings and phenomena here on the lonely planet.

In the last line above surfaces for the first time the phrase which some twelve years later I chose to designate my late-in-life travel reminiscence (2021)—A PLAY OF INFINITE FORMS: THE VENTURES AND ADVENTURES OF A CURIOUS MAN AND WHAT HE FOUND THROUGH THE YEARS AND AROUND THE WORLD—and also this companion volume. Tagore's description came to characterize in a few words how I viewed the odd prevailing given conditions on the lonely planet, where all earthlings carry out their strange experiment in living, and the more remote but no less strange forms Big-Banged into existence in the universe and in the cosmos beyond.

My annual visit yesterday to the Home and Builders Show presented the usual extensive array and displays of products and services for home improvement, gardening, construction, cooking, eating, finishing and furnishing houses and much else, many of the offerings evidencing American ingenuity and creativity. Although uninterested in buying anything, I do get a childish pleasure in wandering through the vast hall to see the exhibits, chat with the vendors, eat the food samples, plus plucking pens, key rings other doodads and hand-outs and (especially) candy. What I most enjoy is observing the energy, productivity, enthusiasm, effort and variety on show at the show, an inspiring scene which evokes to me basic, down-home, down-to-earth regular day-to-day life here in the provincial precincts of America's heartland. On offer are such domestic needs or enhancements as siding, windows, gutter guards, candles, pots and pans, painting/roofing/repair/plumbing/dog care and other services, pest control (probably useful to keep intrusive free-loading non-buyers like me away), fruit and vegetable peelers and choppers, cosmetics, sausages, massage chairs, hair care potions and much else. The vendors try their best to entice buyers, but for the salespeople the three-day show must be a rather tedious and tiring effort to earn a few dollars.

Some lonely souls mistakenly seek low quality relationships or social connections due to an inability to remain alone. More preferable is to value and make use of your solitude and free time than to give those useful circumstances up in order to be with someone who doesn't bring you much fulfillment. Solitude is usually preferable to interactions with other humanimals which involve inappropriate relationships.

As I've learned over many years of reading and writing, the printed word offers a poor substitute for the real world as people experience it. Removed from real life, books serve only as surrogates for reality. Adventure travel attracted me as an alternative to losing myself in wordy activities. I preferred to lose myself in the maze of byways in Venice and the back alleys of Cairo and, sweetest of all, the gelato shops of Rome.

Both the attractions and the disadvantages of the life of the mind reside in how it's an internalized process. Facilitated by reading, observation, contemplation, the thinking man's way of being consists of a dialogue with himself. In theory you need never escape from your mind to participate in the outside world. But such a self-oriented and solipsistic confinement limits you to living an incomplete life. The ideal is to establish an appropriate balance between the active and the passive modes. One without the other leaves you with a poorly executed experiment in living.

When I recently ran into long-time acquaintance he exclaimed, "Where have you been?" The question emphasized to me how much I'd followed my own path for my own purposes and absented myself from the people who normally I'd have interacted with but who I seldom saw. For most people, an unexamined life is much more comfortable than an examined one. For unsettling thoughts and existential matters, "out of sight, out of mind" offers more serenity than does contemplation of basic life and death matters. A mindless way of life may be preferable to a mindful existence in which you contemplate unanswerable questions which bear on how you choose to live.

Time offers no time-outs or time off. It's relentless, continuous, impervious to change. It victimizes living things in a silent stealthy way which slowly decays them. What time lacks in drama it makes up for by its persistence and its long-term effects. As time evolves it never exhausts itself—only us.

AUGUST 2006

Every person is both a humanimal and an individual incarnation of that category. Which of the two elements—the general or the specific—predominates?

For oldsters who often wonder, "When will my time come?" the answer is that your time comes when it's gone.

Time must have a stop, but often that arresting moment comes too early or too late. For a promising youth felled before his or her potential could be realized, the end of time comes too soon. For an unhealthy, dysfunctional person suffering serious and possibly terminal conditions but who lingers on and on, time stops too late. For everyone in whatever state or stage of life, it's wise to assume that your time might end at any time, while at the same time hoping that the future will bring you some more tomorrows.

To diversify my sensory impressions which at home remained narrow and shallow I expanded them to a much wider and deeper dimension by far-ranging foreign adventure travel. The two kinds of experiences gave me a valued balanced and diversified view of life.

Saturation of the senses over a long and active life isn't all bad, as it means you've had your fill of what the world has to offer.

According to the laws of economics an endless free supply of something lowers its value. In that way the limitless occurrence of death—including one's own—represents an event without any value.

In a few previous entries I've noted that by old age many life experiences have become repetitious. Similarly, my reactions to and thoughts about the world have over time become repetitious, which may explain the occasional long gaps between the Journal entries. Habits, routines, rituals, repeats, cycles and other regularities operate with such duplication they leave me with nothing to say about all those recurring sensory impression categories. Here at home few opportunities exist for me to diversify my experiences or expand my horizons (as I did with travel) in ways which interest me.

Science progresses; culture doesn't—it merely accrets. Scientific and technical advances have produced many amazing and important products—M & M's, Levi's, Ex-lax, Barbie Dolls, whoopee cushions—and have shown that the atom can be split, and bananas as well, that time and space are relative and that relatives are sometimes spacey. By way of contrast, cultural products have by now exhausted originality and no longer offer much novelty. Just about everything has already been said, written, painted, sculpted, noted and for a long time most cultural work-products have simply repeated, restated, revised or reformatted previous works, echoes and reflections of the originals offering only variations on old themes.

The different life expectancy in advanced and in underdeveloped countries no doubt influences incentives and how people view their experiment in living. If born in a Calcutta slum with a probable short earthly existence and with little prospect of ever enjoying a pleasant life, your ambition will most likely be quite limited. Why bother to struggle to achieve anything when the odds are against you and if you'll probably disappear before long? Residents of countries which offer a likely extended longevity will deem worthwhile the pursuit of education, professional skills, improved circumstances, and other such enhancements and upgrades as a longer life incentivizes and justifies efforts to enrich an experiment in living. In the end both unfortunates too demoralized to seek a better life and those energized to improve their circumstances suffer the same outcome: non-existence. So perhaps even with a long life expectancy it's not really worth exerting yourself to seek accomplishments, success, wealth, recognition and other admired societal values which in order to attain will deplete much of your limited time, effort and energy.

DECEMBER 2006

Two different but related questions on an experiment in living interact to help you shape your answers. "What is the good life?" is definitional; "How do you live the good life?" is actionable. The "how" depends on the "what," and the "what" without the "how" remains only theoretical.

The purpose of the exercise is not to engage in a thought experiment but to activate decisions and pursue goals which are likely to help you fulfill the "how." "Good" doesn't pertain to an absolute but to the relative elements which characterize your situation, such as age, interests, abilities, resources, realistic potential, circumstances and other subjective and individual factors. The "what" refers to what you believe is good for you, not to some abstract Platonic notion of the Good. One way to decide on your "good" is to imagine that you'll expire after another few years. The question then becomes: How should I live now so as to reduce, in so far as possible, any regrets I might have at the end.

Man versus nature characterizes how life on the lonely planet operates. Humanimals exist as a result of natural forces, and those creatures benefit but also suffer from such forces. People constantly struggle to cope with the ceaseless deprivations inflicted by nature. In the end, nature always wins. In the meantime, mankind develops ways to produce some comfort, security, well-being and various other means to mitigate the often harsh effects unleashed by such natural forces as diseases, climate, weather, earthquakes, floods, volcanic eruptions, fires, cyclones, tornadoes, hurricanes, typhoons. In addition to services, systems and tangibles meant to help earthlings, those creatures also produce works of art to induce some meaning into an otherwise insensate and indifferent cosmos. But, alas, in the end nothing helps as the hostile conditions on the lonely planet and the nature of things defeats all attempts to survive and thrive.

It's difficult to maintain either a spirited or a spiritual attitude when confronted with the random indifferent workings of the cosmos. The sparkling lights during the holiday season represent noble but feeble attempts to signal some fleeting brightness in the dark void. Before long the lights will vanish and darkness will once again shadow human life on the lonely planet.

Every December 31st provokes thoughts of endings. Dawn of a new year somehow seems less promising than does the finality of the old year and the primacy of the past, with its certainty. The only thing known about the years which follow is that at one time or another I will transition into non-existence. This is not altogether a disadvantage, as death destroys death. Once you're gone, mortality no longer threatens you. With death dies death. So it is that the expiration of general time this December 31 suggests how my personal time will also come to an end.

2007

Although I wrote nothing during the first two months of 2007, once I resumed my Journal entries they became frequent and long, as in 2006. This erratic and sporadic pattern I can't entirely explain, other than to suggest that, like Lady Luck, inspiration is a fickle and capricious visitor.

MARCH 2007

A long gap since my last entry, in part because I've been away—two weeks in January in Florida and my just-concluded long trip to London and then to the Emirates in the Arabian Peninsula. My travels so satisfy me that they pleasantly remind me that what I excluded from my life—such as possessions, ambition, a compulsion to accumulate wealth, fame, approval, recognition and other common bourgeois goals—freed me up to pursue activities I deemed represented higher priorities. That which you reject can be as significant as what you choose to undertake.

The advantages of hosting a house guest include: the visit motivates you to clean the place; you get to spend some quality time with your visitor; and you now have a call on a reciprocal visit which will let you stay with the person you hosted. The disadvantages include: presence of someone else requires you to engage with the visitor; the guest intrudes on your privacy and interferes with how you want to spend the day; after the visitor departs you have to again clean some areas of the house.

APRIL 2007

Over time we become accustomed to the cast of characters who people our life. They seem a fixed presence up until the time when they become unfixed by disappearing. After they vanish the known voice on the phone never again speaks, the familiar face and behavior and mannerisms vanish, the shared memories and all the other associations which characterize long-standing relationships lack the bilateral connection. In recent times those losses occur ever more frequently. One of these days I'll join the defunct crowd, leaving my surviving cast of characters to carry on with their roles in the play of infinite forms until, in their turn, those I left behind also disappear, after which both sides of the bilateral link will no longer exist.

Up into their their twenties people remain stranded between experience and format. During that decade they've lived long enough to complete their education, function in the working world, and perhaps settle in with a companion. By then those still fairly young humanimals have something of a grasp on their experiment in living but aren't yet fully equipped to form a coherent attitude on the experience. It's still too early to formulate guidelines, and even beyond that awkward stage many earthlings never develop any workable formats to help reach the end in a desirable way. Such people carry out their experiments oblivious to their fragility and to how time-limited they are.

MAY 2007

One key element in creating "the good life" is the ability to avoid spending time with people you prefer not to associate with. This rare privilege remains unavailable to most people, who face the necessity to engage in associations or relationships which include such possibly unpleasant characters as bosses, colleagues, neighbors, tradesmen, service providers, customers, family members, bureaucrats, salesmen and the like, an often unlikable cohort. Nothing personal, but I'd rather not see my dentist who—apart from his needle and drill—is a personable, pleasant and unthreatening guy. Many outcasts from society enjoy the advantage of being able to avoid unwanted relationships. They include vagabonds, vagrants, bums, tramps, hobos, street people, waifs, drifters, slackers, lay-abouts, recluses, hermits and "himits," loners, drop-outs. Such types are freer than many people who enjoy regular but more confining lives.

To establish any sort of relationship requires an acceptance that you'll be caught up in the connection. Whether initiating and maintaining a romance, a friendship, a commercial undertaking, a marriage, children, a dog, or any other on-going obligation, your freedom of action will perforce be constrained. Whether or not this limitation turns out to be acceptable to you depends on how the relationship develops. Adopting a dog is perhaps the obligation most likely to prove satisfactory.

Inertia and the known advantages and disadvantages of an existing situation deter people from making changes. This eliminates the risk of bringing unknown and possibly more serious unsatisfactory outcomes instead of simply retaining the familiar negative characteristics you're already aware of. But inaction may also prevent you from enjoying the possible benefits of a new and better format. As a two-edged sword, change may cut either way.

The most basic amenities common in my little corner of the world—the Midwestern provincial suburban neighborhood where I live—are completely unavailable to unfortunates all around the world. In my travels I visited many places where the impoverished locals lacked space, peace, sanitation, clean water, plumbing, always-on electricity, a private dwelling, greenery, a car or any other mechanical means of transportation, and even clothes (in Ethiopia some of the children wore nothing). My modest middle-class American way of life at home represents an earthly paradise unattainable for many miserable humanimals in under-developed lands.

JUNE 2007

Each pleasant passing summer day also brings melancholy as the days which remain grow shorter day-by-day. This reflects the paradox that the more fortunate and favorable your life the more you lose when it's over. Something of a bittersweet fin-de-vie mood suffuses every passing pleasurable experience with a mixture of delight and regret.

JULY 2007

Many provisional pleasures come twinned with undesirable effects. Sex is both intensely satisfying and extremely fleeting, and can lead to undesired consequences. While sleep refreshes you, it also steals away your allotted earthly time allocation. Eating brings tasty but transient sensory delights, soon eliminated, and some sorts of savory foods can be bad for your health. On a more existential level, existence itself entails a chiaroscuro experience brightened by many pleasures and shadowed with a number of dark moments. Toward the end, the darkness somehow seems more pervasive.

AUGUST 2007

I recently came across the phrase: "Life is gratuitous: it comes uninvited and unexplained." Never did there exist a mortal who asked to be born, and many earthlings have probably regretted that they were. It's both unsettling and liberating to realize that the world, the universe, the cosmos lack meaning. That disturbing reality forces you to accept that no benevolent or any other guiding force presides over the insensate system, but at the same time realizing how purposeless the system is frees you to create your own experiment in living as best you can, given both your circumstances and the conditions which prevail on the forlorn lonely planet, suspended in space and spinning its way on to oblivion.

After a recent performance of "Oklahoma!" I attended, the words and rhythms of "Surrey With the Fringe On Top" continued to sound in my mind. I saw/heard/felt the clip-clop pace of the music, which matched the lyrics. The players wished that the surrey would go on forever, go on forever, go on forever and never stop, but this is a wish unfilled as the surrey always comes to a Full. Stop. Like Time's wingèd chariot, which always catches up with you and stops your advance, the surrey clip-clops to a stop. The ever-forward-moving wheels—time on the roll if not on the wing—spin motion to evoke passing time. The fringe flaps on the top as the wheels underneath spin on and on, and there's no forever but only the now, a present which slips and slides like carriage wheels on a storm-swept road, the wet tracks soon to vanish as they're washed away by the rain after the surrey moves on.

SEPTEMBER 2007

The coolness of autumn seemed to arrive suddenly this fall, as if nature jerked away the summer to hurry along the seasonal cycle.

It's easier to visualize the world at is was before mankind existed than how it will be after humans are gone. Evidence of the pre-human era has left clues about that long ago time when the lonely planet, lacking the swarm of humanimals which call the place home, was especially lonely. It's more difficult to imagine how the earth will be after people no longer populate the place. History informs you about how life was before your time, but the history to be created by the future as it becomes the present and then fades into the past remains obscure.

A friend my age suffers from various ailments, none of them life-threatening but some life-style threatening.

OCTOBER 2007

Writers who address the topic of mortality seem to believe that they can present some original ideas about a subject long ago exhausted. Whatever can be said about death has long since been discussed. My many Journal references to the matter represent not an attempt to throw new light on the dark subject but simply to come to terms with mortality in a personal way.

The path of least resistance is simply to continue on with the same format which currently applies to your situation and to adopt the prevailing value systems, beliefs, rituals and behavior of the society which defines where you happen to exist. I dissented in many ways from that convenient and comfortable path. One way was to change my settled and conventional life by diversifying my experiment in living with adventure travel to remote and exotic foreign lands. My compulsion to travel both bewitched and bedeviled me. This change of "seen-ary" greatly diversified and enriched my life, while at the same time bringing me many challenges, anxious moments, dangers and often ominous uncertainties. While out in the world I at times wished that I had remained on the convenient and comfortable familiar range-bound path at home.

A few days ago when in Paris I took some old-form photos with a simple throw-away Fuji camera, flew home and within 48 hours the developed film showed me the images taken 4,400 miles away. The seemingly ordinary elements of contemporary life involved in the process I've described—the camera, the flight, developing the film—depend on remarkable technology and complex infrastructure, modern-day marvels little appreciated and most often taken for granted by almost everyone who makes use of the systems which enable such miracles. Well, call them wonders—I don't believe in miracles (except that it was truly a miracle my writings got published.)

DECEMBER 2007

At a nearby church where I attended a performance of "The Messiah" cut-out paper stars, tinsel, holiday trimmings and other festive decor decorated the sanctuary. The concert, setting and religious rituals represent an effort by humanimals to endow the season with some sort of transcendental significance in the belief that such activities can bring meaning to an essentially meaningless holiday. Christmas symbolizes a failed attempt to endow nothing to make it something. No presiding cosmic consciousness is aware of these rather sad and puny earthly doings, meant to wrest from the void some enlightenment and belief. Although I failed to participate in the devotional parts of the occasion, I enjoyed the music and, especially, the delicious buffet offered by the church sisterhood following the concert. I thank the Lord that Christmas brings me so many pleasurable unintended consequences of the religious observation.

Existing as a humanimal thrown unwillingly into the nuisance of being an earthing on the lonely planet is inconvenient, intrusive, dangerous, brief, uncertain, confusing, threatening, bewildering, baffling, purposeless—all elements of the terms of engagement the creature faces while it's alive. You must either accept those terms or opt to disengage.

Reading the diaries of Thomas Mann prompts me to wonder why anyone, even prominent figures like Mann, would bother to record daily trivia. A compulsion to record passing routine day-by-day events never motivated me to keep a home-based diary, which would have been boring even to its author. However, during my foreign travels I did maintain a detailed diary of the particular play of infinite forms which happened to come to my attention while away. Mann includes far too many mundane passage in his diary—shaved, took a walk. But if he shaved while walking, that would be noteworthy. Much of what Mann mentions applies to routine habitual behavior common to every humanimal but, thankfully, very few write about such truly insignificant matters.

Whatever anyone may think or believe in the way of non-verifiable views may console the individual who holds such often improbable and unprovable beliefs but they mean nothing for anyone else. Accepting the doctrines of Marxism, Freud, religion, atheism, anarchism, existentialism, surrealism, mysticism, free-love, vegetarianism and any of the other arbitrary constructs imposed by humanimals to order messy and chaotic reality enables the true believer to establish a framework to deal with his or her own experiment in living. but none of those systems necessarily offers any guidance for anyone else. Although Thomas Mann recorded in his diaries some of the beliefs which formed his *Weltanschauung*, one Mann's worldview doesn't necessarily inform another man's. Whatever I've written in the Journal to express my opinions, beliefs or attitudes pertains only to my own experiment and aren't meant to suggest that my thoughts represent valid or relevant guidelines for anyone else.

Although familiarity may or may not breed contempt, it usually eventually induces boredom. Families which gather on every possible occasion overdo togetherness, a habitual proximity likely to lead to relative fatigue. Because the familiar guests interact with one another so often, there's little or nothing new to discuss. The closely-knit group in such a hermetic (and "himetic") cluster is reduced to engaging in inane chit-chat and chatter. At the same time, there's something heart-warming about a family so close that its members enjoy being in frequent close even if mind-numbing contact.

Whenever I become peeved, impatient, irritated, dissatisfied or disappointed by one of my good friends I think of what they sometimes have to put up with from me, and my grievances about them immediately cease.

JANUARY 2008

By now I've most likely reached the stage of life when just about everything of significance—except my final decline and demise—has already occurred. I've met all the people I'll ever know, visited almost all the places I'll ever see, read just about all the books, seen the museums and performances, experienced the events and happenings, cycled through the rather repetitive news cycles, thought about and reached conclusions on most of the matters that mattered to me for my experiment in living, and experienced all the rest of what will comprise my life. Although, as always, uncertainties and surprises lurk in the future, and luck and chance will have their way, it's probable that little more of substance remains to add to my already long familiarity with the infinite forms I happened to know.

For some people possessions serve as an identifier: you are what you own. Part of my identity lies in what I don't own. Other than the most basic, functional and necessary things, I possess very little. I felt that possessions would own me more than I them. Stuff would stuff my life with irrelevant and burdensome baggage. I valued intangibles much higher: travel, experiences, friendships and other relationships, memories, reading, thinking, momentary pleasures and passing delights. I have very little to show for my life as most of it consisted of what doesn't exist as dimensional objects.

Deep heartfelt romantic relationships inevitably end one way or another in heartbreak and tears: if separation and a final break doesn't rupture the relationship, for sure death will

NOVEMBER 2008

A very long gap since the last entry on January 21st. Not that I stopped thinking, but for some reason I stopped writing. My failure to record passing ideas during the year relegate them to the obscurity from which they originated. I apparently deemed none of them worthy of inclusion in the Journal, a consideration which may also apply to many of the thoughts which did find their way into the notebooks.

Regrets: for what you hoped to accomplish but never did; for what you wanted to experience but left undone; for what you ventured but which proved ill-advised; for what pleased you but ended far too soon; for opportunities which you rejected but which, as you later realized, would have turned out well. How do these regrets rank in order of severity?

DECEMBER 2008

My house has treated me better than I've treated it. Except for the problems which must be dealt with to prevent further problems, I ignore most of them. Deferred maintenance applies to houses as well as to oldsters. The two of us—manse and me—have grown old together. One day in the not too distant future new homebodies will occupy these familiar spaces, ones I'll soon be forced to vacate.

At a recent dinner in a Chihuahua, Mexico restaurant filled with objects, artifacts, photos, antiques (including me) and other decorative items, I asked the proprietor how she managed to accumulate such a large collection. She replied, "Dinero."

On New Year's Eve old people wonder less what the new year will bring than what it won't bring—all you'll miss out on if you expire during the year.

JANUARY 2009

New Year's Day brings yet another year filled with annual repetitions of the same familiar rituals: holidays, birthdays, death days, Mondays and more days, and on and on. Humans track time by such markers, which serve to distinguish the otherwise blurry passage of the diurnal cycle. Without those delineations time would seem seamless and even more unseemly and seamy, killer that it is.

One way to gain a perspective on another person's experiment in living is to assess how curious they are. Without a sense of curiosity, a humanimal's experiment is more likely to be quite limited, mundane and conventional. Sometimes I envy the settled and less bothersome way of life enjoyed by the incurious.

So remote to us in time and often in place are our ur-ancestors we can scarcely imagine them as real people who in their day faced the same sort of personal and existential concerns as do those of us who are their descendants. Like everyone who has lived, suffered and enjoyed many of the same kinds of experiences known to all human beings, defunct, present and future generations share much in common. But while our own engagement with life seems so vivid, immediate and real, what past earthlings experienced in similar ways—and future generations will experience—remains abstract and insubstantial. It's only the present play of infinite forms we know which presents images and events sufficiently granular and real to inform us about how it feels to be a living humanimal.

APRIL 2009

I've always tried to interact with the older and the younger generations. The different age groups brought me new perspectives. By now almost all my senior friends have died, leaving me a member of the older generation. Left for me now is only the younger group. Yesterday dawned as the first day of my life without the existence of my life-long friend who died two days ago, age almost 98 [also referred to in the very last entry, September 2022]. His disappearance affected me less than I'd imagined it would. Given his age, I expected his passing at any time. Also, I've by now lost so many friends I've become somewhat inured to their demise.

On Easter Day it's comforting to realize that death has its advantages, as without it resurrection isn't possible. But you have to be quite an unusual dude to accomplish that revival trick. The rest of us get no curtain call—only the mortuary shroud which curtains our performance.

MAY 2009

I've always followed the advice of Ted Williams, who in his *The Science of Hitting* wrote that young baseball players should be very selective in choosing which pitch to swing at. All through the years I've been careful in deciding which activities to undertake and which to reject. Nonetheless, it surprised me that last week I kept my bat unswung by deciding not to embark on a trip to Mongolia. This decision to let pass the kind of pitch I usually hit represents something of a turning point for me, as up to now I've almost always taken every opportunity to travel and especially to distant, remote, exotic and possibly even dangerous areas. Never before have I undertaken such detailed preparation, only to renounce the trip to stay at home. The road not traveled attracted me more than the venture which would lead to adventure. Perhaps I've now reached the saturation point for trips which require long flights, high energy, great effort, Third World conditions, grueling itineraries and being distanced from my home comforts and conveniences. If so, my life will now be easier and in many ways more pleasant, but in some ways by far less interesting.

Many hazards threaten returns on capital. Capital remains ever vulnerable to any number of depredations, among them radical social change, unsettled political and geopolitical conditions, taxation, predatory politicians and governments, regulation, systemic distortions and failures, foreign attacks, economic turmoil, natural disasters and much else. Capital presents an inviting target for those who don't have any. In its vulnerability to all manner of risk, any form of wealth can be considered risk capital. Asset values depend not on their intrinsic worth but on how markets price various components of wealth, which fluctuates based on opinions—that is, on the prices. Any attempts to predict values lack credibility. Forecasters, market commentators, portfolio managers, wealth advisers, economists, business journalists and other such characters make a living telling people who seek guidance what the future holds. If those sages knew, they wouldn't have to continue to make a living giving such advice. B.C. Forbes, the founder of *Forbes* magazine, said the way to make money from the markets is not to invest in but to write about them.

JUNE 2009

The world conspires to rob people not only of their wealth but also of their time. The thievery originates with both individuals and from more general distractions. To a greater and a lesser degree in each person's situation, other people in your life—friends, family, relatives and such—have a claim on your time. How you respond to each claim will determine how much of your time you choose to devote to the person who wants some of your limited moments. As for outside influences, those which attempt to capture your attention include such attractions and distractions as media (social and otherwise), digital sites and gadgets, vamps and gold-diggers, gigolos, hobbies, entertainments, advertising, marketing, demonstrations, spectacles, sports, museums, festivals, presentations, commercial operations, the works of authors and other creative types, high and pop culture, consumer goods and bads, regulations and rules, politicians, bureaucrats and governmental demands, salesmen, solicitors, bosses, associates and colleagues, dogs (never-fail attention-getters). Just as OPM (Other People's Money) remains attractive to all sorts of predators and subject to many risks, so does OPT. Other People's Time, which to its possessor is limited and valuable, represents to outsiders a free resource which can be taken with no consequences for those who exploit it.

While time is a valuable resource, at the same time it's corrosive as eventually all the experiences, relationships and memories its passage enables disappear when your time runs out. This makes you wonder whether it's worth going to all the trouble to create what time brings you in the first place.

It seems to violate the natural order of things when your life-span exceeds the age of your parents when they died. While alive, parents are always older than their child, but now I'm quite senior to both of them.

JULY 2009

A cool mellow yellow Midwestern summer afternoon as the day's waning sun casts its fading gold hue upon the greenery, the shifting shadows gradually forming slowly changing patterns. It seems a Vermeer-like moment suspended in time, except that there's no suspense in the inevitable outcome as no suspension holds time still. The light continue to fade away, the shadows creep across the foliage and everything changes in slow but inexorable motion. Such a fleeting interlude seems all the more enjoyable for the evanescent and impermanent nature of nature these moments reveal.

AUGUST 2009

Although my now limited longevity as compared with much younger people seems to be a disadvantage, I believe that my situation is better than my juniors. It's preferable to enjoy the certainty of the past and be out of harm's way if you've enjoyed a satisfactory experiment in living. The younger generation faces many threats, risks and such capricious forces as luck, chance, fate and happenstance before the youngsters can reach the possible benefits of a contented old age. Better to have attained that serene stage than to cope with all the uncertainties which stand between a young person and his or her eventual satisfaction.

Although I still enjoy the regal fare at Dairy Queen, Burger King and White Castle as well as treats like M & M's, Tootsie Rolls and peanuts, after you've consumed some 82,000 meals (three a day. plus countless snacks) over, say, 75 years eating seems rather repetitious, as do many other life experiences. At a certain age you reach a saturation point, bloated both from food and from life.

For someone who possess enough monetary resources to live in a satisfactory way, as you age the time value of time becomes as important as the time value of money.

Setting priorities and making decisions is in a way easier in your old age than in earlier years. Toward the end the limited remaining time eliminates many options, so allowing you to focus on the highest and best use of the brief interlude until your demise. By then your "to-do" list is much smaller and more like a "to-don't" agenda, as no more time exists for long-term undertakings and in any case your long experiment in living includes almost all the content it ever will.

DECEMBER 2009

My month-long trip to Europe, ending September 7th, accounts for some of the long interval since my last entry back in August. Perhaps being away weakens my sporadic habit of writing in the Journal.

~PART THREE~
LATE YEARS

VI. Entries As I Neared the Exit: January 2010–December 2019

This last section which covers 12 years accounts for only some 23 percent of the time I maintained the Journal but more than 80 percent of its content, much of which remained consistent with my viewpoints, opinions and conclusions reached in earlier years. If it's true that you can't teach an old dog new tricks, it's probably the case that a new dog can learn some tricks usually understood only when the animal is older.

JANUARY 2010

A fresh new year. The show—the spectacle produced by the play of infinite forms—plays on. To my surprise I still go on as part of the show, my surviving friends go on, most everything continues on as before, in that way presenting the illusion of stability and continuity. Routine daily life, as it creeps ahead dawn to dusk, night to morning, repeats with all the familiar people, surroundings, routines, rituals and settings which make the play of forms seem as if nothing changes. But over time everything steadily and stealthily mutates and eventually disappears.

Snow-bound at home, not a range-bound confinement but a delightful retreat from the outside world. For me the icy isolation brings me not down-time but useful up-time.

"Know thy language" can be as as challenging as to "know thyself." I never learned English; it taught me. So deeply embedded is my native language English seems completely natural to me. But occasionally I become aware how complex and opaque my language is for foreigners trying to make some sense out of what for them is a foreign way of speaking. The construction "to make"+ a preposition (or other add-ons) produces baffling expressions which offer no clue to their meaning: (a) "to make up a story"; (b) "to make up a face," which differs from "to make a face"; (c) "to make up" (conciliate) or "to make up" (to finish an uncompleted task) or "to make up" (to fib); (d) "to make up to" someone (ingratiate yourself); (e) "to make out" (to discern something or, with a lover, to cuddle and pet); (f) "to make merry" or "to make Mary" (also merry, unless you must marry); (g) "to make hay while the sun shines" (even city slickers can do this); (h) "to make over"; (i) "to make time" (would that we could) or "to make up time" (j) "to make fun" of someone (not to give them joy but to ridicule them); (k) "to make good" (which implies not goodness but restitution); (l) "to make over" (re-do) or "a make-over" (a cosmetic improvement); "to make-do" (but there's no "make-don't"). A "make-work" project doesn't create real work but only a non-productive busy-work activity; "make-believe" doesn't make people believe but entertains them with usually unbelievable fantasy; a "makeshift" solution doesn't shift but stabilizes. It's all far too confusing to explain to students. English as a second language is much more challenging than learning that eccentric tongue as your first one.

Apart from those who people our lives, almost all the other 7.5 billion terrestrial humanimals [by now some 8 billion such creatures, but I've retained here and elsewhere the figure I entered in the Journal] are to us only an abstract general category: a vast herd of indistinguishable creatures. Although we realize that each and every such animal behaves, thinks, feels, acts and reacts and eats, drinks, sleeps and procreates in ways common to all of humanity, to us all those strangers exist only in an impersonal and indistinct way, unlike our familiars who form part of our existential DNA. So it is that when components of the strands are cut—the double helix becoming at various places single—we feel some part of us has been removed. The death of strangers—"Thousands killed in Java earthquake," "Hundreds roasted alive in Pakistan fire," "More than twenty thousand in Outer Mongolia felled by epidemic," "Countless numbers in Inner Mongolia yurts dead from yak attacks," "Plane crash in Afghanistan leaves no survivors," "Zulu king and his 33 wives die in bed," "8328 perish in Indian train wreck"— doesn't affect us in the same way.

"Escape to Oblivion"—a book title which could denote not just a living escape to obscurity but also how mortality allows us to depart into an eternal state of nothingness.

Although (as Don Quixote says) a man is the son of his acts, we're all step-children as humanimals are also sons and daughters of their thoughts. Which better defines the creature's essential being—its acts or its inner life? James Joyce spent years trying to present a detailed and inclusive description of one man's mind during one day in Dublin—a doublin' of the sensory impressions which the outside world happened to deliver that particular day to a particular individual. To picture a life in full, it's necessary to know both acts and thoughts, but apart from yourself only actions and other externals are apparent. This implies that we can never know another person all that well.

FEBRUARY 2010

That was fast! Already the second month in the new year and decade and of the twenty-first century now one-tenth gone. As time spins on, oldsters like me wind down. The law of entropy applies to the elderly but not to ageless Father Time, who never becomes a Grandfather. Unfair: why shouldn't He suffer over time the same fate as humanimals do?

No matter how simple a person's life, many impositions and intrusions deplete his or her time and energy. Even a full-time beachcomber occasionally faces sand flies and sand fleas and must somehow get hold of a sandwich, perhaps made with whole-grain bread to continue the familiar grains of sand feeling.

Two kinds of life events which seem unnatural: to live longer than your deceased parents did, and for a child to die before his or her parents do.

MAY 2010

Three months since my last entry in mid-February. But now, for no explicable reason, a noteworthy thought suddenly occurs to me: One way to judge the amplitude of a person's life is to measure it by the number of habitations he's occupied. One category pertains to owned or rented houses where a the person has lived. Serial transients have resided all over the map, while deeply rooted characters like me have remained in just a few houses, each located close to one another. A second category relates to the number of places where you've been a house guest, a measure which indicates a person's social network. Then there are the number of hotels a person has transited through. Over a long lifetime of wide-ranging travel I've occupied hundreds of hotel rooms, most of them soulless and forgettable. They gave me only a roof over my head and a pillow under it, while visiting friends and family brought me an inside view of their way of life. However measured, I've slept in many different beds all over the world—none more restful and cozy than my own berth here at home.

Nature hasn't singled me out as the only fall-guy fated to fall into oblivion. If by some sort of miracle I were an exception I'd probably resent not being included as a participant in the vast cohort of departed souls, one reason being that never could I satisfy my curiosity about that life experience. Although a humanimal may experience dying, the creature won't be aware of death as once it occurs the animal becomes oblivious to its non-being, to its former existence, and to everything else. Only the survivors are left with the aftermath of death and the implications of that passing happening. I believe it was Archibald MacLeish who wrote in "The Young Dead Soldier," "Our deaths are not ours ... They are yours: They will mean what you make of them."

Time's versatile scythe operates with two edges as both a grim-reaper and a sower of benefits. For convicts, convalescents and those mourning a loss the passage of time usually brings relief. But for those who mourn a lost spouse, child, close friend or dog, time may be a "faux ami" as its corrosive effect has operated to destroy the deceased. In archaeology, age-old discoveries often offer more significance than more recent findings. By their age Lucy, Neanderthal Man and King Tut brought to the play of infinite forms ancient characters who play major roles in the history of mankind. In that way antiquity, as created by a long elapse of time, brings benefits to civilization, even at the expense of destroying earlier empires.

JULY 2010

This last day of July marks two months since my last entry. But somehow two Journal-worthy stray thoughts have now suddenly occurred to me: (1) "Good evening" and " Good night" seem to represent similar social salutations, but each denotes quite different sentiments. "Good evening" serves as an open, welcoming, anticipatory greeting: the evening ahead hopefully offers some pleasures. "Good night" conveys a sense of closure, an ending of the day with only dreams or nightmares to fill in the hours until morning. (2) An oddity related to the above has for years baffled me, and no one—native Spanish speakers, professors of the language, or anyone else— has ever been able to explain the curious format. Spanish uses the plural to greet people during the various day parts: "Buenos dias ... buenas tardes ... buenas noches." Such a salutation applies only to the singular moment in time—"Good day, good evening, good night"—so why the plural? Perhaps such expressions are meant to wish people good days, evenings, nights in a general way to include not only the present but also future periods—a kind of good luck incantation. People who speak Spanish as their first language have never given me a reason for this rather strange practice. As is common, you seldom think about the language you learned as a child, one which seems so familiar, logical and normal to you but which to students trying to learn a foreign lingo represents a mysterious and often incomprehensible set of letters, symbols and forms.

The penumbra of mortality which shadows my existence brings certain advantages. Approaching mortality liberates you from many previously concerning matters. Limited choices and fewer options now eliminate complicated and confusing decisions. Whatever ambition possessed you no longer exerts a hold. The kinds of uncertainties which young people face no longer confront you. By old age the operation of luck and chance will affect your now short life less than when you were younger. Near the end you needn't try to make up for lost time. Living to a ripe old age can bring you many benefits, as long as you don't survive to an over-ripe infirm old age.

Unfulfilled desires: to learn how to play the piano; to have enjoyed additional pleasant relationships, even though I had a lot more than my share; to have spoken more than just four foreign languages, such as adding Arabic, Russian and Chinese; to have bought Microsoft on the underwriting. Oh well, you can't win 'em all. Content is the person whose regrets are ones like those I've mentioned.

Given all the obvious disadvantages of being thrown unwillingly into existence, I wonder if the experience is worth the hassles. If left unborn you'd wouldn't miss what you never know. Non-existence presents no disadvantages at all, as you completely avoid such fearsome consequences as disease, decay, disintegration, death, and those are just the "d's": many other "a" to "z" threats, hazards and risks afflict humanimals. As an incarnated creature you exist momentarily between two eternities, but it would be preferable to cut out the middleman by by-passing the problematical earthly phase in favor of remaining an eternally un-created and disembodied nothing.

Test of a satisfactory experiment in living: if you'd prefer to revert to earlier years for a second chance with the hope of an improved outcome or if you accept how the experiment turned out and wouldn't want to risk another try.

SEPTEMBER 2010

Even though it's only early September I can already feel the season beginning to turn. Occasional cool days and rain hint that autumn will soon dethrone summer's reign. The aging year seems an analogue to my own life.

The trio of components—health, wealth and time—which represent essential factors to enable a satisfactory experiment in living possess varying characteristics. The first two depend partly on personal behavior but largely on chance random factors, while time exists in an absolute way as a mechanical force which is the same for everyone. Health and time inevitably decay away, while wealth can wax or wane or disappear. Time always becomes more scarce, but wealth can become more abundant. Without time neither health nor wealth can exist. With chronic bad health the gift of time comes as a poisoned chalice. Without wealth time offers few opportunities and often brings about bad health sooner than normal.

A lack of curiosity usually operates more as a blessing than as a curse. Being incurious allows people to live in peace, content with their own familiar little world and focused on their immediate concerns. Compulsive curiosity distracts and unsettles you, effects which brought me many exceptional experiences and memories, and so for me my inherent inquisitiveness represented more of a benefit than a disadvantage.

OCTOBER 2010

A paradox of old age is that every decision is both highly meaningful, because you have so little time left, and at the same time of little importance, as so little time remains. With a poor decision you suffer the consequences only relatively briefly, while a good choice will bring you the benefits you sought for only a short time.

What happens represents actual and known outcomes, but the negative elements of life also influence how your experiment in living turns out. What you avoid, non-events, rejected opportunities, what never occurs shapes much of a humanimal's life, but counter-factuals based on potential but non-existent happenings are impossible to assess, so you remain ignorant of how such important influences like omitted factors affected your experiment.

NOVEMBER 2010

Crispy, crunchy, crumbling leaves now litter the lawn, signaling autumn's end and the onset of winter.

Since my last entry a month and a half ago the season has turned and I've returned home after traveling many miles to Libya, across the desert sands there, and then back to where I began. All is once again familiar following my far-flung travel adventure to a land where many things are different—customs, habits, practices, government, language and even the concept of time in that age-old land littered with ruins from ancient civilizations.

DECEMBER 2010

Toward the end time shrinks as if a self-sealing plastic wrap which gradually starts to suffocate me. A December always makes me wonder if I'll continue to have some breathing room to see the new year through to its end, before mine.

JANUARY 2011

New Year's Day marks a beginning quite different for the young and for the old. For youngsters the new year arrives with promise; for oldsters, with nostalgia and foreboding. The young savor the possibilities the year offers and look forward to benefiting from new opportunities; seniors wonder both how much of the new year they'll see and how, when and where they will come to an end.

What effect would a shortened average life span exert on the willingness of a humanimal to pursue a long and difficult education, to undertake long-term projects, to engage in challenging time-consuming endeavors, to try to excel in their chosen field, to attain high professional accomplishments? Society, civilization, culture, politics and government, the economy, personal relationships, scientific and technological innovations, research and development, capital investments and much else would be affected if people's normal life expectancy were, say, only 40 or so years. But what if humans could expect to live and function well until age 100—would that extended period incentivize the creatures to be even more ambitious than many earthlings already are?

"To be or not to be" represents a Plan A and a Plan "Be." Once a humanimal is thrown unwillingly into life and then soon becomes aware of its terrestrial existence a powerful survival instinct takes hold. Being alive becomes a habit, one which, like many habits, you resist giving up. So compelling is existence, once being is inflicted upon an earthling almost no one wants to abandon Plan A (to remain Alive) for Plan "Be," a misnomer as it designates not to be. "Be" includes both ceasing to be and never having been born. But once you happen to exist it's too late for "Be" and, unless you decide to end A, you're stuck with that option, to which most people cling for dear life in spite of its many obvious disadvantages.

Random observations which, as such, reflect how life for the most part comes at you randomly: (1) English is sometimes too subtle for words. Note the difference between "hands-on" (to deal directly with a situation) and "to hand on" (to avoid dealing with a situation by passing the problem on to someone else). Also, between "wrong" (which implies a mistake} and "wrongful" (which denotes an injury or an unlawful act). (2) Recently someone told me of an M.B.A. degree entrance exam asking for a one-page essay on the three people the applicant would most like to dine with. The best answer would obviously be: the dean of the school, the admissions director, and someone willing to pick up the dinner tab. (3) Who, then, would I most like to spend an evening with? Apart from Snoopy and a femme fatale (my first choices), I'd choose Montaigne, Shakespeare, Goethe, Mark Twain, Churchill, Hemingway and a scribe (maybe Samuel Pepys) to record the conversation. I'd also include Vermeer, but since he's not known as a wordsman like the others it's difficult to know if the artist would have anything to say; perhaps the painter would simply brush off all attempts at conversation.

Over time, what's distinct becomes extinct. What exists desists. "Is" mutates into "was." Integration decays into disintegration. "Now" almost immediately becomes "then." Tomorrow is simply a briefly deferred yesterday, the next generation soon the senior one, the current era history, the earth eventually a lifeless sphere spinning in the void and devoid of any human presence. And now—time for lunch.

The snow which now covers the landscape will soon melt away to reveal the seemingly solid terrain below. But the ground beneath our feet remains vulnerable to tremors, eruptions, tectonic plate shifts, earthquakes, sink holes, collapse, displacement and other random natural forces which can reshape the land, which appears to be stable and invariable but which can suddenly disappear.

Apart from nature (which, as discussed in the last entry, can bring about sudden and substantial changes in the land), mankind also often intervenes to alter the configuration of the topography. The landscape around my house no doubt looked different before the subdivision was developed. Builders felled trees and removed overgrowth, and perhaps somewhat reshaped the land to construct the 50 or so houses in the neighborhood. Years before that, much wildlife probably frequented the creek which flows past the yard behind my house, and perhaps some tribesmen occasionally camped there. Arrowheads, bones, pottery shards and other evidence of human life might lie buried beneath the soil on my property. Like the previous passing humanimals on the terrain I now occupy, I'm only a transient here.

Just like my own extremely brief and transient tenure on the ground I now occupy, everything which exists—the entire cosmos and all within it—has assumed a passing form which represents an unnatural state of being. Whatever happens to be formulated is an aberration, as the norm is non-existence. The likelihood of any particular form being created is almost nil, while the certainty that all forms thrown by chance into existence will disappear is absolute.

FEBRUARY 2011

It seems something of a paradox that while nothing is really worth anything, something is worth more than nothing. Although all terrestrial accomplishments lead to nothing, many earthlings somehow strive to create something. Such ultimately meaningless efforts represent both the glory and the grim destiny of the humanimal.

So tenuous, uncertain and chance-permeated is human existence, one should try to make the best of the situation without taking it too seriously.

My belief in the controlling factors of chance and luck perhaps originates from a sense of inferiority. If only random forces influence outcomes, this suggests that whatever I managed to accomplish derived not from my ineffectual efforts but from luck. Perhaps I should attribute to my own agency a little more credit for what happened to endow my experiment in living with its favorable characteristics.

MARCH 2011

The physiology of functioning well: establish a protective membrane which allows you to isolate yourself to some extent while also retaining the ability to transcend the barrier and interface with the outside world.

When it comes to the supply of creative works and so-called "art," more is less. Most of the stuff which aspires or purports to be artistic exemplifies a variant of Gresham's Law—the bad creative works drive out the good.

I shunned many of the prevailing values, practices, beliefs and ways of life common in my area and among my friends. Instead of a Descartes-like mantra, "I do, therefore I am," I favored "I don't, therefore I'm my own man."

Being "busy" reflects in part the kind of conditions which prevail where you live. Unfortunates in underdeveloped areas are truly busy, as they engage in a life and death struggle to carry out the menial tasks necessary to survive. A "busy" life in advanced countries includes many frivolous and useless activities which often contribute little, if anything, to society, such as the "insubstantial motion" of computer games, social media, web-surfing and other digital distractions, consumerism, bureaucratic red tape and many official regulations, much social science research, all too many investment adviser and financial industry money-spinners (but not for the spun-around customers), unneeded services and products, and other such redundant and unproductive matters which keep people"busy" in ways quite different than for the down-trodden in Third World countries.

When it comes to writings which appear in a Journal, context influences content. Although some of my observations might apply in a general way, my thoughts all derive from my own narrow perceptions and perspectives. As for everyone, my own situation has shaped how I view the world, a quite limited circumstantial frame of reference which denotes that little or nothing I've written pertains to anyone except to the author himself.

A dollar bill is a ticket of admission far more useful than other types of tickets good only for a specific flight, performance, sports event, museum or other event or service. As I observed all around the world, money opens all sorts of doors—no questions asked. People who try to sell you things want your money, not your life story or an account of how you happened to acquire your purchasing power. These rather obvious thoughts were inspired by the following comments on money, in a biography by Joseph Patterson of his cousin, offered by Colonel Robert R. McCormick, one-time owner and publisher of the *Chicago Tribune*: "Money is power and dominion. It is wine and women and song. It is art and poetry and music. It is idleness and activity. It is warmth in winter and coolness in summer. It is clothing and food. It is travel and sport. It is horses and automobiles, and silks and diamonds. It is books. It is education. It is self-respect and the respect of others."

At a recent funeral attended by the deceased's four daughters, their husbands and their children and by many other relatives, I reflected on the copulative evidence of the departed man's late terrestrial existence as shown by all the related humanimals present at the service. Those animals seem driven to produce incarnate remnants of the progenitor's earthly presence. Such a reproductive instinct leads to a plenitude of beings which violates the dictum, "Less is more."

APRIL 2011

Although many characters and events during your time may seem larger than life, after an era ends everyone who then lived and everything which happened during that time becomes smaller than life, almost to the vanishing point. After our time our present-day experiences and conditions, dramas and traumas will seem as remote to our successors as to us appears what occurred when our predecessors lived. How we happened to experience the world and its vivid play of infinite forms will be as if nothing to those who follow us. Those later generations, each in its turn, will have their own realities.

For anyone who happens to enjoy the potential to excel, how much a person so endowed should exert himself to achieve noteworthy accomplishments, praise-worthy success and other recognition bears some thought, given that the more you manage to outperform the more you have to lose in the end.

To have faith that being born brings you a desirable state and then to believe that it's worthwhile to remain alive requires a willing suspension of disbelief. To justify your existence you need a strong pair of rose-colored glasses. It's necessary to suppose that your unwilling being presents an opportunity rather than a disaster. This unrealistic but useful view will enable you to get from crib to bier without letting the futility of an experiment in living damage the experience.

Modesty of ambition and moderate expectations is more likely to produce a satisfactory result than a reliance on exaggerated hopes and aspirations. One way I achieved what for me represents success is the lack of it in other than the most measured and minor way.

JUNE 2011

The designation "spring" perhaps originates from the way many living things spring forth during the season to produce a renewal of life. Enormous energy and ingenious processes by an insensate nature oblivious to its effects creates a spectacular show whose performers, and viewers, will soon disappear.

After winter's cold there then arrive the winds of March, April's rains, and the year's longest day, then the days start to shorten as the light gradually wanes and earlier twilights and longer nights darken the world. As you grow older the endless seasonal cycle somehow seems shorter. Before long the changes will carry on without my awareness of the seasons.

The irises which briefly bloom in my yard every spring are fair-weather friends. The flowers leave me very quickly and disappear for an entire year before once again making their brief appearance. Like flowers, humanimals live only briefly; unlike them, we never reappear. We're annual animals, not perennials.

JULY 2011

My relative lack of ambition served me well. I managed to remain somewhat productive and engaged without distorting my life in pursuit of achievements beyond my capabilities. My few modest and ordinary successes were sufficient to satisfy me. Contrary to driven types, I avoided driving and just walked along at a slower pace, opting not to devote my time, energy and effort to goals which meant little or nothing to me, even if highly valued by society.

Although an acute awareness of mortality operated to blunt my ambition, for a few especially gifted and unusual figures the finalities of death and oblivion served to inspire some great works. Without mortality Shakespeare might never have put pen to paper, or parchment; Vermeer, brush to canvas; Bach or Beethoven, notes to music; medieval builders, stone into cathedrals; believers, faith into rituals; Greeks, philosophical speculations into words. Thanks to death, the world is a lot more culturally rich.

I was unlike Robert Musil's Ulrich, a "man without qualities," as I had qualities but they in some ways differed from those of my contemporaries, friends and peers. I was by no means a drop-out but continued to drop in to engage with the conventional world while at the same time refusing to adopt all the prevailing beliefs, values and ways of life in my corner of the world. This half-way position suited me well by letting me participate in some of the regular local activities and also allowed me to avoid many of the standard procedures and practices common in my context.

An always-on cell phone seems to me a phony way to live. Why make yourself available for a conversation and at the beck and call (literally) of someone whenever they want to reach you? I have no cell phone, but even my land-line is at times intrusive. Although a ring-less phone means no one is thinking of me I'm for the most part content if the device remains silent most of the time. An infrequent bell suits me well.

Hyper-"busy" people often engage in their frantic activity, ceaseless insubstantial motion and kinetic behavior because of a *horror vacuo,* a desire to evidence purported importance, a need to show that you're in demand, and a lack of imagination which would serve to suggest some other less frenzied and more productive and meaningful activities.

Just as for people, no day is identical but each is in some ways similar. The repetitions arise from enforced behaviors, which require daily food, hydration, elimination, sleep, hygiene, dressing as well as other periodic activities such as buying food and other necessities, household and administrative chores, and managing the details of ordinary every-day life. All days and humanimal lives are both the same and different.

What happens to be takes its place in time; what could be but isn't has lost its potential for being; what was exists in discarded time. Every form which by chance enters existence—an animal, an event, whatever can produce a sensory perception in a receptor—forms part of the one and only one version of reality which happens to come into being. All the other possibilities which ahead of time might have entered existence never ripen into reality: their time has come and gone.

AUGUST 2011

Summer scurries, scampers and skitters on—or so it seems. But that kind of observation incorrectly endows a natural process with an anthropomorphic image. Time, the seasons, the cosmos and all in it—other than humanimals—operate quite oblivious to the effect those elements exert on earthlings. To attribute to summer human traits mischaracterizes an insensate natural force which unfolds completely oblivious of and indifferent to humans.

By now my life is for the most part a set piece, so for me there remains only the need to tie up some of the loose ends, wind down, wrap things up and prepare for the end. Those pressing final matters are not oppressing or depressing me, as I view an exit strategy in a matter-of-fact way.

Time's cumulative nature never gives us a break or a brake. Time never relaxes or relents, as at all times it insists on greedily accumulating ever more content to form the detritus deposited as the past. In the next iteration of a terrestrial-like format, produced by a hopefully improved Big Bang effect, perhaps the new format will include a more user-friendly system of time. But perhaps not.

A revised format for time might include the convenience to allow humanimals to choose to shift their lives into different periods so that the creatures need not live only in a cumulative way. You could opt to fracture unbroken chronology, as it now operates, by living some of your later years earlier and then earlier years later. This system would allow you to draw on your time bank to allocate various periods of your life in an order different than the present "time's arrow" rigidity. I will leave it to others to reconcile all the confusing elements of such a system and to design it properly.

Art represents a man-made response to creation by letting mankind show that, like nature, humanimals can also be creative. Both forms of creation represent arbitrary and ultimately meaningless constructs.

Human consciousness serves not only to perceive the world but also to filter it and reduce sensory impressions to a manageable flow. For that reason, almost the entire play of infinite forms remains beyond our ability to experience the great spectacle.

Just as far too many natural forms exist for any humanimal to absorb, the vast number of works thrown together by those busy-body and busy-mind creative creatures also defies assimilation of other than very few examples. The mind or hand of man is never still. Some innate force compels the animal to scribble, scrawl, carve, smear, note or otherwise produce new forms to supplement the infinite number which nature has already formatted. It's as easy for humans to fabricate forms as works of art as it is for nature to proliferate natural forms, so both categories—man-made and the systemic versions—include far too many individual components. Only very few of the human products merit existence, with most of the rest (including this book) of little or no long-term value. Thankfully, no teacher ever told Shakespeare that he couldn't write and should give it up and get a real job, or advised Vermeer that he should stop dabbling and daubing on canvas and become a house painter, or Beethoven that he'd do better to give up composing and just enjoy himself drinking wine at the neighborhood *heuriger*. But for the vast majority of creative people, such advice would have spared humanity of a lot of awful offal.

As Pascal observed, the inability to remain in your own room can lead to many problems. I tempted fate by traveling to many unruly and dangerous areas. By now there's nowhere in the world I'd rather be than on my back porch savoring the pleasant but quickly passing days of summer, a gem-like offering by nature but, unlike jewels, fated not to endure.

Over the summer the play of light and shadow held constant, as if time were suspended, but now toward summer's end the pattern has changed as light begins to fade earlier in the day and the shadows shift into new formats which show how the season is beginning to change and the year moving on to its end.

SEPTEMBER 2011

Although Beckett states that the whiskey resents the decanter, it strikes me as strange that humans begrudge how the world continues on without them after they're no longer part of it. In life troubles are certain, pleasures problematical. Nature has bestowed on mankind a great benefit by giving human beings an exit strategy which allows them to escape from existence. Immortality would be insufferable. We should not resent the decanter but simply appreciate the whiskey as we drink it.

OCTOBER 2011

Autumns in the Midwest endow the region with some of its most delightful characteristics. A pleasant coolness permeates the recently summer-warm air. Trees display their colorful but fleeting hues as leaves begin to amputate from their limbs and litter the ground with wind-blown abstract changing patterns. The play of light and shadow offers a chiaroscuro moving picture which plays across the lawn, and the pleasing fragrance of evanescent wood smoke perfumes the air before evaporating. Birds on the wing streak across the sky heading for warmer climes. Before long all these passing pleasures will end as another Midwestern autumn mutates into winter.

As pleasant as autumn is here in my part of the world, for an oldsters like me fall evokes my own coming fall from life into eternity.

Although I'm now a member of the senior generation, that status will last only briefly as before long the next group of seniors will replace those of us now serving.

States of being include never was, was and no longer is, now is and then not. Of the billions of people who happened to have existed, countless numbers of other potential humanimals were never incarnated into being, escaping existence by chance and by good or bad luck—which is it?—in favor of remaining in their natural state of eternal non-being. Those of us who, fortunately or unfortunately, happened to have been thrown into being to become part of the play of infinite forms face a short melancholy and bittersweet passing opportunity to engage in the strange experiment in living. We should be thankful that the opportunity is brief.

Although science serves to explain in part how the play of infinite forms operates, that insensate system functions mainly by unknown and in some cases unknowable forces. The predictability of science goes only so far because beyond explicable natural phenomena hides a twilight zone of opaque factors which influence the entire cosmic order and disorder. These include fate, luck, chance, destiny, happenstance, coincidence, serendipity and other such random and capricious elements more akin to black magic than to scientific methods and proofs. Like an experiment in living, scientific experiments leave much undiscovered and fail to solve many mysteries.

The World Series now being played as part of the ceaseless play of infinite forms symbolizes the world-wide practice of mankind to establish rituals, ceremonies, holidays, festivities, festivals, traditions and other such repeating events, all constructs which impose artificial markers on the otherwise amorphous passage of time in order to civilize it. This attempt to establish some order in a fundamentally disorderly world represents a make-believe process which gives mankind the illusion of regularity. Regular events like the World Series present only a false positive which wrongly suggests that life on the lonely planet offers predictable regular, cyclical and organized forms when in fact chaos rules the lonely planet.

NOVEMBER 2011

Earthlings are stranded in their terrestrial habitat as strangers in a strange land. Nature has endowed those exotic creatures with enough consciousness to enable them to function but not enough intelligence for humanimals to comprehend much about their place in the cosmos.

Although we can experience a few scenes in the play of infinite forms, we never know enough about the plot of the play to understand the performance. Life on the lonely planet seems to be a cosmic accident, the result of a randomly created mechanical process involving a meaningless dance of molecules. If you begin with a huge chemical stew which simmers for millions of years, all kinds of strange things can emerge. By a highly unlikely fatalistic development, the cosmic stew cooked up a recipe to produce conditions on one planet, the lonely one, which by chance happened to be favorable to enable life—animal, plant, bird, insect, viruses, microbes, many of the forms feeding off one another. The fantastic puzzle this odd system presents will ever remain beyond the comprehension of the humanimals on whom existence has by chance been inflicted.

"Mankind" is a misnomer, as the word designates a creature which is not particularly kind. Is the humanimal essentially human or beast? Does the creature function as a thinking animal, with mind over matter, or only as a bundle of brutish instincts? The animal's split personality typifies the way life on the mysterious lonely planet somehow seems some sort of deeply flawed experiment by nature.

It seems quite odd that any sentient force would go to all the trouble and effort to create such a strange place as the planet which hosts mankind. The obvious explanation is that the creative force involved was not at all sentient but operated in only a mechanical, insensate and capricious way with no purpose in mind. Or perhaps some malevolent presiding consciousness decided to produce the terrestrial spectacle to entertain its creator, a sadist amused by a play of infinite forms made toxic by trouble, turmoil, confusion, conflict, disorder, war, greed, misery and death.

Each human life is only a mimesis of life in general. So vast is the entirety, an individual experiences an infinitesimally tiny fragment of reality. Virtually every element of the play of infinite forms lies beyond our perceptions.

"Lot" explains a lot about man's lot in life: from beginning to end it's a lottery. Unlike his wife Sarah, Lot luckily managed to escape from Sodom. There's a lot to be said about luck, chance and fate as the determining factors in life. The cosmic casino happened to create the games of chance which typify the play of infinite forms. The system toys with its forms. From conception at the inception on through its earthly tenure and up until death a humanimal remains subject to the luck of the draw. An agitated chaos of combinations, collisions, clusters, clones, clashes, convolutions ceaselessly brings random forms into existence and destroys them in a vast insensate lottery with no winning tickets.

DECEMBER 2011

The darkest days of the year now shroud the earth. Mankind perhaps invented Christmas to bring some light into the world at the time of mid-winter's deepest darkness. But my solipsistic observation shamefully fails to recognize that in the Southern Hemisphere these days are the longest and brightest of the year. This suggests that Christmas is really of no general use to combat the prevailing darkness, and also that each individual humanimal's perspective on life is quite limited and focused only on a creature's immediate circumstances and experiences.

For me Christmas means nothing, with two exceptions: one, as a marker to indicate that now the cycle again begins to lengthen the days so that in a few months spring will arrive; second, that on the Day I get a large and delicious home-cooked family meal with friends who host the holiday.

After a certain age, a stage I reached some years ago, special events no longer seem very special and lose their power to delight. I am now all too familiar with the rituals: Easter means bunnies, eggs, ham and lamb; on July 4th the sky cracks, crackles and lights up as fireworks burst overhead; Memorial Day brings few memories of the departed but many cook-outs, school closings, pool openings; on labor-less Labor Day more holiday eats as schools near reopening and pools soon close; on Halloween we give a treat or get tricked; Thanksgiving offers turkey plus the traditional trimmings and the usual pumpkin or apple pie (or both), followed by the inevitable belt-loosening. Wedding weekends, birthdays, graduations, funerals—I've seen them all, participated in some, and all include similar rites, rituals and routines by now familiar to me. So what's left? I will for sure be present at my own funeral, even if not in a position to enjoy that traditional exit strategy, which for some of the survivors in attendance is often a festive social occasion.

Christmas dinner today with the same large family which for years has hosted the gathering. A plenitude of humanimals spanning three generations fills the rooms. Apparently the creatures are instinctively programmed by nature to want to reproduce. But if that's the case, why is it necessary to motivate such behavior by imposing on the animal such a powerful, pleasing and pleasurable physical imperative? What if the procreative act was accompanied by pain, discomfort, agony (as often is birth)—would the animal still be driven by instinct to copulate in order to engender offspring? Perhaps an Immaculate Conception, such this Christmas day celebrates, would be better for all concerned.

This evening the year reaches a dead-end and in a few hours will end dead. Does time—or any and all of the play of infinite forms—need human consciousness in order to reify reality? Will the spectacle which continues on the lonely planet after mankind's time still exist without the presence of sentient beings to observe the show? How many Dairy Queen cones and M &M's will I consume in 2012?

JANUARY 2012

New Year's Day initiates a *tabula rasa* for a time unit humans designate with the latest in a series of arbitrary numbers based on different starting dates depending on the event from which time is measured. Not everyone would call this year "2012." On this day I wonder how many of the pages of my "*tabula*" (the Journal) will be filled this year and how many will remain "*rasa*" if I'm no longer around to fill them. At my age each day ticks away like a time-bomb which at any moment could explode.

Whee! Away we go—the new year already a day old, to be followed by yet another day and on and on until, before long, yet another New Year's Eve. As time flies it earns a lot of frequent-flyer miles.

The ingenuity of man, that clever but in many ways ignorant creature, has created an overlay of many superficial layers atop the basic ones needed for an effectively functioning civilization and society. Frills, frivolities, conspicuous consumption and many excesses beyond people's relatively simple needs bring about unnecessary complexity and wasteful practices. New Year's Eve afternoon I walked by an Eve-filled beauty salon where woman sought Adam-tempting make-overs and make-up. Attendants embellished customers' hair, nails, skin and other show-off areas with superficial (or superfacial) cosmetic touches, the artificial layered atop the natural just as society has added superfluous glossy veneer onto the basic essentials. The vast array of consumer goods, now produced in all too many versions and varieties, make many so-called developed countries seem over-developed. Few amenities are required to enable a humanimal to lead a reasonably comfortable life: simple food and clean water; a safe and decent place where the creature can sleep away a third of its life and function as needed when awake; some frill-free garments; health services; a functional but not flashy vehicle, or at least access to transportation—not much else (unless you'd also include a pet dog). Such is the sort of world I will not live to see, and nor will anyone else.

None of my mentions of mortality relate to "man's fate" or to "the human condition" or to any other such solemn and unfathomable concepts. Such abstract generalities don't concern me, and in any case I have no opinions about those kinds of all-encompassing existential matters. When it comes to mortality I prefer to contemplate only my own. Although death is an equal opportunity destroyer, it kills each person one-by-one-by-one and, as such, its significance is always an individual matter.

Viewing in different ways received wisdom, commonplace perceptions, cliches, conventional attitudes and widely-held assumptions and opinions can offer some useful new perspectives. Reversing the parental identity of Mother Nature and Father Time brings new insights about those two old geezers. "Mother" Time seems an appropriate designation because she's so fecund. Out of nothing she unceasingly births offspring in the form of moments. Just as the dream of every cell is to replicate, so it's said, so Mother Time in a mechanical and relentless way reproduces endless replications of temporal units. But she doesn't nurture her young, as they live only for an instant before dying a natural and painless death. It's left to Father Nature to provide the infinite play of forms, the cosmic spectacle which originated by hyperactive insensate forces. Father Nature functions as an indifferent parent. He lacks any paternal interest in what he's created. Father Nature operates as a hands-off dad who never disciplines his offspring. Nature functions in a way indifferent to purpose or niceties. Poppa cares nothing at all about all the atoms and molecules and the rest of the ceaselessly agitated components he's created—the forms which spin and clash, combine and separate and mutate, reconnect and disconnect in a random kinetic chaos of motion. Both Mother Time and Father Nature operate as wicked step-parents, a forbidding pitiless mommy and daddy who treat their children in unfeeling, uncaring ways.

Although it's tempting to believe that mankind is by nature essentially kind, much of the evidence suggests that the humanimal is more animalistic than human. Nature may in fact have programmed the creature to behave in violent, contentious, belligerent ways. Clashes over resources and reproduction opportunities, the seeking of pleasure, power and wealth, self-preservation, contests for control, domination and territory, and many other needs and wants dominate the animal, so relegating altruism, generosity, kindness, caring and compassion to a lower order of behavioral traits. The creature's default behavior in many situations seems to display human nature in its most raw, untamed and uncivilized forms. Wars, violence, crime, aggression, killing and the fragmentation of populations into clans, bands, tribes, sects, cults, religions, ethnic groups, family networks, classes and other such splinter units reflect how much of the world functions, or doesn't function. Racists, fanatics, revolutionaries, tyrants, dictators, militias, guerrillas, terrorists, anarchists and other violent operatives add to the toxic mix, as do weapons, bombs, bellicose behavior, atomic and biological and chemical killers, torture devices and many other such fiendish murderous instruments of pain and death invented with great creativity and imagination by humanimals. It's an ugly scene here on the lonely planet, as if some sadistic cosmic force with a perverse sense of humor wanted to create a nightmarish joke. First you establish a pristine prelapsarian world, then introduce mankind into the system and watch from afar as the unkind animals fight it out.

Travel once motivated me in a compulsive way to undertake wide-ranging adventures, so I'm somewhat surprised that this trip-grip now seems to have lost some of its hold on me. Perhaps this represents an indirect way of saying that as I've gotten older I've become wiser, at least in regard to the somewhat nonsensical process of giving up my comfortable home-life for the often uncomfortable rigors and challenges of hard-scrabble but exciting and rewarding scrambles, scurries and scampers in far off and sometimes dangerous lands.

A vast sub-stratum of workers supports the fortunate few at the top who enjoy stimulating, interesting and lucrative jobs. Every practicing physician benefits from a large corps of underlings such as assistants, technicians, orderlies, hospital and office staff, clinical workers, lab specialists. Other high-level professionals and executives also function with extensive support systems. A scientist I once briefly encountered when traveling abroad told me, "It's better to be the beautifully embroidered tablecloth atop the table than the dust underneath," but he failed to add: dust to dust for all concerned.

Degeneration and eventual dissolution afflict everything which exists. Possessions and people wear out. Cars, appliances, household systems, machines, buildings can be maintained for a time but over time become dysfunctional. Similarly, a person's family, social circle and support system all gradually wither away, reducing the circle to a dot. Although you can trade in an old car for a new model, move into a newer house or buy updated appliances, you can't replace the departed who once populated your life. One by one they disappear until, if you live long enough, you're left with few, if any, of your valued friends and family who so greatly enriched your now impoverished life.

FEBRUARY 2012

The upcoming month-end leap-year adjustment adding a day to February doesn't represent a freebie as if a gift of time. In the big scheme of things, a February 29th brings only another construct imposed by man in an effort to delineate time units.

A fine balance exists between striving too energetically to achieve success, fame, wealth, recognition, status, prestige, acclaim and other such rewards valued by society and a more modest way of life which allows you to remain connected and participate in the world without excessive ambition. The most appropriate equilibrium lies in exerting enough effort and productive activity to be part of the system without distorting your life to pursue accomplishments society may value but which mean little or nothing to you.

Each humanimal sees itself as special and worthy but to the outside world those creatures represent targets and sources of exploitation. To a lion, alligator, vulture, hyena and other such predators a human body is meaningless other than as a menu item of savory meat. Human predators often include politicians, bureaucrats, government officials and agencies, regulators, taxation authorities, functionaries who issue permits and licenses, tyrants and dictators, salespeople, marketers, many wealth managers and financial industry operatives, various service and product providers, slickers in foreign lands who exploit visitors, and many other characters who seek rents and benefits from people vulnerable to being euchred or victimized. You and your intimates may think highly of you, but to many outside that charming if not charmed circle you're simply another humanimal in the crowd ripe for the taking.

Today, February 29th, begs for an entry because this is the rarest of all days. Christmas comes but once a year, but a leap-year day even less frequently. If you live for, say, 80 years you'll experience during that long lifetime only 20 leap year days. It's a long leap to the next one: will I be around that long to make the jump from the end of February to March 1st in 2016?

MARCH 2012

To fear the process of dying, which can be quite uncomfortable, makes sense, but less so the fear of death. In spite of all the disadvantages of remaining alive, humanimals cling to existence even though they should welcome relief from the turmoil and misfortunes of being. The creatures prefer the devilish state of their earthly presence to the unknown possible demons of non-existence. Although some devout religious believers fear death because they imagine hellish conditions in the afterlife, others suppose that after life on earth they'll end up in a postmortem paradise. If true, then why not depart sooner rather than later so you can reach the heavenly promised land as quickly as possible?

Is it preferable to be possessed by a questioning and seeking mind and a sense of compulsive curiosity or to live in a mindless way indifferent to many of the nuances, implications and subtleties intrinsic in the play of infinite forms? Remaining oblivious to those less obvious elements frees people from noticing and contemplating many bothersome and unsettling matters, but also diminishes an experiment in living. In any case, it's not possible to choose one's temperament, personality, mentality or other randomly endowed personal characteristics.

In my mainly unstructured way of life, if I happen to find myself at loose ends I can always tighten them, like shoelaces, by any number of pleasant activities, including writing in my Journal.

I've tried to keep the printed word—both reading and writing it—in its place, but my respect for that form of communication has impelled me to save many articles and clippings from periodicals which would otherwise be discarded after being read. I somehow found it disagreeable simply to throw away newspapers and magazines, condemning them to the recycling pile without salvaging at least a few of their author's hard-earned writings. My pack-rat habit seems an analogue to my practice of trying to salvage in my Journal a few passing thoughts which would otherwise disappear like abandoned print materials.

In recent years people occasionally address me as "sir," but that unsought title seems more benighted than knighted. "Sir" suggests a seniority which denotes not authority or status but only old age. In a few cases youngsters have seen me as old enough to give up their seat on a crowded bus. Although I accept the offer, I reject the title as no oldster can stand (even if seated) to be reminded of his age.

MAY 2012

Man is both a social animal and an unsocialized and uncivilized ferocious beast. Which of the two opposing traits best defines the creature?

The cosmic play of infinite forms plays out in a theater of the absurd, a spectacle performed as an ad lib plotless drama acted by characters for whom no audience is present and with no encores, curtain calls, revivals or road shows.

JUNE 2012

The names of some months designate people. I recently noticed that a woman is called January Jones. "March Jones" would be too commanding an imperative. More common are April, May and June, while August does double-duty as "August" and "Augusta." September, October, November and December perhaps evoke too much of an autumnal or cold personality to suit people who might who prefers a more sunny designation. "December Jones" suggests a frigid woman and the sense of an ending. It seems that other than Tuesday (Weld), no days of the week serve as peoples' first names. As to years, "2012 Jones" seems odd but might work as a little-used middle name: "January 2012 Jones." "February 29 Jones" would offer a special, rare date as a name.

One function of humanimals is to receive reality fragmented into minute units so that each individual consciousness can absorb a few elements of the vast play of infinite forms in a way comprehensible to sentient beings. Without all those very finite individual sensory impression receptors known as people, the totality couldn't express itself in billions of tiny formats the many different discrete brains receive.

An especially pleasant June day like the brief passing interlude I now enjoy seems to make the lonely planet here just now a welcoming and hospitable place, but in truth random mechanical forces indifferent to earthlings happened to bring about this balmy spring day. "Nothing personal," is the insensate system's motto.

As these delightful spring days ease by I cast my thoughts ahead to summer, then to on autumn and winter. Contemplating the four distinct seasons where I happen to live makes me wonder if residents of areas with an unchanging climate realize that they're missing one of the best acts brought to mankind by the play of infinite forms.

Time seems to move slowly for creative types whose work has been submitted but not yet accepted, or accepted but not yet issued; for elected officials awaiting inauguration; for school children anticipating summer vacation, or kids looking forward to Christmas; for medical or Ph.D. students engaged in long courses of study before receiving the desired credentials; for guests invited to a special event, such as a gala wedding, a fun party, an exclusive gathering scheduled for months in the future; and (I must admit) perhaps for my readers who find this book advances too slowly. After Jenny kissed him, Ben Jonson said that time's a thief but it's more in the nature of a rascal who plays with our sense of time.

One advantage of being comfortable with your own company is that it's always available.

AUGUST 2012

A great curiosity about other places motivated many of my travels. Somehow I felt uncomfortable carrying out my experiment in living without visiting the great cities such as London, Paris and Rome, as well as others designated with such exotic names as Timbuktu, Ougadougou, Chichicastenango, Samarkand, Ponca City and many more. At my advanced age I'm comforted by the fact that I missed only a few places with names as compelling as those I mentioned, the main omission being Cox's Bazar in Bangladesh.

What Mother Nature gives with one hand—time and life—she soon takes away with the other, as each gift the perfidious mommy soon re-gifts to eternity.

Time's an Indian-giver, as over time it takes back the life it gave you.

So complicated is the corporeal system which enables human life and its homeostasis, it's a wonder that such a complex organism even exists or that it continues to function for so many years before breaking down and wearing out.

For the young whose past is brief the future looms ahead in a remote and indistinct haze, while for the old the past seems an insubstantial nearly vanished reality. Times to come and those come and gone thus resemble one another in their misty dream-like quality.

"Was" and "will": two little words which represent big differences.

What I avoided or eliminated influenced my life almost as much as what I actually experienced. Both my doings and my don'tings played important roles in my experiment in living.

Death's true insult is not that it removes us from life but how little our absence makes a difference to the world we leave behind.

OCTOBER 2012

Looking ahead at time to come, Shakespeare's "life's petty pace" indeed describes how the days seem to advance in a slow cadence. But looking back toward the end, the cadence appears to have advanced at a race pace much faster than when you look ahead and perceive how slowly time seems to move on.

In contrast to the billions of people who have lived, now live, and will live, an untold number of potential human beings never materialize as incarnated creatures. Fictional characters offer some surrogates as examples of types who might have existed but never did.

NOVEMBER 2012

Halloween last night, one of those arbitrary constructs humanimals impose on duration to attach some meaning to the flow of days—a trick which treats those creatures to the illusion of order. Although earthlings can't dominate time, at least they can denominate it.

The absolute and eternal certainty of the state of non-being would seem to be greatly preferable to existence, and yet few humanimals would choose never to have been born.

Many conventional types would do their best to avoid being labeled a fish out of water, out of step, going against the grain, a renegade, a dissenter, eccentric, an exception, an outlier, a loner, a weirdo, a round peg in a square hole (or a square peg in a round hole) and similar. Any and all of those characteristics serve to diversify, expand and enrich an experiment in living.

Today I voted in what for me will perhaps be my last presidential election. But that finality wouldn't in the slightest bother me. What I'd really miss are Dairy Queen cones, M & M's, friends, family, comic strips, reading, travel, people laughing at my jokes and much else. As for politics, politicians, campaigns and public policy matters, I'm quite content to give those up at any time and, in fact, for the most part already have.

Even if generations—grandparent, child, grandchild (maybe even "greats" at each end)—overlap, the oldest and the youngest have little in common, other than their consanguinity.

However, one quite common element is the oldest generation 's wealth, which the younger age groups eye and wait—patiently or impatiently—to inherit.

Over many millennia Mother Nature no doubt engaged in a lot of experimentation and fine-tuning to configure in a satisfactory if not perfect way the human corpus, now probably in its final version. But it's possible to imagine any number of other kinds of formats for the body's morphology, physiology, anatomy. biology, organs, genes, cells, physical, chemical and other organic components. Some such variants might even enable the humanimal to function better in response to the challenges presented by the creature's presence on the lonely planet. As playthings of nature, earthlings could well benefit from a replay of their physical format to produce a new and better model.

At home in my rather repetitious regular familiar setting time seems to pass in a constant orderly flow, while when I travel in distant exotic areas time moves in kinetic, jumpy and lumpy, jerky motions. But at the same time in every place and for every earthling time always actually passes at the same measured pace.

DECEMBER 2012

My mid-December Caribbean cruise thankfully enabled me to escape for a time the frantic commercialized holiday consumer frenzy which dominates what originated as a religious celebration but now includes all too many presents rather than the intangible gift supposedly represented by what the devout believe Christmas celebrates.

Year's end reminds me—as does much else—that by now I'm in a race with time, one I can't win. But I hope that before losing the race I'll at least manage to bring to closure, before mine occurs, a few matters which still need attention.

JANUARY 2013

The useful general principle of Occam's Razor enabled me to simplify my life by shaving away many distractions, but a Norelco might have been more efficient to cut out extraneous matters as that shaver comes with a more finely calibrated trimmer.

The law of supply and demand applies not only in economics but also in other matters, such as the huge current over-supply of words. In the modern age producing and distributing writings or spoken thoughts has become easy and largely cost-free, which has greatly increased the supply. Old-form print-on-paper publications, which had to be written, revised, reviewed, processed, manufactured and then distributed, all time-consuming and costly operations, have to a large extent been replaced by friction-free technologies. This over-supply of news, opinions, comments and other palaver created by all too many un-lettered writers and commentators has greatly devalued words, whose supply now greatly exceeds the demand for that commodity.

Any arbitrary designation can be used to describe the names of months. Examples include Brumaire, Germinal, Messidor, Thermidor. Replacing the names of months with their number would be more informative, and especially if they were quantified in an order which reverses the present format so that January as "12," February as "11" and so on would indicate not expired time but what remains, until finally "1" represents December. The same would work well for weeks—a time unit mankind has somehow refrained from naming—by designating them as

"52" and on down to "1," the last week in the year, a system which would inform you of how many weeks are left.

Books and other reading materials flatten to the dimension of the printed page the much more vivid three-dimensional outside world and, as such, mere wordy versions of reality should be kept at arm's-length.

MARCH 2013

The night has a thousand eyes, the lonely planet's humanimals some 15 billion. If you could somehow combine all the sights those eyes have seen plus the other sensory impressions accumulated by the creatures' hearing, taste, smell and touch you could piece together a more complete, even if still rather limited, picture of how earthlings experienced their collective experiments in living.

If a knave stabs you, you feel pain; if a woman caresses you, you feel______ (fill in the blank); if a dog barks you hear, and if the animal bites its teeth marks will pattern the victim's skin. To everyone, roasting chestnuts produce pleasant aromas, and horse chestnuts a stench. So are humanimals more defined by their herd-like similarities than by their individuality?

As you age you might as well reduce your curiosity, as the time remaining to assuage it grows ever shorter.

On this Easter Sunday true believers celebrate the (claimed) miracle that a humanimal was resurrected, a trick very few other such creatures (Lazarus lives!) ever supposedly accomplished. An extraterrestrial visitor to the lonely planet would most likely find such a belief quite unbelievable, as do many irreligious terrestrial inhabitants. Religious faith and many other beliefs, practices, rituals, routines, interests and behavior by earthlings seem like playful jokes the play of infinite forms inflict on hapless humankind.

APRIL 2013

Today features another imposed time marker, but in this case with a description which characterizes much human behavior—April Fools Day. For once some earthly beings happened to invent a time unit identifier which accurately depicts how people often act.

If occurring within the same seven days, both Easter Fools and April Fools Day suggest yet a new time marker which might be called April Foolish Week.

Instant gratification for me, as I've been informed that millions of Americans are celebrating the newly designated April Foolish Week by acting as they do normally. Full disclosure: for some unknown reason, Guam and American Samoa residents have chosen not to participate in the April Foolish Week foolishness, perhaps because word of the new holiday couldn't cross the international date line.

MAY 2013

English language oddities: (1) "Resign"—to bow out, renounce. "Re-sign"—to opt in again, sign up for a new period. (2) "Is X still alive and, if so, where does he live?" requires two different pronunciations of the same four letters.

An ability to entertain yourself produces a performance which never gets a bad review.

JUNE 2013

Although time never relents, what if it could be re-lent? Surely the fantastic creative force which produced the cosmos could have recast time's format into a different way of operating. Since humanimals are never given time to keep but only lent (Lent being a religious holiday which accurately describes time and life), the creatures could opt to put aside some of what's loaned to them to save and then spend at a later time. At age 40, say, you could skip the next decade and advance immediately to 50 and then, when you reach 80, retrieve the foregone ten years and enjoy your forties. Maybe that option will be available in the next version of organic life following the present rather inconvenient one.

The supposed wisdom of the old is something of a myth. Although experience is cumulative, understanding is not. A centenarian may understand little more than he did half a century or more earlier.

Humanimals often behave by aping others. This copy-cat (or copy-simian) behavior offers a short-cut as following the crowd reduces or eliminates the need to think for yourself. Herd-like—or, if we listen for cues, heard-like—behavior saves time because you can simply adopt group-think beliefs and practices. Monkey-see, monkey-do is a much more convenient way to pursue an experiment in living than monkey-see, monkey-doesn't. If you politely and passively take your cues—minding your peeves and cues—from society as you find it, you can avoid the bother of thinking about things in an independent, skeptical and perhaps eccentric but more satisfying way.

I could just as easily have been someone else or no one at all. The "me" which happened to be cast into being resulted from a random process which by chance brought into existence a passing form which will before long pass out of existence.

On this first day of summer I already start to think about its last day.

JULY 2013

Children, church, charities, clubs, schooling, sports, entertainments, amusements, hobbies, shopping, social life, politics, meals: those kinds of everyday activities and elements represent how most humanimals experience their experiment in living.

My waning sense of curiosity may expire before I do.

Of all living animals, only humanimals realize and lament their mortality. Dogs and frogs, rats and cats, ants, butterflies, roaches, baboons, aardvarks and other critters and creatures don't know and don't care that they will before long pass away. The definition of all animate living things, other than humans: a being for whom *carpe diem* represents the only way they live.

Chance gave to humanimals a pristine and bucolic terrestrial setting with more than enough resources to provide a comfortable way of life for a limited population. Even if not Edenic, such circumstances, if preserved, might have led to a much more pleasant and benign kind of experiment in living for the creatures than how things actually turned out for earthlings. As shaped and degraded by humans over the centuries, the lonely planet became both less livable than during the original conditions but also more endurable, thanks to the advances produced by science and technology. On balance, all things considered, were earthlings better off back in the pre-historic era when they first appeared on earth or now?

AUGUST 2013

By acts of will—or, better expressed, "won'ts"—I rejected many of the values and practices common in my provincial suburban context. As a substitute for some of the conventional pursuits and practices favored in my home setting I opted to expose myself to a variety of the infinite forms of play in places unavailable at home and wildly different from my native habitat, a decision which helped me diversify and enhance my experiment in living.

Being thrown into existence brings an unsought bargain: we get a life, nature gets a death.

When young you usually don't realize as you go along what in the distant future you'll regret, an omission which prevents you at the time from remedying the actions or inactions which will eventually bring you remorse. By old age it's too late, as by then few if any timely remedies exist to enable you to reduce or eliminate regrets.

At any stage, and especially in very old age, a humanimals's continuing being hangs on a thread. Like a spider on its web, a human exists by a slender connection with life which might at any moment be severed. Remaining alive depends on intricate and delicate internal systems, fragile functions, coordinated components, a web of receptors and connectors, on deep-seated and obscure processes and interactions which enable the body to function and our consciousness to continue to absorb sensory impressions. It could all go wrong at any time. A tiny vessel here, a minuscule chemical malfunction there, a missed beat or throb, a blocked or surged excretion or elimination, a rogue microbe or bacterium or virus, a stumble-tumble and other insults, intrusions and failures can distress or destroy the operating system necessary to sustain life. Oldsters constantly wonder what fatal bodily function will in the end cut the cord which, for a brief time, keeps you connected with life.

The "is/was" of what happens and then what constitutes the past offers specific information on the content of your life. But it's impossible to assess how all the possible events which might have occurred but never did would have affected your experiment in living. You know only that what didn't happen played some part in how your experiment turns out, but not exactly how the non-events influenced your outcome.

Although you can never be sure how a counter-factual—what didn't happen—might have influenced your life (as noted in the last entry), one way to get something of a notion of the effects of non-events is to observe in other people situations which affected them but not you. This gives you some idea how such a similar situation, unknown to you, might have impacted your life.

The gift of gab is a present that keeps on giving, often to a fault. Modern-day society spews out a torrent of words, a vast and ceaseless chatter, clatter and clutter of opinions, beliefs, viewpoints, arguments, claims, demands in a noisy sound and fury which for the most part signifies nothing. Any puny voice can now be amplified, any claim to authority or expertise enlarged and widely disseminated. It seems that observers and commentators with the least sense or valid claim to well-informed and reasoned views talk the most. The vast flow of so easily and indiscriminately contrived present-day communication by every Dick and Harry (the Tom's are all okay) greatly pollutes the public dialogue, these days most often a monologue.

How nature happened to create the existing system, after countless years of experimentation and trial and error, most likely developed erratically in arbitrary and fortuitous ways. It's not difficult to imagine better formats. One might be to allow each humanimal to redistribute its lifetime total of sleep requirements as the creature determines. Instead of a pay-as-you-go arrangement which requires you to set aside one-third of each day to sleep, you could choose how to allocate your mandated withdrawal from wakefulness. This would allow you, say, to sleep for lengthy periods to accumulate a sleep credit you could draw on to stay awake for longer periods. You might even sleep for a solid year so that the 24 hours a day you banked would give you three consecutive years of continued wakefulness. Similarly, it might be convenient to impose a stop-action order on time to freeze-frame its passage—a kind of cryogenic time-out without the chill—until you decide to reactivate its advance.

SEPTEMBER 2013

A late-in-life high school reunion inevitably prompts you to assess how you fared in your experiment in living as compared with your classmates. The gathering of your surviving peers, and memories of the many missing disappears, recalls Christopher Wren's tomb inscription in St. Paul's Cathedral: "*Si monumentum requiris circumspice.*" Judging your life by looking around at how your contemporaries extant and extinct lived may not bring you monumental pride but will offer a way to gain a realistic view of the quality of your own experiment.

OCTOBER 2013

Death is the absence of time, and as such non-being offers a permanent respite from the relentless forward thrust by which time pressures your existence. Without humanimals to victimize, time would lose some of its toxic effect.

Living near the Equator where the cycle of seasons doesn't distinguish each one with distinct characteristics may alter how humanimals in such areas perceive time and the rhythm of life the local creatures experience. Lack of contrasts—whether based on time, terrain, routines, personal circumstances—provides fewer opportunities to perceive and distinguish the variety of infinite forms as they ceaseless play on.

Money which burns a hole in your pocket may provoke you to engage in wasteful spending; even more unfortunate, wasting time will burn a hole in your experiment in living.

NOVEMBER 2013

Time operates both as friend and foe: it endows us with the medium necessary to exist and at the same time eventually forces us to give up our existence.

People tethered to a conventional life with family obligations, an on-going work-a-day routine, repetitious and narrowly focused rituals, a lack of variety and other such limiting constraints may experience the passage of time differently than do more adventurous characters who engage in wide-ranging and varied ways of life. For which category does time seem to pass more quickly?

Free-time isn't really free; you pay for it because however you use time you spend it.

Before his 1946 rematch (after the first bout in 1941) with Billy Conn, Joe Louis taunted his opponent, "He can run but he can't hide." In old age I can hide by retreating from the world but can no longer run around as I once did to see that strange place churning and seething with infinite forms.

Time-greed represents a common old-age affliction. Many oldsters wish for just a little more time, and then more and more. No matter how much time remains, it's always too short. This longing for more is like a low-grade infection which over time becomes more acute, as the shorter your time the more feverish your desire to prolong it.

Asking for more time is like requesting more money. In both cases, it's better to live within your means.

Charles de Gaulle said that old age is a shipwreck. Maybe so, but before the vessel sinks you should enjoy the cruise and especially the buffet, its wide array of foods suggestive of the more general infinite play of forms which offers a smörgåsbord of sensory impressions and food for thought.

Demands on my time always exceeded the available supply. Because I couldn't increase the supply I did my best to limit the demands. But people, the system, the nature of things constantly imposed intrusions on both my time and attention. Best as I could, I responded to such impositions only to the extent that they conformed to my own agenda, but all too many unwanted demands inevitably operated to drain away some of the time I tried to preserve for myself.

Inhabitants of underdeveloped lands enjoy no spare time as they devote all their time and energy to the endless (until ended by death) struggle to stay alive. Many residents of developed areas, like my own country, have too much time on their hands and use the surplus in frivolous, wasteful and non-productive ways. A better arrangement would be to distribute some of the excess time in the one place to those elsewhere who seldom or never have a chance to benefit from some free time. Exporting time to time-starved lands could represent a lucrative business proposition, an innovative concept whose time has come.

Unlike time, which ineluctably disappears, money may or may not slip away, depending on good or bad luck and on the behavior of people who possess either inherited or earned wealth. Inherited fortunes are especially vulnerable to attrition because heirs often abuse unearned wealth received from predecessors who produced the assets. Even riches produced by one's own efforts remain vulnerable to threats, risks known and unknown, bad decisions, poor handling, adverse developments and many other depleting effects. Such damaging influences include demands, dissipation, desertion and divorce, drink, drugs, debt, default, destiny, decay, decline, destruction, Danegeld, deadbeats, debauchery, derangement, depreciation, deception, degeneracy, distractions, personal and economic depressions, despotism, difficulties, digamy, disease, diminution, disputes, disagreements, discord, dishonesty, disturbances, double-crosses, dupery plus unavoidable disappearance due to death. And those are just the "d's." It would take a complete alphabet—from absconding to zamindar—of possible threats to wealth to list all of the many ways good fortune can become misfortune for those who happen, by luck or effort, to possess assets.

Apart from the "d" factors noted in the last entry, many other forces can operate to dismantle a person's capital. Predatory governments, confiscatory taxation, radical social movements, systemic changes, wars, natural disasters, rampant inflation or deep deflation and economic panics can wipe out wealth much faster than the time it took to create the assets. Expropriation, appropriation, extortion, licensing, regulation and other official takings move other peoples' money into the hands of new owners. Nice work if you can get it, and even better if you can keep it. In the end, every fortune loses its owner, as even if the wealth isn't taken it eventually passes on to the successors.

Stuff-stuffed shopping malls always make me uncomfortable. Surrounded by so many things, none of which I want, I feel a sense of claustrophobia. Instead of the mantra adopted by consumers, "Shop until you drop," I favor "Drop before you shop." But I don't begrudge or denigrate those addicted to consumption. Many of them would no doubt consider my rather thrifty and frugal way of life just as undesirable as I view their consumerism.

Externals—such as possessions, extravagant spending and conspicuous consumption—offer objects and practices much less opaque and more evident than the less visible characteristics of people who pursue internalized activities and experiences imperceptible to outsiders. That intangible way of life includes reading, contemplation, memories, relationships, travel experiences and other such insubstantial but highly enriching pursuits which other people can't easily perceive.

DECEMBER 2013

Whether organic or inanimate, each form which happens to come into being represents a brief exception to the norm, which is non-being. Whatever kinds of life or things nature creates in its capacious and capricious meaningless experiment will end in ex-existence—the same state as before the forms existed. Human beings are more accurately described as human non-beings, as such creatures who momentarily exist quickly disappear and the countless number who might have been thrown into life never were.

Humanity can be divided into various categories, one of which is that a few people often divide their fellow earthlings into two categories while most other people don't. Closely observing nuances, distinctions, subtleties, differences and gradations motivates you to categorize humanimals into affinity groups. This helps to put some order into an otherwise rather amorphous and messy world.

People I encountered on a recent trip to New York City and Philadelphia illustrated the contrast between humanimals with sedentary, settled and rooted lives as compared with other such creatures who by choice or by necessity somewhat frequently change careers, cities, activities, spouses and other personal activities and behaviors. Long-term stability, regularity, familiar surroundings and routines characterize the settled group, while the restless types often enjoy change, sometimes carried out with a sense of adventure which includes establishing new connections and different routines in an alternative context. For me, wide-ranging adventure travel served to bring me many new kinds of experiences, but otherwise I remained unmoved by the prospect of altering my life by living in a different city or pursuing new ways of being. I was content with my old ways.

With its vast cornucopia of stuff and the way the bonanza stirs consumers to buy, the holiday season evidences the workings of the great American economic machine which so efficiently produces a huge outpouring of mostly affordable goods. It's a fantastic system, perhaps mostly un- or under-appreciated by the people who enjoy or benefit as members of the consumer society.

The seasonal cycle which inhabitants in their own corner of the world view as normal differs greatly in other regions. Australians may dream of a white Christmas, but the holiday season Down Under remains upside down compared to the December snow-whitened regions in the Northern Hemisphere. If Lewis Carroll had by chance lived in the Southern Hemisphere, in a place like Christchurch (New Zealand) rather than at Christ Church College in Oxford, he'd probably have versified a kind of Christmas Carroll version, "Autumn frosts have slain December," rather than "Autumn frosts have slain July." Down South the seasonal climate is reversed; or is it up here in the North where it's reversed? But in whichever wonderland the dreamy scholar happened to live, for sure he would have retained the closing line of his 1891 poem "A Boat Beneath a Sunny Sky": "Life, what is it but a dream?"

When visiting the Museum of Modern Art in New York City earlier this month I saw many people using their phones to take pictures of the art works. Especially popular for photos were iconic works and those by famous artists. Brands are even more influential for creative and cultural products than for consumer stuff and other goods and services. Those widely-known labels verify the supposed utility, merit and validity of intangible intellectual offerings whose value depends on so many subjective factors consumers of the artistic artifacts find them difficult to assess. Brand names confer status and endow the chosen works and artists with authority, so assuring the otherwise clue-less and beguiled public that the anointed works and creators represent the pick of the litter, much of which litters the cultural landscape.

As digital images of unique items become common and easily distributed, this wide availability of copies may dilute and devalue the originals. Years ago Benjamin (Walter, not Franklin) pondered the significance of art in an age of mechanical reproduction. (Maybe Benjamin in his time did, too.) If people can conveniently view high-resolution images of famous works of art, does this lower the motivation to seek the originals out in their authentic and unique form? And, when the real versions are seen, is the effect of the originals diluted after the viewer has previously seen such realistic copies?

Prolific and profligate reproduction of artistic objects by mechanical or digital means finds an analogue in how humanimals also reproduce themselves. Does adding ever more of the creatures to an already over-populated world reduce the value of each animal?

This December 31st I by surprise find myself alive for the advent of yet another year. I've now survived to see a new year, a new decade, a new millennium: how much longer can this keep going on? Time will tell, at which time I will not be around for the tale.

2014

The 2014 section includes more than 100 pages, one of the Journal's longest. Subsequent years also number among the most extensive, as my conversation with myself expanded. It seems that the longer I lived the more I had to say. Perhaps my ever more limited time inspired me to record my thoughts before they vanished when I did. In conducting a dialogue with myself through the Journal my interlocutor never gave me any backtalk, criticism or arguments.

JANUARY 2014

My working hypothesis at this late date in my life assumes that whatever I experience in the way of desired or beneficial happenings may be the last of those favorable episodes. If my assumption proves incorrect, so much the better as the bonus of additional pleasant experiences will deepen my appreciation for those extra chances to enjoy what someday is bound to be my final version of various valued events.

With two days of 2014 already history, this 3d day of January now operates to deplete nearly one percent of the entire year. As the future gives way to the past, each passing day bangs another nail in the coffin of ambitions, hopes, aspirations, possibilities, expectations and other such forward-looking perspectives which the elapse of time gradually diminishes and eventually buries.

A very thin membrane supports the upper crust of humanity which functions above the billions huddled below. Poverty, disease, crime, oppression, servitude, violence, intractable problems, unfavorable circumstances and other disadvantages with grave (often literal) effects afflict the down-trodden. Tough luck for them. As for the elite fortunate few at the top, somehow good luck, chance, random effects and other capricious factors have favored some humanimals as much as and probably more than the contribution of their own skill, will, agency, diligence, merit, intelligence, energy, effort, cunning, hard work and other personal traits. The exalted few who enjoy high status may lose their position much more suddenly and easily than those mired below can rise into the top tier.

Many people on the lonely planet live like dogs, but the similar morphology of all animals means that in many ways dogs—especially pampered pets—also live like people, and often with a standard of living higher than the unfortunate earthlings who live like dogs. After millennia of experimentation, once nature settled on effective solutions to enable animal life to function those formats were used for most living creatures. In the animal kingdom menagerie humans rank as top dog, but they're simply one version of how nature formatted most beasts.

Raising a child gives its parents as much of a learning experience as what a new-born gradually learns as the youngster develops. I recently overheard an observant six-year-old refer to an angled snowplow as "broken," an original perception of the V-shaped object which never would have occurred to me.

The initial circumstances nature and chance endow you with and which represent your opening situation often bear little or no relationship to what follows. Luck, chance and randomness intervene to affect your every step, and misstep, along the way.

Viewing humanimals as those creatures actually are creates a perspective which reduces life to its bare-bones reality. The animal consist of a skin-bag filled with pulsating, churning, throbbing, pumping, excreting, agitating processes along with chemical interactions and reactions as if some sort of random autonomous laboratory experiment. Such a purposeless project will win no Nobel Prize as the operation yields nothing of value for mankind and is of questionable value for the specimen (or speciwomen) who are the subject of the experiment.

Although every mortal realizes that death is inevitable, some humanimals live as if they've never heard of that part of life. Ignoring the fact that every beginning leads to an end, those death-deniers seem to behave as if time doesn't exist. Earthlings oblivious to finalities assume that what's not done today can be taken care of tomorrow; that words left unsaid or deeds unperformed can later be done or said; that postponed matters can eventually be handled in a posterior way. No urgency animates those time-immune mortals, content to remain unmoved by the ceaseless advancing moments. Those lucky time-oblivious souls whose time-frame bears no borders and who exist in a timeless world act as if there's no time like the present to ignore the future. Passing time brings passivity and inactivity rather than action, and for the dilatory a time-out isn't just a pause but a continuing delay. Those who endure duration without concern and are lost in time never find their way out to face the finite nature of pressing passing time and in the end, as time continues on its way, they run out of it.

At a certain point in time, perhaps around age 30, a person's life takes shape as its general outlines and direction become somewhat apparent, even if always subject to change and to the operation of such capricious forces as luck and chance. By about age 30 you've developed your adult personality, completed your education, begun your career, perhaps found a mate, maybe become a parent (or, perhaps better, adopted a dog), and reached some assumptions and conclusions about how you hope to carry out your experiment in living. By about that time you're old enough to have settled many matters which at a younger age remain unresolved, and some of the uncertainties and unknowns which prevailed earlier have been clarified. If by about age 30 you've failed to establish some basic principles and procedures for how to live, you'll be poorly equipped to deal with the play of infinite forms which impose on the lonely planet the confusing and chaotic conditions faced by every earthling in residence there.

Investing and writing may seem completely different fields, but in fact they resemble one another in various ways. Both use common everyday methods to operate. For writing language, so familiar and natural, represents the raw material which produces the product. For investing numbers and opinions—both easily manipulated and expressed—represent the factors many people use to make financial decisions. Self-deception often leads would-be practicioners to believe that if you're fluent in and adept with words you can easily write for publication, just as an unrealistic self-assessment persuades many investors to suppose that being numerate and engaging in market "research" (mostly sources available to anyone and everyone) will enable them to develop informed and actionable opinions. As I learned over many years by trial and error (mostly error), neither writing nor investing so easily lend themselves to success, which for those endeavors bears no relationship to facility with words or numbers

One characteristic of a great metropolis is that the city can feature as a leading character in a creative work. Few cities pass this test as most never get the call-back following an audition for a starring role. Stories set in a "Wonderful Town" or recounting "A Tale of Two Cities" or adventures during a "Roman Holiday" and similar classics use their locales as marquee players. So vividly does Vienna feature in "The Third Man" the city almost acts as a fourth man. Not many cities qualify as world-class performers who can play major parts in novels or movies. Lesser places provide only supporting roles or bit parts.

Other features of great cities are their diversity and unpredictably. The vast variety of attractions and distractions, the constant kinetic motion and energy typical in lively urban scenes, the sheer amount of activity and activities all contribute to the city's greatness. At every turn appear unexpected sites, sights and happenings. A festival of surprises constantly stimulates and often over-stimulates residents and visitors who witness or participate in the spectacle.

Almost the entirety of the play of infinite forms escapes our attention. The vast play greatly exceeds the very few details we manage to perceive. Even the most observant and receptive earthling misses most of the available sensory impressions which develop on the receptor's watch. The senses of a sentient terrestrial animal absorb little of what's offered. As the moments pass the creature will notice and remember almost none of the incalculable number of available forms. So it is that almost everything in life passes us by. The tiny residue we happen to perceive represents the content of our very brief and limited experiment in living.

FEBRUARY 2014
No matter how prominent or well-rooted a family, the crop eventually fails.

By their behavior, some of it unavoidable, some senior citizens give elders a bad reputation. All too many retired and tired old folks have become sleep-walkers (even if not needing a walker), layabouts, zombies, nappers, inactive couch potatoes or nuts, idlers, babblers about their past, all in an effort to kill time before it kills them.

Being Roger

At a Chinese restaurant for dinner last night a waiter from the old country who gave his English name as Roger served us. Apparently just off the boat from China, Roger spoke only very basic waiter English. Given the language barrier (not only his but also mine), I quickly realized that the two of us wouldn't be able to engage in a discussion of Confucius and his philosophy and beliefs. But I was there not for food for thought but for the Americanized chicken dish (disdained by most Chinese) named after General Tso. I found it hard to imagine how Roger fared in daily life as an apparent recent arrival in a new completely unfamiliar country where he couldn't speak the language. I wonder what Roger's life will be like in, say, 20 years. Will he then be settled into his once foreign land and be able to discuss Confucius in English? But for now his life consists of waiting—he waits for customers to show up, waits for them to decide what to eat, waits for the food to be prepared, then waits on the table, and at the end waits for his tip. Customers otherwise ignore him: he's just an anonymous service animal. Meanwhile, how does Roger live and with whom? How does he function in a society he doesn't know where people use a foreign (to him) language? Does he regret his decision to leave his native land for a new homeland? Roger is most likely untraveled (except to get from China to a provincial U.S. city), uneducated, unsophisticated, untutored, unfortunate, unsettled and perhaps unhappy—or is he a jolly Roger?

MARCH 2014
Unfortunates like Roger (described in the last entry) are forced to live as they must, not as they wish. Life-long toil to survive confines many people to struggle from paycheck to paycheck. Largely beyond reach for such disadvantaged underlings are art, music, books, culture, comfort, travel, luxurious living conditions, education, intellectual pursuits, wide-ranging experiences, life-enhancing social connections and many other benefits of the kind enjoyed by humanimals more favored by luck. Like wealth, luck is unevenly distributed in mysterious and often random and undeserved ways.

If you return to a university classroom for a latter-day lecture where you attended a class more than half a century before it seems as if nothing has changed—same seats, walls, blackboards, windows. But for me almost everything had changed over those 50 years, even though the room looked exactly as it did before.

Local Travels in Time and Place

(a) The Metro light-rail line took me on a journey heavily weighted with memories as I traveled from the leafy suburbs to downtown. On the route we passed many landmarks familiar to me, sights which evoked bygone times of my by now long life here in my hometown. (b) Along the way we also passed many latter-day constructs which form some of the infrastructure common in big cities. Humanimals devised and constructed that complicated built environment to help the creatures cope with the many oppressive and pesky intrusive conditions imposed by nature on mankind. The present-day inventive and recently invented cityscape changed the formerly empty areas from how I remember them, still empty of human additions, in times past. Now a chaos of buildings, structures, constructions, equipment, machinery, containers, vehicles, boxes, alleyways, side streets, towers and other man-made forms, many of them mysterious to me, lined the route. I saw coarse industrial areas, odd looking clusters of metal boxes, valves, wires, funnels, connectors, barriers and all sorts of other strange objects whose purposes I couldn't fathom, but each form represents a tangible example of man's ingenuity in the creature's endless struggle with nature.

The Once Beautiful Woman

One of the most poignant effects time's passage exerts on humanimals is how a beautiful woman ages into an old lady men no longer notice. But recently I did notice the remnants of such a once striking and now faded beauty, and imagined how her long ago formerly attractive features no doubt attracted much male gazing. But for her those days are gone forever. The former fine features of the woman's once striking looks were now on permanent strike. Now in her mid-fifties—a 'tween time after her beauty bonanza faded but before it all completely sagged and wrinkled away—the woman was less a male head-turner than an out-of-date and now date-less face and form from which men turn their head away to look at younger women. As I closely examined the aging specimen of lost looks, my male gaze was probably the only stare focused on her in a long time. For years the woman enjoyed good looks, both her own and the looks of men captivated by her beauty. Now it's all over for her. Unlike other more enduring benefits which sometimes endow people with advantages, beauty is only skin-deep and soon vanishes. Most likely plain women men seldom gaze at face fewer adjustments, as those little noticed females age more gracefully than do beauties who lament the loss of their perishable looks.

Just as there's a certain art to living, so too ceasing to exist requires some thought and preparation. The process of winding down, bowing out, arranging for the end, dealing with terminal matters and departing gracefully imposes obligations as meaningful and necessary as does deciding earlier how to proceed with your life. Both an experiment in living and an experiment in dying benefit from some planning.

Both a "no" and a "yes" bring many consequences, most of them unforeseeable. An affirmative decision to proceed activates a chain of events which a "no" would have blocked. Such a negative choice eliminates forever the specific outcomes which a "yes" would have produced but initiates other developments based in part on what's rejected. Negatives involved in the refusal, deferral, rejection, decline of options play a significant role in how an experiment in living turns out, but just how a "no" affects your life is unknowable. In general it's wise to limit structural life-changing decisions as much as possible, as those kinds of major matters can lead to undesirable and perhaps irrevocable outcomes you're unable to remediate.

Human beings seeking to establish a close emotional connection often make major compromises which in some cases lead to only mediocre results. It seems that for some people anybody is preferable to nobody at all.

MAY 2014

During the month-long gap in my Journal entries while I was in Europe I recorded daily events in my travel diary. The diaries, kept while I was away, and the home-based Journal record the active and the passive formats of my experiment in living, and in those ways present what I did while traveling and what I thought while in my native habitat. Both elements—the doing and the thinking—are necessary for a well-rounded experiment in living.

JUNE 2014

A long life is easier to leave than a short one, as toward the end you've experienced enough and much has become repetitious.

Reflections On A Wedding Weekend (Not Mine)

Of the 150 or so guests at an out-of-town wedding I attended, a few (like me) were old, many mid-life, and some younger contemporaries of the bride and groom. Apart from the oldsters, most of those present will continue on to see how the newly married couple's story evolves. Their children (if any) will carry the family on to the next generation, which in turn will perhaps also procreate, and then on and on down the line. Unlike me, the children present at the wedding will most likely survive long enough to know the entire story of the newly-weds. I envisioned how the youngest wedding guest, an infant (but not for long) now a few months old, would look when old, as am I now, and on the brink of extinction. More quickly than she might suppose (when she's old enough to think such thoughts) that little baby will reach the late premortem stage I'm at. I then put such meditations aside and helped myself to a second slice of wedding cake.

Today's designation as "the longest day of the year" suggest an elasticity in time which in fact doesn't exist.

It was 110 years ago today when my father was born, truly a seminal event in his life and also eventually for me.

JULY 2014

The biggest cause of death is life. To death, life is crucial. Where would death be without life? Without a living victim, death's sting wouldn't be toxic. Life creates death. Without life death would die. Living on life, death is a parasite. Never does life disappoint death, as it always continues to live off of life. Death survives on what's alive. Life without death is an impossible as death without life. "Long live death," they shouted during the Spanish Civil War in the 1930s. No one shouted, "Death to death," for the end of death would change the nature of life.

Financial markets follow what has been called a random walk, a description which also applies to life.

Traffic from the nearby highway zooms along at noisy speeds as the vehicles rush on to somewhere, driven ahead in a kind of insensate and mechanical frenzy as if trying to outrun time.

The following sentences in English would no doubt confuse unfortunate victims struggling to learn a very challenging language: (1) "We project that in one month the project will be completed." Confronting the content of the sentence wouldn't easily content the students. [I also noted the content of this last sentence in December 2020.] (2) "I hope the wind will soon wind down so by this afternoon the weather will wind up being pleasant."

Although time can't be destroyed or captured, people sometimes say, "I need to kill some time," or "I've got some time on my hands." But you can't grasp time, and the only way to kill it is to die as death destroys time for you.

Viewed from the perspective of the closing years, the pieces of a long life all seem to form something of a ragged whole. The specifics give way to the general and from the individual components a kind of pattern emerges. Many of your accumulated sensory impressions knit together like a sampler, a crazy-quilt with patches sewn in but not altogether grown together. Toward the end most everything has been settled. Nearly all of the specific forms from their infinite play you'll ever know will have reached you and to some extent coalesced into a somewhat ordered life experience, in contrast to how the erratic, confusing and chaotic random kinetic forms entered your consciousness. Although you experience your experiment in living piecemeal in a day-to-day catch-as-catch-can way, near the end you gain a more integrated even if not a complete or necessarily accurate perspective on the whole. What you happened to fit together in your backward look represents only one of many possible patterns which the forms you experienced could fit into.

A humanimal exists only as an individualized creature while at the same time belonging to a general category. Which predominates? Is the nature of a person primarily his or her uniqueness or as a member of a genus? Medicine treats both a generalized animal and a creature with idiosyncratic characteristics. How do clinicians delineate between treating a person and a herd member? A humanimal is both a very common creature and a one-off specific example of the category; which of those two characteristics best defines the animal?

Recently I read the claim that "People who oppose journal keeping fear it contributes to self-absorption and narcissism." This suggests that you can't be reflective or introspective without being self-absorbed. In my Journal I've tried to dilute any self-absorption by the solvent of remaining focused on the far more interesting outside world and all the vast not-me play of infinite forms beyond my own quite finite existence. The Journal entries deal not in self-analysis but in non-self matters from the outside world. Once I settled on a general understanding of myself and my strengths and weaknesses in order to facilitate my experiment in living, I no longer looked inward. I think (and record some of my thoughts in the Journal) to help me live; I don't live to think.

The inevitable pessimism of realism—a view any rational person will hold—should be leavened with at least a few pinches of positivism so as to make life seem worthwhile. A true view of human life on the lonely planet deprives life of all meaning, a perspective which will diminish or eliminate a humanimal's ability to function, persevere and at times enjoy whatever satisfactions and benefits life happens to provide. Although realistic, a negative attitude robs you of pursuing and appreciating potential pleasures. As unfavorable as the terms of engagement with life for an earthling are, with the right attitude the unfortunate creature can salvage at least a few positive experiences during its quite strange, brief, baffling and all too often disadvantaged terrestrial interlude.

Keeping at arm's-length as many unwanted and undesirable experiences as possible will shape an experiment in living almost as much as pursuing and creating wanted ones.

Many and perhaps most people who enjoy favorable starting conditions end up in unfavorable circumstances. Misfortune chronically threatens good fortune. Often a person advantaged at the outset fails to retain the benefits luck and chance happened to provide. Rather frequently the more favorable the initial endowment, the more likely those desirable given benefits will be abused, misused, wasted, lost. Many times entitled people who inherit personal or financial resources often take those assets for granted. Equipped by chance with unearned advantages, the lucky few fail to gain a sense of reality which conforms to the way the world really works. That flaw in many cases causes the fortuitous original good luck to degrade into bad luck.

As a Doubting Thomas I always tried to carefully look a gift horse in the mouth, and usually what I saw was a lot of needed dental work.

SEPTEMBER 2014

Very few birthdays of earthlings who once lived remain known to or celebrated by subsequent generations. Even the most accomplished, renowned and admired figures of any era are soon forgotten. One obvious exception is Jesus Christ, who in many modern-day lands has become Jesus Christmas. He also features in His rebirth—a double dip for the guy—celebrated at Easter. Americans remember George Washington's birthday, less to honor the first president than to give themselves a holiday. Although Mohammad's exact date of birth (in the year 570 A.D.) is unknown, he died June 8, 632, which perhaps most Muslims know. But apart from a few very rare exceptions, a person's birth or death date is remembered by no one.

The span of remembrance for family members extends only about 50 years or so, from the grandparent's generation to the grandchild's. The "greats" usually aren't known or get remembered as the time separating those four-tier removed generations is too long for any familiarity. Remote ancestors and far in the future descendants represent to one another only an obscure leaf on the family tree.

Like a person, time expires—but does it die? Resurrecting some recollections of the experiences you collected serves in a way to keep expired time alive up until the time when you disappear, at which time time for you dies.

NOVEMBER 2014

Received wisdom is a gift much easier to acquire than what you earn learning lessons by your own efforts directly from life.

The skills of so-called creative types who produce works of art (or what's claimed to be "art") pale in comparison to the truly creative people who function as entrepreneurs, small business operators, risk-taking venturers, originators of innovative new products and services. The intellectual works of writers, artists, composers and similar creators of cultural artifacts derive from subjective sources based on personal taste and many such products of the mind are of questionable quality and little utility. Because such works lack objective standards to judge their validity, they're assessed with opinions—not facts or proofs of concept—offered by reviewers, critics, academics, interested parties, promoters and self-serving operators, many with a vested interest in publicizing art products regardless of any possible merit. Artistic creations often succeed based not on quality but on such flimsy factors as publicity, hype, promotion, advertising, fashion, word-of-mouth, blurbs, uninformed opinions and other such tenuous and subjective influences. By way of contrast, business people face a more demanding environment which requires them to deliver products and services to fulfill needs or wants at prices consumers are willing to pay. To meet those rigorous requirements, owners and managers must operate in efficient and proficient ways. The judgment of the market-place out in the real world—not of taste-makers like critics, reviewers and academics—forces commercial enterprises to produce useful problem-solving offerings. Creativity and originality in business far exceeds those same characteristics claimed by artistic characters who pretend that their works of the mind are of a higher order than the work-product of mere commercial types.

Many of the arty types I encountered who produce creative works struck me as pretentious, self-absorbed, narrow-minded, impractical and unfamiliar with how the world operates. Other than that they're likable, as evidenced by the fact that they like themselves a lot. Many of those sensitive souls I occasionally met, but didn't befriend, focused on and talked mainly about their own insubstantial works of the mind divorced from experiences out in the great wide world. I avoided interactions with other writers, whose little interior world wasn't the kind I sought. The entrepreneurs and small business owners and managers I knew professionally and worked with taught me a lot more about creativity than any of the supposedly refined artists who make up cultural products.

Although money plays a leading role in the cultural world, as in almost all human affairs, the relationship between wealth and taste is tenuous. Buying, funding or owning cultural works bears no connection with refined taste and keen sensibility. Financial considerations have tended to degrade popular and even "high" culture in modern times, and maybe in earlier eras as well. An excretion of artistic products seeking attention and financial success competes in the cultural marketplace. Money in and of itself is tasteless, and so are many of the people who control wealth and make decisions about the merits of what is claimed to be "art."

Much could be written about the psychology of money. Regardless of its source—earned, inherited, extorted, stolen, or however else wealth happens to be gained—money becomes a magic substance which out in the world performs many tricks, no questions asked. Counter-parties you deal with want to know only if you have money, not how you got it. Irrelevant is the source of your spending power: no seller cares if you acquired the means to buy by luck, chance, hard work, inheritance, gift, theft, extortion, appropriation, embezzlement, marriage, divorce, lottery winnings, investment acumen or other methods. Money endows its possessor with a halo effect, one people may admire and envy but which they seldom question.

Each individual life is both everything and nothing. To be alive certainly seems like something, but in the end it's nothing. Every momentary passing sensory impression, so vivid in its immediacy, immediately mutates from something to nothing, leaving only an insubstantial and often soon vanished residual impression in the form of a memory. Enter: religious belief, an invented concept meant to console people that in fact meaning does exist for earthlings unwillingly thrown into existence on the baffling lonely planet. As for non-believers, those poor souls are forced to toggle between the realization that human existence is both everything (all there is) and nothing.

A range-bound view of human existence such as imposed by religious belief both consoles and limits the devout. From religion believers gain purpose and meaning, while at the same time lose an accurate perspective on reality.

The marginal value of staying alive another year or two after you've already enjoyed a long, lucky and satisfying experiment in living is small. Additional longevity will add little, if anything, to your experiment and may in some ways damage it.

Somewhere between stasis and inertia, as contrasted with momentum and hyperactivity, lies a suitable balance. Habits, routines, familiarity, a settled way of life and apparent predictability operate to preserve a person's status quo. Euphoria, excitement, high expectations agitate over-activity. How to enjoy the best of those two extremes requires you to keep busy and involved without engaging in busy-work or manic activities which represent motion but not action.

Wealth, freedom, independence and other such favorable elements come with responsibilities not readily apparent to outsiders. If used properly privileges require careful, conscientious and disciplined handling. But all too many people endowed with fortunate circumstances behave in frivolous, wasteful, extravagant, self-indulgent ways. This sort of behavior gives good fortune a bad name.

An annual ritual such as Thanksgiving draws together people who often have nothing in common except their family relationships. Because the gathered guests have little to say to one another, they go through the usual routines by rote, and no one stands out as the life of the party as the forced togetherness lacks life. Many in attendance wish they were elsewhere.

It's common for people dissatisfied with some of their current circumstances to believe that changes will somehow improve their life. The discontents think contentment will follow with a new job, hobby, house, spouse, city, dog, friend, car, outfit or whatever. But often change makes things worse or at best changes little or nothing.

DECEMBER 2014

As usual the year end reminds me of my end. To avoid that soon to occur fate I (a) could never have existed or (2) gotten death out of the way earlier by not surviving until now. Would either of those options be preferable to my present death-defying (so far) status?

I was to some extent out of place in my native habitat as I didn't subscribe to many of the values, beliefs and practices common in my setting. Similarly, when away during my far-flung adventure travels I was always and everywhere just a stranger, passing through as a curiosity-seeker who belonged nowhere. Both forms of displaced estrangement pleased me.

Sometimes compared to a lottery, life is not really a game of chance as unlike gambling in life you can never win.

To imagine the world as it will be after I'm gone requires a leap of the imagination, and in that way every year-end reminder of an ending is a leap year.

Many people seem satisfied with small talk, trivia, trite comments, banal dialogues, idle conversation, empty chit-chat and other rather meaningless and insubstantial exchanges. I willingly participated in these sorts of inane conversations as they enabled me to avoid talking about myself—which in large part decribes kind of chatter I just described.

An idealized image dominates what people expect by getting what they lack in the way of family life. All too often such fantasies don't survive contact with reality. I've heard childless aspiring parents or an only child who wants a sibling long for offspring or for a brother or sister. What they really wish for is a winning, pleasant, lovable, compatible and companionable additional family member. But fulfillment of the wish often brings a problem child who fails to fulfill those idealized hopes, so resulting in disappointments and headaches because of unrealistic unmet expectations which motivated producing the new arrival.

For seniors, people who have seen it all before, a New Year's Eve and New Year's Day seem more like Old Year's Eve and Day.

As I wrap up the Journal for another year I'm increasingly aware that the opinions and conclusions expressed in my writings are not at all meant to serve as guidance for how other people should carry out their experiment in living. Descriptions of my own experiment I recorded in the Journal only for the purpose of helping me carry out the experiment. Far too many opinions already infest human society, which really doesn't need any more wise-guy views. Many assertions are ill-informed or originate for self-serving or professional reasons, common motivations for the purported authoritative statements of such characters as politicians, bureaucrats, government agency operatives, academics in non-science fields, economists, social scientists, social activists, social critics, social media, commercial operators, newspaper columnists and their fellow journalists, tweets, internet blaming, shaming, explaining, exclaiming and claiming, investment managers and financial commentators, and many other opinionated so-called experts. The arguments and viewpoints many of those sages propose often lack facts, data, analysis, knowledge, reason or other elements which might support the stated conclusions. Such is my opinion of many of the opinions and their originators who speak loudly and with great certainty about highly uncertain matters as if shouting can endow opinions with an authority they mostly lack.

2015

Just as for the year 2014, the length of the Journal's 2015 section greatly exceeds those for most previous years. During the 45 years since I began the Journal I'd grown old, and as a senior senior citizen I'd already experienced most of what I ever would and by then knew just about all of what I'd ever know. Because of the accumulation of repetitive similar impressions, some of the entries in the late Journal contain variations on previous themes. Those additional angles of vision both confirmed my earlier ideas and brought me some reformatted new perspectives on old thoughts, so expanding my earlier views, making them more complete and more useful.

JANUARY 2015

The annual cycle of familiar repetitive events, holidays, celebrations, rituals, seasons now once again begins. Although all those regularities which I've experienced so many times before no longer hold much interest for me, I appreciate the new versions of old forms as they bring a certain imposed order to what otherwise is a disorderly incoherent world where the only certainty is that chance and luck will continue to operate in their unpredictable random, chaotic and capricious ways.

Time operates as the greatest story-teller of all time. No earthling can imagine or human agency create stories more dramatic, surprising, incredible and memorable tales as can Father Time, along with Mother Nature one of the two most creative characters known to man. We depend on time to fill in the blanks of our otherwise empty lives. Without time, nothing can happen. With time, anything can happen. Time will tell, but whatever the story it always ends in the same way.

A fortunate few occupy the very small platform atop the symbolic pyramid which represents the human hierarchy. The luck and chance wild cards which enabled most people to occupy the heights can also at any time topple the top-dwellers from their high perch and cast them into the depths. The dizzying view from the top can induce a vertiginous feeling of vulnerability to a sudden fall, a concern which haunts all the topsters. Not only their high position but also the entire support system of what appears to be a solid structure can collapse and bring everyone and everything down. Nothing is as stable as it might seem. Even the Pyramids will some day crumble into the desert, there to be lost in the sands of time.

People seek and enjoy sleep, which refreshes them but also robs humanimals of a large part of their sentient daily existence. A more appropriate attitude toward that intrusive necessity which depletes one-third of the creature's life would be to resent sleep.

The effect of mistakes you avoid are impossible to assess. Imagining a life other than the specific existence you actually experienced is a thought experiment which adds nothing to your experiment in living.

It's unsettling to imagine other people living in the familiar house I've occupied for many years. Here in my obscure little corner of the world of no importance to anyone but me I've lived out my days, withdrawn nightly into sleep, seen the seasons come and go, and carried out much of my experiment in living. Before long, strangers unknown to me and I to them will live in the spaces which once sheltered me. In my turn, years ago I replaced the previous occupants who I didn't know—they were just names on the warranty deed—and who meant nothing to me. Each generation gets its chance at tenancy and for none is the lease on life or where you live permanent. In the end you don't re-lease but only release your right of occupancy.

Humanimals cling for dear life to their completely unnatural state of being, an exception to their prenatal and postmortem nothingness which represents the norm.

Even the most obtuse and incurious person hopes to remain alive long enough to witness how many on-going personal stories will develop. Parents wish to watch their children mature, elders want to know how their grandchildren fare. Friends enjoy observing how each of their lives evolve. But often you don't survive long enough to see how the various experiments in living play out in the great play of infinite forms. On and on continue the stories, even if the spectators don't.

The past's settled immutability is both comforting and unsettling. The fixity of what's occurred consoles because finally future uncertainties have been eliminated and reduced to a single unalterable reality. But the irrevocable nature of the past also forges iron-clad and sometimes unknowable restrictions on what might happen in the future, which limits or eliminates possibilities. As the past accumulates it lies heavy on the future, but just how previous unalterable events might weight down scenarios to come is for the most part unknowable.

Your family and friends who one by one gradually disappear seem to represent a kind of tontine (in my context perhaps better called a "tomtine") but unfortunately a lottery without a payoff to the ultimate survivor, just another poor mortal who ends up not with a fortune but with the misfortune of having lost everyone meaningful to him.

The loss of familiars suffered by old people gradually dismantles and dis-"womantles" the human infrastructure which once stood to support the foundation for an important part of your experiment in living. As the years go by the fissures grow ever wider until the damage eventually threatens the entire structure. In your younger years you could repair some of the gaps by filling the openings with new relationships. In old age little time remains for such maintenance or remodeling, and near the end the structure becomes quite dilapidated and near collapse.

My disdain for the opinions of other people no doubt saved me from many errors, while at the same time causing me to make mistakes from relying on my own opinions and conclusions. Nonetheless, I was content to suffer poor consequences based on my own views rather than to follow recommendations or opinions from outsiders, even if such advice might have led to better outcomes. I kept an open mind for my internal dialogue and at the same time a mind largely closed to outside influences.

Although the play of infinite forms plays on and on in random and chaotic ways, for individuals their past may make them in some ways immune to the operation of chance. Both a person's accumulated personal history and history in general operate with considerable but largely unknown effects to set the limits of what can happen in the future. How much the past controls in a deterministic way and how much remains free-form and subject to the influences of chance, luck and other capricious forces is unclear. Both chance and inevitability somehow mysteriously shape what emerges from the possible to become forever set as reality. It may be that the past influences less what actually takes place than by delimiting or eliminating what might happen. If that negative influence predominates, then what doesn't occur depends to some unknown extent on the past while what does happen remains subject to the uncertainties and randomness of luck and chance.

In my entire Journal (by now 663 hand-written pages) there's not one original thought. The only originality is the very limited one that the thoughts happened to come to my attention and that I've expressed those perceptions in my own way. Many of the ideas contained in these notebooks over the past 46 years have surely also occurred to other people, but I found it useful to formulate for myself the observations, opinions and conclusions recorded in the Journal, all of which helped me carry out my experiment in living.

Self-deception comforts many people whose illusions allow them to believe in notions which don't conform to reality. Those believers often prefer to see what isn't there and fail to notice what really is. This leads the fantasists to overrate their own capabilities, skills, knowledge, importance, standing, reputation and place in the world. Those confident in their self-perspective judge their likability, behavior, accomplishments much less critically than how they view the same characteristics in other people, and they ignore and justify their own faults. Such a solipsistic attitude seems part of human nature, in which case nature—as in many other cases—has done the humanimal no favors.

Pascal wondered—Why here and not there? Why now and not then? Good questions, to which there are no answers, so why bother to ponder them? A similar useless query, but one I've occasionally passingly contemplated, is—Why me and not him? As I've traveled all around the world and seen so many unfortunate humanimals trapped by chance and bad luck in oppressive circumstances, I've wondered why those mired in misery and hopelessness happened to suffer such ill-fated conditions of the kind I somehow escaped. The opening situation which by chance applied to me, along with the circumstances—economic, social, political, geopolitical and others—which by chance prevailed during my time were for the most part favorable. What fate endowed me with that capricious force denied to the benighted struggling and suffering masses I saw during my passing visits to places filled with disadvantaged masses disfavored by luck.

So vivid, granular and real seems the reality of what actually occurs we sometimes forget that an infinite number of other possibilities could have taken form rather than the specific versions which by chance actually came into being.

It's sobering but gratifying to realize the random and capricious ways luck and chance operate and how they so profoundly affect your experiment in living. Timing, place, happenstance, coincidence, serendipity and other similarly random influences determine much of how the experiment develops. The slightest variance in those wild-card factors can lead to substantial differences in outcomes, positive or negative and sometimes both with a reversal of fortune as things continue to develop. Because human agency plays a much less influential role than many people assume, there's always a chance good luck will remedy any shortfalls in how your own efforts work out, and an equal chance that bad luck might damage any successes which somehow happen to come about.

Of the "where-when-who" triad which pertains to three of the most influential random factors imposed on a person's circumstances by luck and chance, the "when" may be the most misleading. If the specific era in which one is alive happens to be particularly favorable, as has been the case for my generation, the fortunate group which by chance enjoys the benefits of such a propitious time may assume that those benign and advantageous conditions represent the norm. In fact, the opposite is true: seldom do political, geopolitical, social, economic, cultural and other societal factors coalesce to establish for any generation circumstances as exceptional as those which prevailed during my time. Normally, much less favorable conditions exist. Chance and luck just happened to endow my era with the good times which helped to enhance my experiment in living. Other generations aren't so lucky.

Some humanimals forget to die. Those creatures live oblivious to the inevitable end-game, as if for them death doesn't exist. As a result, the deathless fail to account for mortality when calculating the way to live. Death seemingly takes the deniers by surprise because somehow those carefree and time-gainsayers don't expect to disappear. This devil-may-care attitude ignores the reality that the devil does care, as every mortal must give the devil his (or her) due.

To imagine your ultimate fate long before mortality becomes personal to you, rather than just an abstract concept applicable to other people or in your distant future, allows you to prepare for the end. Living a satisfactory existence depends in part on leaving it in a premeditated and well-curated way. The aversion to confronting mortality arises in part from an unwillingness to face the fact that in the end a humanimal is a nobody, a nothing. No matter how ardently such creatures aspire to be somebody, the human animal is simply a nothing pretending for a brief time to be something.

Active and productive members of the human race who enjoy engaging with the play of infinite forms are in a race with time to accomplish all they hope to achieve. But "race" fails to accurately describe the experience, as the race faced by the human race doesn't really represent fair competition: the contest always produces the same winner.

To sustain my longevity over by now many years brought or required many gallons of drinkable fluid and thousands of meals; one-third of my days lost to sleep; large quantities of such necessities as gasoline, natural gas for heat, electricity, water; constant maintenance to assure reliable mechanical and bodily functions; torrents and mountains of personal excreted waste materials; receipt and processing of countless sensory impressions; innumerable encounters and conversations with other people; an untold number of thoughts; thousands of air/car/bus/ship/ train miles traveled and hundreds of hotel beds briefly occupied; plus all the other inputs and outputs necessary or desirable for me to survive long enough to produce this Journal entry. To be born and continue to exist seems like a lot of trouble, an experiment probably not worth the effort. Why bother?

Essentially a receptor of fleeting passing sensory impressions, a humanimal absorbs and retains very little of what happens to come to the creature's attention. Only a tiny residue of what we experience forms our experiment in living; all the rest is wasted on us.

MARCH 2015

As a short month, February ends more quickly than the others, but once over they all also seem short.

Only a few fortunate humanimals possess the freedom to decide if they prefer to live as an outsider looking in or as an insider looking out. The outsider functions largely as an observer, passively watching from a distanced perspective; insiders participate as activists, doing rather than simply looking. Outsiders may occasionally wish that they were more hands-on activists, while at times insiders would perhaps prefer to remove themselves from the hurly-burly of the outside world. The most desirable format is some sort of synthesis of the two modes so that you can function as an outsider while still retaining the many advantages enjoyed by an insider.

We can thank nature for creating the specific conditions necessary to enable human life while at the same time blaming nature for establishing the very same conditions. Although chance-given natural factors enable earthlings to exist, nature's terms of engagement have imposed on mankind many inconvenient and oppressive problems and an untold number of hazards and threats. Animals face all sorts of internal mishaps and failures as well as intrusive accidents and traumas from the outside, all of which subject the body to disease, damage, decay, decline and disappearance. External threats include disasters from inner space (earthquakes, volcanic eruptions, sinkholes, quick sand, collapsing terrain) and outer space (meteors, Martians) and everywhere in between (extreme weather, pandemics, famine, floods, drought, pestilence, many other systemic intrusions), an endless number and variety of assaults and calamities inflicted on earthlings by the cosmic system. Mankind's terrestrial home is not only a lonely planet but also a dangerous one for the mortals in residence here. Nature gave humanimals quite a mixed bag: food and famine; water and poisoned chalices; electricity and the electric chair; ease and disease; time and eternity; life and death. As a force of nature, nature operates in diverse ways which both enables and disables human existence.

Wise-cracks, jokes, gags, the fun of making fun of whatever target attracts ridicule, derision or humor, provoking laughter, teasing all serve as good ways to deal with conditions as they exist on the lonely planet. You really have to laugh at the entire ridiculous terrestrial play of infinite forms. Heine could have used some of that comic relief to cheer him up when he wrote, "*Ich weiss nicht, was es soll bedeutet,/Dass ich so träurig bin.*" ("I don't know what it means that I'm so sad.") Don't be sad, Heinrich—cheer up and laugh at it all.

When someone recently asked me if I had "independent money" I found the question poorly phrased. There's really no such thing as "independent" wealth, as what you own always depends on constant oversight, management and care. Making and retaining money requires diligence and attention to detail. Absent such due and often overdue diligence, wealth will disappear. The fortunate few who happen to be endowed with financial assets, whether inherited or earned, don't really enjoy monetary independence as the wealth depends on how its owner handles the benefaction. Anyone with financial means who supposes that means they possess "independent money" sure to remain without close attention will eventually become dependent on other sources of income, as the ignored and soon vanished assets will no longer support such carefree characters.

A marriage of convenience may in many ways become inconvenient, but so can any marriage.

APRIL 2015

The better you get to know someone, the more obvious appear their defects. This means that if you attempt to "know thyself" you're likely to see many faults you'd prefer to ignore or deny.

Finding a true soul-mate—that elusive and perhaps unique person who could also be described as a sole-mate—represents one of the major challenges for an experiment in living. Because such a find is so rare, many people pair off in relationships which involve quite contrasting, incompatible and ill-matched personalities. It seems that the many compromises, adjustments and burdensome conditions required in such a relationship outweigh the perceived disadvantages of living alone. One way to resolve this kind of trade-off is to get a dog, a companion who seldom if ever provokes in its service provider any complaints or resentment for the obligations which come with the pet mate.

Death isn't the only ending but just the final one, a determinative termination which eliminates all other endings. In that way, mortality may be not simply a blessing in disguise but a favor of nature clothed in full parade dress very evident to all concerned.

Some losses can also brings gains. When a grown child leaves home to establish an independent life the departure may please both the parents and the child. Perhaps the most difficult trade-off which involves both gain and loss is when a father gives his daughter away in marriage. He loses his adored daughter, who for her part gains a husband.

Every humanimal exists within two worlds, the creature's smaller one within the vast all-encompassing totality. The larger realm includes the great play of infinite forms derived from what nature and mankind have activated. Subordinate to this general setting which affects every earthling lies a small mini-world limited to each individual. The greater world where the nature of things sets the terms of existence for every humanimal remains largely impervious to reshaping. This leaves an earthling with the possibility of attempting to cultivate his or her own little experiment in living, a great challenge in that luck and chance, part of the nature of things which intrude on individuals, determine so much of what happens.

Operating within the realm of your own little individual circle of competence to try to shape what little you might be able to control involves proceeding with a realistic sense of things as they are. This includes understanding the motives, agendas, incentives, interests, needs and wants of people you deal with. An unruly confusion of ceaseless demands, requests, requirements, suggestions, offers, pressures, impositions, seductions, opinions and other importune behaviors constantly confront you with decisions which lead to expenses, time depletion, commitments, obligations, burdens, entanglements and various other complications. Apparent opportunities are often simply opportunism on the part of your counter-party. Failure to carefully assess what's presented to you as a supposed benefit is likely to damage your ability to make informed decisions in the few ways which offer you agency in managing your experiment in living.

Not only needing but also being needed motivates people to establish close relationships. Owning a pet represents the most basic and probably the least complicated format to satisfy the human need to be needed. The animal is absolutely dependent on its human master, who in turn benefits from the faithful pet's devotion, even if based primarily on the many services the animal receives from its owner. The motivations of both doggy and daddy are self-serving. As for human relationships, to hear the words "I need you" represents both intoxicating and toxic implications. To be needed is to enjoy a deep emotional connection while at the same time charging you with your partner's tremendous hopes and expectations which task you with the related implied obligations and responsibilities. A true bond with another animal, whether human or canine, entails the two dimensions of needing and being needed, with the difference that ideally a human relationship is reciprocal, whereas with a dog the pet runs the show and gains most of the benefits.

Thousands upon thousands of well-made and worthy creative works of merit have over the centuries fallen into obscurity. Writers, artists, musicians have invested tremendous amount of time, effort, energy, thought, ingenuity, skill, emotions, feelings, patience and other mental and sentimental ingredients to produce clever, amusing, profound, entertaining or otherwise useful and desirable cultural products. Few of those hard-earned creations remain known.

Experiencing the final version of each kind of life event you've known over many years characterizes the state of being old. Whatever specific events happens to take place in your late years may well be the very last such occurrence you'll ever encounter.

The lively mind and the limited mind each look at and deal with life in completely different ways. Narrow mentalities settle for a technical and procedural approach with decisions based on relatively few factors based on immediate and obvious circumstances rather than on less apparent, more subtle and nuanced implications and considerations. By way of contrast, a more supple and aware active mind enables you to imagine collateral effects and diverse factors which bear on a decision. That sort of approach depends on a hinterland of facilitators based on a diversity of experiences, judgment, intelligence, imagination, awareness, sensitivity, perceptions and other such granular factors which allow you to consider many of the relevant elements which bear on a decision. The broader your perspective, the more advantaged will be the process you use to carry out your experiment in living.

The longer we live the more mellow and pleasing our earlier years seem. Remote yesteryears season over time and bring us heart-warming memories tempered by regret for how distant in time those treasured vanished years are. Although recent experiences seem much more vivid than older happenings, many of the remote events from the distant past offer the advantage of having at the time been new to you rather than, as in old age, simply repeats of what you've already known.

MAY 2015

Ego, pride, self-importance, hubris and various other such characteristics motivate many humanimals to try to stand out and display individuality. Some people will go to great lengths to avoid being just another face in the crowd, only to end up as just another corpse in the cemetery.

The happenstance of being thrown into life unwillingly produces early on-set mortality. From first breath to ultimate death, every humanimals suffers from a terminal condition. Some people deal with this ailment with dis-ease, as they find the notion of non-being unsettling and prefer not to confront that eventual inevitable outcome. But whether you contemplate your mortality or not, the fact remains that life is a sickness unto death.

To "know thyself," as the ancients advocated, is okay for openers but after you assess your personality and the various perspectives for how you perceive the world those views should then be used to proceed effectively with your experiment in living. Once you establish the framework for your experiment it's necessary to move on rather than continuing to focus on the self and dwelling on your inner-being, a self-referential activity far too narcissistic, introverted, narrow minded and removed from reality to help you much with your experiment.

The great play of infinite forms (as Tagore put it) creates a ceaseless chaos of images. The never-ending spectacle plays on and on in the terrestrial theater, its stage the lonely planet. Becoming a living animal operates to plug the creature into some of the sensory impressions the performance offers, only a few of which come to the animal's attention. At the end of the show when the lights darken and all the delights fade the final curtain descends, never again to rise. What we happened to experience during the brief time our sensory receptors remained active came to us mostly by chance. The play of infinite forms follows no script, as the free-form drama/comedy/farce is almost entirely improvised and ad lib.

Individual humanimals face the same conflict between order and disorder as do countries. Without some self-control the creature will most likely experience turmoil and confusion in its experiment in living. Similarly, anarchism or simply extreme license and freedom may well lead to unsettled, chaotic and dysfunctional conditions in a country. A controlled dictatorial society brings stability, civil order but without civil rights, a managed but usually mismanaged economy, and the benefits of a more predictable even if less dynamic system. A free-spirited democracy and a suppressed "demoncracy" represent opposite ways of arranging society. For people, impulses, passions, emotions, instincts and other such irrational forces vie with logic, reason, premeditated considerations, contemplation and similar governing characteristics to determine if a humanimal acts in an impulsive, spontaneous rather animal-like way or in a more deliberate and thoughtful human mode. Ideal would be a balance between a free-for-all and a free-for-none format, but that kind of equilibrated system seems to be rarely attained, either for governments or for people.

A cautious, rational mind-set can be set in such a rigid way the fixed mentality blocks you from enjoying many pleasant experiences, but a controlled and carefully curated attitude can also save you from impulsive decisions and their often undesirable consequences.

Why any specific event occurs or why any particular thing exists lacks interest. The significant element regarding what comprises reality relates to the "what": what the actual happenings or beings are. One exception to the uselessness of a "why?" pertains to the need to assess why other people you deal with behave in certain ways. This involves asking yourself why someone is motivated to offer you suggestions, proposals, seeming opportunities, deals, bargains, specials and other propositions meant to activate a positive response from you. The "why?" of those people can enlighten you as to their interests and how they'll benefit from persuading you to respond as they wish.

My relative lack of ambition suited me well. Possible noteworthy successes and admirable accomplishments failed to motivate me. I was content to stay off the fast track and confine my efforts to a slower more measured pace. I performed my role in the play of infinite forms as a sideshow rather than as a featured act under the big top; the little top satisfied me. My modest life brought me sufficient minor achievements meaningful to me, even if to no one else. Such was my experiment in living, an experiment whose proof of concept wasn't peer reviewed but a way of being I viewed as fit for purpose.

As time goes by the Second Law of Thermodynamics operates not only in the realm of physics but also for human relationships. Over time the woven fabric of your most material friendships fray. Circles narrow, links break, contacts lapse, ties untie, networks lose strands, couples unpair, knots untangle to become nots, knits unravel and become seamless, connections disconnect. Familiar faces eventually fade into a blur and gradually dissolve; long-standing bonds disband (or disbond); presences become absences. Slow-motion changes gradually alter previously long-settled and on-going togetherness. Marriages end, by death or divorce; children age and move away; long-time service providers retire; close neighbors leave and become ex-neighbors; long familiar neighborhood shop-owners bow out; beloved dogs bow-wow out as they depart for canine heaven; and even cats, creatures endowed with nine lives, finally reach their limit and vanish without a tenth life. Entropy also operates on you, gradually sapping your energy and unbalancing your homeostasis until finally you, too, no longer recognize yourself because you're a mere shadow of how you once were, a ghost-in-waiting.

A moat-like gap to separate you from the outside world from time to time serves the useful function of allowing you occasionally to retreat into solitude. But it's necessary to bridge the gap with a drawbridge so that you can emerge and rejoin the world after your solitary interludes.

Both the personal and the systemic preexisting conditions which define your terms of engagement with the world operate as a kind of tar-baby to which you bit by bit stick, so limiting your flexibility and ability to carry out an unimpeded hands-on experiment in living. Your own particular circumstances, the nature of things, human institutions and the restraints imposed by your accumulated past all constrain your freedom of movement. Those sticky tar-baby effects restrict and tarnish in a hellish Tartarus-like way how you handle your experiment.

A very senior senior citizen exists as a ticking organic time-bomb which may at any moment explode.

JULY 2015

Each particular humanimal represents just another meaningless experiment in the billions randomly produced by nature as that capricious force incessantly rearranges genes into new and temporary differentiated forms. The creature exists at the intersection of the macro endless play of infinite forms and the micro specifics of a one-time never-before and never-again incarnation of an animal both unique and an archetype of its category.

One purpose of an established system of law and order is to provide that a contract rather than a gun represents the means to transfer property. The advantage of the gun method is that it avoids lawyers.

An American man and a Japanese woman joined together as a newly married young couple I once briefly encountered many years ago. Apart from a few words, he spoke no Japanese and she no English. Lacking each other's language, the two of them were not on speaking terms. Is this an advantage (no arguments) or a disadvantage (no communication) in a marriage? Are the two of them still married? Can they now converse, or are the two of them content to remain incommunicado?

Although blue collar workers and blue-blood heirs each experience their experiment in living in quite different ways, at the end of that brief experience both blues are fated to face the same blackout.

Three invariable constants common in every country and society I saw around the world: family life, religious belief, and red-yellow-green traffic light signals. Each of the three serves to establish a structure to order human conduct. Without families and religion the lonely planet would be even more lonely, and without uniform traffic signals auto body-shop owners would be millionaires.

A leopard may not know that it can't change its spots, but at least the animal doesn't try. Humananimals often suppose that change might solve various problems and will otherwise be beneficial. But after the creature establishes a new way of being his or her old self usually continues to haunt the animal and continues to predominate, so in an existential way the changes change nothing.

Very old age is just one stage away from no age.

Short of mortality partial death represents a death-in-life state. This premortem status typifies how such zombie-like earthlings function. Those ghosts-in-waiting seem oblivious to any of the play of infinite forms which don't immediately affect the living dead. Lack of curiosity, self-orientation, narcissistic behavior, solipsism, disinterest in the world and other such introverted characteristics operate to turn some humanimals into the walking dead. But pre-death, which anticipates the real thing, may offer the advantage that death's sting may be drawn for people who have already mostly died while still alive.

Although your past, as viewed from a late-in-life perspective, may appear to be a set-piece which seems coherent and an integral whole, in fact nothing which happened to comprise your life had to form a part of it.

As those in your social circle one by one disappear you wonder who will be the last to survive. If not you, you'll never know who.

Toward the end, when it comes to when, where and how you'll meet your end, you start to think, "The suspense is killing me." But it's time, not suspense, which will kill you.

Because such exceptional traits and factors as originality, daring, a sense of adventure, effort, energy, risk tolerance, persistence, intelligence, good judgment, diligence—plus the capricious forces of luck, chance and randomness—represent the operative elements to produce wealth, it's understandable why most people lack money.

Digital technology magnifies the consumerism and the narcissism typical of many Americans. The internet makes buying stuff easier than ever, while also providing the means to distribute at almost no cost self-referential and exhibitionist video, blog, chat room and other presentations characteristic of a selfie culture.

Because so much is now available on the internet the proliferation of data, information, interpretations and opinions makes it nearly impossible to gain any advantages by seeking facts, useful news, insightful perspectives or other actionable perceptions. Moreover, much of what passes for information is only misinformation. These days the ability to tune out all the static and discern which sources represent the very few which provide the most relevant and reliable information and interpretation represents about the only way anyone can get a competitive advantage. For that reason I often ask highly successful people not the secret of their success—which anyway many of them can't precisely define—but what sources the over-achievers use to equip their decision-making with the best possible considerations.

To the common refrains, "Time flies" and 'Where have all the years gone?" my answers say that for me time didn't fly but simply crept along day to day, and as for the years they went to fill and fulfill my experiment in living with the kinds of experiences I hoped to accumulate.

In chapter 25 of *The Prince* Machiavelli considers "How Much Fortune Can Do in Human Affairs and How It May Be Opposed." He states his belief "that fortune is the ruler of half our actions, but that allows the other half or thereabouts to be governed by us." It would indeed be comforting to suppose that as much as half of our lives depend on our own volition, but I suspect that we govern much less than that portion, with chance and luck playing the dominant roles.

As from my younger years I based much of my behavior on how my life would appear to me when viewed looking back on my experiment in living from old age, which is now. That forward-looking theoretical retrospective perspective allowed me to get old with few regrets.

No matter how fit an oldster may be, old age is a terminal disease. But when you're near the end the hazards of fortune will negatively affect you for a much shorter time period than when you were young.

As for every mortal, I owe nature a death-debt, one which my deceased friends have already paid. Their accounts are closed. For me, the balance due is yet to come.

Some of the most pervasive and common human practices and institutions depend on emotions, instincts, intuition, opinions and subjective views rather than on rational considerations. Creative works, love, many political and economic theories and positions, the social sciences, investment management and market commentary, cultural presentations, artistic reputations and perceived merit in many fields all represent examples of how people often formulate evaluations based on mainly illogical and unprovable considerations not subject to experiment or objective standards.

To contemplate "the road not taken" which might have led to more favorable outcomes greatly limits the thought experiment, as an almost infinite number of routes—not "the" road— always fork off from the path you happen to be following at any particular time. Of all the roads you might take, one and only one will in fact lead you onward and from that way forward there's no turning back.

SEPTEMBER 2015

As civilization advanced over the centuries science explained many of the mysteries of nature which puzzled ancient mankind. Scientific developments have also served to mitigate many of the natural world's harsh effects. A time-ticket to travel back to prehistoric times to see how early-day earthlings managed to cope with nature in that long ago era would be a worthwhile journey, provided that the ticket included a round-trip and not just a one-way excursion which leaves you stranded in the distant past, truly a foreign country.

For humanimals death isn't the problem: life is. The system blessed mankind with a natural way for life to end, a process which will extinguish all of the many concerns and ominous portents and nightmares which haunt the human mind: anxiety, dread, disappointment, regret, disease, old age, bad luck, poverty, misery, misfortune, failure, the thousands of other shocks mankind is heir to and, perhaps above (or below) all mortality. Releasing the decedent from all difficulties and worries, death provides complete relief like no other remedy.

The devout who believe in an after-life hold perverse views, as earthlings should cherish oblivion rather than hoping for some sort of new and improved state of being. That idealized version of postmortem existence represents fake views as the postmortem context might well bring even more problems and difficulties more severe than the vexations already faced by earthlings during their brief tenure on the lonely planet.

Although Americans view Labor Day as summer's end, nature ends the season at a different time. A child of nature, mankind plays with that strange and capricious force while at the same time nature toys with humankind. Between the two players the overwhelmingly dominant natural cosmic play of infinite forms wins out in the end.

If the past is another country, the future is even more so. At least we know something of the past, even if we perceive the remote yesteryears only through a glass darkly. Of the future we know almost nothing. We expect the near future to proceed on a continuum such that what happens will follow from what has recently occurred. But in the long run, over time, the future brings into existence another country which would indeed seem quite foreign and strange to inhabitants of long ago previous eras.

Like time, humanimals migrate from one state to another—from non-being into existence and then into the past. An earthling's first stage occurs when suddenly the creature leaves the eternity of prenatal non-being to enter the world, a foreign place where the new arrival is a stranger in a strange land and then, after a brief presence on the lonely planet, the human transitions back to non-being to complete the round-trip from nothing to nothing. The being gains nothing by this journey.

The arbitrary nature of creation—of infinite forms and of events—depends on random chance factors. Almost anything might have developed in a different way. Grass might have been red, blood green, humanimals equipped with four or six fingers, three ears, more or less teeth. There could have been one less Journal writer (oops—just kidding). Nature might have developed in ways completely different than those known to humanimals, and perhaps even without producing such creatures. Would that have been preferable?

"Only" doesn't necessarily mean lonely, as some sole souls enjoy their solitude.

Culture transmits a sense of past eras to future ones, but artistic creations can convey only a vague idea of yesteryear life. The vivid granular play of forms unique to each period in history never seems the same when described or depicted in words or visual forms. A person's own time is real and authoritative; times past, only dead history and derivative. As for the future, speculative science fiction attempts to divine what years to come might bring but, just as for the past, how earthlings will live centuries from now is such a remote and theoretical matter any imagined scenarios represent only sketchy and indistinct concepts of eras no one now living will know. Our by then long gone era will appear the same to future generations.

Of all the billions and billions of written and printed words, only an infinitesimally tiny few will remain, among them—most likely—are such valuable writings as (if found) a few Shakespeare holographic manuscripts, the secret formula for Coca-Cola, the instruction manual to manufacture M & M's, the code to access the Fort Knox gold vaults, books containing "Peanuts" cartoons, Chinese fortune cookie fortune slips, tell-all memoirs by Lady Gaga and Madonna, and perhaps Victoria's Secret catalogs. All other written materials and everything else created by the hand of man and mankind itself will vanish without the slightest trace as the play of infinite forms plays on and the cosmos spins on and on, motion devoid of meaning and indifferent to whether anything exists or doesn't.

Since the time of the ancients, thinkers have suggested that life is a dream and that we are such stuff as dreams are made on. But maybe the reverse is true: dreams are life. Perhaps dreaming represents a way to access real life, a kind of netherworld or hinterland embedded in our consciousness and which comes to life only in our sleep. IF true, then a third of our terrestrial time would be connected with real life and two-thirds in the dream world of what only appears to be reality.

It strikes me as strange that even at this advanced age I compulsively continue to pursue my curiosity-compelled reading and travel and such truly odd practices as looking up the meaning of a foreign language word new to me. Why bother? Of what possible use would yet another word in French, German, Italian or Spanish be? Yet, somehow I persist.

After millennia of experimentation, nature finally settled on a standard morphology for members of the animal kingdom. The lower orders fared better than mankind, which didn't enjoy such efficient operating systems and practices. Humanimals have produced a babble of languages along with a baffling number of sects, cults, religions, beliefs, heresies, denominations, doctrines, canons, scriptures, all based on a search for meaning. Folks, take a step back, take a deep breath and take a tip from nature—don't overthink and complicate things: accept a workable prototype and let that model function as intended without formatting additional complicated and far-fetched line extentions.

OCTOBER 2015

A mellow autumn day, part of the annual natural cycle which brings some regularity to an otherwise mostly chaotic, confusing and random play of infinite forms.

After a magician's sleight-of-hand makes one of his associates disappear, the helper later returns for a curtain call. When nature makes humanimals vanish the curtain drops forever and the players never return to the stage.

Although experts and advisers benefit and make a living from domain knowledge, those service providers also suffer from their expertise. Their deep familiarity with a particular field induces them to try to fit all sorts of different situations into their specialty. Because the professionals focus on their own limited field, to the exclusion of a broader view, the experts offer technical opinions which fail to account for factors beyond their specialized training. Expertise in one area prevents people from taking a holistic view to consider a diverse range of elements. As a result, narrowly-crafted expert opinion often fails to offer much help in the way of useful and actionable advice.

Human society is so set in its ways people tend to resist most attempts to change what already exists. Only a few determined and exceptional individuals can bring about substantial changes. By way of contrast, constant change characterizes the cosmic play of infinite forms. For humanimals, most significant changes are not initiated by but are imposed on the creatures.

Engendering a child is primarily for the benefit and amusement of the progenitors, but to the disadvantage of the humanimal created by the parents. The procreators enjoy the passion which initiates the process and then get pleasure from what follows—gestation, birth of the little bundle of joy, nurturing the new-born, caring for the child, raising and educating the creature, then observing the mammal, one of billions but to the couple a one-and-only unique specimen, develop and mature. Kids provide a sense of purpose, a means of entertainment, an heir and then descendants (roles only partly fulfilled by a dog). Of what use is all of this to the child? Life unwillingly inflicted on the kid becomes the new arrival's continuing problem after the parents have had their fun.

To build a life requires years of thoughtful and constructive construction, and then at the end you need a similarly careful process to dismantle with an appropriate exit strategy what it took you a lifetime to build.

An authentic experiment in living depends on a participatory rather than just a surrogate and derivative format. Only through experience, trial-and-error, and hands-on practical engagement with the world can you manage to understand and function properly on the lonely planet, even if only in a limited and basic way. Wall Streeters call this kind of process "suck it and see." A more literate and complete description comes from Charles Koch, CEO of the huge Koch Industries conglomerate: "You get a lot of losers. What all this comes down to is, you need an experimental discovery culture and model. You can study these things till the end of time and not know, because the future is unknown and unknowable. We try to do experiments at a level that we can afford to lose." What you can know about the future is that the main influences which will shape outcomes include luck, chance and randomness, uncertain factors to which you must react by flexibility and improvisation.

Time now Octobers its way on toward the first chill of winter, just as millennia ago when the same seasonal cycle played out in the area where I happen to briefly live. Perhaps thousands of years from now someone alive here on the land I now momentarily occupy will wonder how things were in this little corner of the world back in my time.

From a young age I somehow became aware of the skull beneath the skin, and all through the years I was grateful for my recognition of mortality early enough so that I could adjust my life with time enough to deal with my ultimate demise. Some years ago during a spring visit to Cambridge (England) I happened upon a student reception out on the lawn in "the Backs" by the Cam River behind one of the colleges. Among the guests I noticed an especially pretty co-ed, endowed with rose-pink cheeks in the English way, slim limbs, a pert face, a ripe and nubile form. Engaged in young fun with her fellow upper-class fresh-men and women classmates, she was perhaps lost in the moment and oblivious of what was to come. Observing from the sidelines the attractive fresh face and figure as shadows slowly crept across the lawn and moved the party to its end, I couldn't help but envision the young beauty grown old and perhaps one day in the far distant future taking a few moments to look back on this long-vanished festive day in the Backs as she contemplated her soon-to-end earthly existence. But the good-looking Cantabrigian wouldn't be thinking of that just now, there on the immaculately tailored Cambridge college lawn that spring day, nor would any of the other students visualize the time when they'd all be long gone from that serene scene, or imagine how they'd all rather quickly age, and one day late in the day a long time from now perhaps give a brief passing thought to their brief young years when once upon a time they gathered there on the lawn by the flowing river.

Although both happy and lucky, fortunately I wasn't a happy-go-lucky type. I didn't frolic through life as a "good ole boy," nor did I suffered from any of the many psychological "disorders" listed in the professional manuals, although a somewhat exaggerated sense of order, no doubt based on my Germanic heritage, characterized my attention to detail and a perhaps too precise mentality. My somewhat frequent references to mortality in the Journal don't evidence a depressive or morose personality. Quite the opposite: my awareness of death from an early age brought me an opportunity to factor an eventual certain disappearance into how I decided to live. My thoughts of final matters greatly advantaged me, as by facing the realities I could engage with them in ways which would best enhance my experiment in living. Cemeteries, tombstones, obituaries, funerals, burials, the Day of the Dead, Halloween, ghosts, skeletons and the like never spooked me, as I viewed those morbid evocations as useful reminders and vivid precursors of my own eventual fate.

NOVEMBER 2015

Today brought both the Day of the Dead (which, in truth, for humanimals is every day as they are essentially walking dead) and the death of daylight saving time. That temporal change extends my life by an hour, at least as measured by human rather than physiological time, thus postponing my Dead Day by 60 minutes. But if I survive until spring the time change will then set me back by an hour. What time gives it takes away.

The essence of many of my thoughts about time, mortality, life on earth and other existential matters Santayana summarized in just 13 words: "There is no cure for birth or death save to enjoy the interval." I can condense that to just two words: "Have fun."

A compulsively curious person who exists in the present age fortunately enjoys a vast variety of things to be curious about, as well as many ways to satisfy the curiosity.

A local small town newspaper recently reported on an 85-year-old man who for 66 years worked as a barber in his shop in the village. Charlie spent his entire life cutting hair in a picture-perfect Norman Rockwell "Our Town"-type pleasant down-home Midwestern suburb. Trimming thousands of heads of hair, many multiple times, he knew heads better than the most accomplished phrenologist. Charlie enjoyed the benefits and satisfactions of a steady job in which he was his own boss with repeat customers and a hands-on low-tech profession invulnerable to offshoring (or off-shaving) or to rapid technological change. He lived as a known and appreciated character in a friendly small town with a sense of community, and had a stable and satisfying personal life. Charlie the barber's experiment in living was definitely a cut above that of most humanimals.

When someone asks your opinion about an already concluded matter—"Did I do the right thing?"—they don't really want an objective appraisal. They're in effect seeking not a reasoned opinion but approval, validation, praise, support, understanding, compliments. This wished-for response applies especially for people who have produced creative works, as the merit of those intangible and mostly unnecessary products of the mind always remains uncertain until subjected to public scrutiny. Creative types who ask you about their cultural creation want to be assured that it's a worthy work. If you criticize the creation or otherwise offer a realistic view which doesn't entail approval, the person who inquired will ignore your views, may even start ignoring you as a friend, and will probably never again ask for your opinion.

In theory, before whatever happens to exist comes into being that particular form is almost impossible up to the moment when, out of the infinite number of possibilities, one specific event or thing chances to be thrown into existence. What is then seems normal and natural, as if it had to be.

Health, relationships, money, jobs, family represent the source of almost all the personal problems which afflict humanimals. It's difficult to feel any sympathy, empathy or compassion for strangers or for humanity in general who suffer such problems. Only specific cases pertaining to family, friends or people we know elicit emotional responses to misfortunes. This inability to sympathize with strangers is reciprocal, as they don't sympathize with or care about our problems either. Similarly, those kinds of afflictions which affected or will affect our ancestors or our descendants—all strangers to us— lack the power to elicit empathy from us.

So unsettled, kinetic and changing is the ceaseless play of infinite forms, at any moment the spectacle presents only a transient version of reality, one of many possible realities. Such is also true of whatever happened in the past: it could have all been different.

It seems perverse that much of what's pleasurable can often produce unwanted and undesirable consequences. Food brings taste treats, but overeating or consuming unhealthy grub leads to excess calories, fat, sugar. Good health will abdicate if you stuff yourself with too much regal fare at Dairy Queen, Burger King or White Castle or other more plebeian such stuff. Alcohol and narcotics may give you a temporary high, then degrade you to a low. Passion's pleasure risks especially unfortunate outcomes as sex can inflict existence on a humanimal who didn't request or want to be alive and create a creature you didn't intend to engender.

Borrowed money restructures time in that consumers can buy today what they'd otherwise have to postpone until later. This displaces consumption by moving it from the future to the present. Perhaps more than in any other society, Americans have been conditioned to acquire goods or services which will be paid for over time. The reverse process, deferring consumption until it can be fully paid for when bought, seems less common for Americans. In our system, the time value of money benefits lenders more than it does savers.

All the departed people I once knew will suffer a second death with mine. Although I couldn't create any new memories of the deceased after their death, at least I retained some residual impressions of the vanished characters who played a part in my life. But when I disappear so will all my memories of those friends and in that way they'll undergo a second death, one which will destroy how for a time a survivor remembered them. The deceased will then be only a name from the dead past inscribed on a forgotten tombstone, as will I after the death of my survivors who knew me.

Our place in the world derives from two perspectives. First, how we see ourselves formats one view of where we fit in. That perception may or may not be completely realistic, but in any case it represents the way we suppose ourselves to be. How others perceive us provides multiple perspectives which offer more objective and perhaps in many ways more realistic views of our actual presence among our fellow humanimals. If you live as a hermit or a recluse and remain unknown by other people you are alive in an organic way but otherwise don't exist. If man is a social animal, a humanimal without any relationships is less a human than an anti-social animal.

The way other people know us forms a large part of how we belong to the world. If no one knows us, we exist only by how we view ourselves. Take the case of a tenth generation 50-year-long resident of a village of 100 inhabitants who leaves for a year or so. While he's away an epidemic kills everyone, so that when the once well-known local returns he's a stranger in his own home town as the new residents never heard of him. Because all who once knew the new stranger are gone, no longer does he exist in the memories of the current residents. If no one knows the former long-time townsman, does that change the nature of his existential place in the world? The perceptions of us by other people represent to a large extent how we're present in the world.

Although some people may wish to be young again, for anyone who's enjoyed a satisfactory experiment in living it would be foolish to turn the clock back so revived seconds and minutes could bring you a second chance to carry out your experiment. I'd enjoy repeating the tasty Chinese dinner I ate last night, and maybe the recent bag of M & M's but nothing earlier. Regaining expired time risks losing everything which transpired after the point at which you begin again. For me, I prefer the "déja do," "déja vu" and "déja done" pleasures of having lived as I did and now recalling past delights than tampering with time in the hope of creating an even better experiment.

Herd behavior, heard attitudes you adopt, copycat beliefs, accepting conventional wisdom, conformity, follow-the-crowd and other such lazy follow-the-leader practices serve to eliminate the need for independent thinking, which offers a convenient but mindless way to carry out an experiment in living.

Character, temperament, personality, intelligence, will, effort, energy, volition and other personal characteristics all play a role in one's life, but in the end chance and luck operate as the determining factors. In that way every earthling is condemned to be a prisoner of fate, with parole possible only when released by death.

I've avoided in the Journal metaphysical speculations as I prefer to concentrate on matters derived from and connected with the world we live in, not one beyond our knowledge. My comments here on the soul represent one of the few and perhaps the sole example of contemplating a subject for which no evidence or personal experience is available to discuss with at least a few shreds of realism a purely speculative matter. Apart from doubting that a soul exists, if that elusive intangible substance in fact occupies a role as one of the forms in the infinite play of terrestrial forms I wonder how the thing finds its place in the scheme of things. Is the soul inserted into a person randomly from an amorphous inventory of preexisting souls awaiting incarnation, or is each such component specifically formatted to suit the particular person who gets it. Perhaps all prenatal souls placed into a fetus begin the same but then mutate during gestation as the cell-shuffle evolves. After the bodily container in which the soul supposedly resides dies, does the soul also cease to exist or does it return to the great inventory in the sky to await insertion into another humanimal? For me the purpose of the soul is clear:

meditating on such a mythological construct created by religion enables me to produce a Journal entry. I thank the Lord for His, Her or Its inventive, ingenious and fanciful phantom-like phenomenon which inspires these comments.

DECEMBER 2015

Only a truly remarkable process activated by some very strange forces and developed through their peculiar effects could have created what happened to produce life on the lonely planet which mankind calls home. A witch's brew of ingredients by chance operated to stir up in the cosmic stew- pot a stew of cellular, molecular, viral, bacterial, fungal, chemical, physical and other elements which somehow enabled life on earth, creating in animal, vegetable, insect, fish and fowl forms all manner of beasts and bugs, plants, nautical, earthly, domesticated and wild familiar and strange living things. All those manifestations of life play a role in the great spectacle produced by the play of infinite forms, a performance the likes of which the cosmos had never before seen and never again will.

Being alive forces you to come to terms with the extreme contrast between the everything your life represents to you and the nothing your being means to the totality. Although your specific unique existence is for you the center of the universe, to the universal environment the fact that you're alive is a matter of complete indifference. How to reconcile those two opposite realities causes earthlings many existential problems. My solution: don't sweat the details.

The balance between what a person produces during his lifetime in the way of wealth—not just financial but also such contributions as cultural, social, familial, relational, professional and otherwise—and how much he consumes of those same elements can never be precisely assessed. In some cases, such as the fortunate few who inherit financial resource used to maintain a standard of living far beyond what such heirs themselves earn, it's clear that what beneficiaries of chance produce by their own efforts falls far short of what's consumed by those profiting from good luck. By way of contrast, some people contribute far more to society than they ever take from it, a category which perhaps includes someone who invests a lot of time, effort and energy to write and then publish their diary or journal without receiving much in the way of royalties, credit or notice for the effort.

Because a realistic self-image helps to establish a useful perspective which can improve a person's engagement with the world, it puzzles me why so many people resist having their attention called to faults, inconsistencies, mistakes, failures, poor decisions, misbegotten ventures, defeats and setbacks.

Earthlings often refuse to acknowledge even their most obvious faults and errant behavior. It seems that many humanimals prefer to proceed as if crowned by a halo of self-righteousness rather than submit to self-criticism or to justified critiques by outsiders. For my part I always greatly valued and expressed appreciation for well-reasoned constructive criticism offered by friends who know me well and had my best interests at heart. I sought rather than shunned such useful correctives for the all too many matters which I handled poorly. Comments, opinions and criticisms from judgmental observers who didn't really understand or care about my circumstances or way of life I for the most part ignored.

It seems something of a paradox that in a time of selfies self-knowledge and self-criticism are rather rare, an anomaly which might be explained by the fact that a selfie produces only an image with no substance, a format which in this day and age suffices for many purposes.

Just as my hometown continued to serve as my native habitat my entire life (so far), so my starter house bought more than half a century ago will be my finisher residence. My domestic setting seems to blend into my very being, with all the mementos, furnishings, fixtures, possessions and other contents along with the dust, wall splotches, paint defects and other blemishes by now intrinsic elements of my daily life. The house is a fixer-upper (as I'm getting to be) or maybe even a tear-downer (as I will soon be), but whatever the fate of the place my haven will soon house strangers who never knew or cared that I lived here.

The ways oldsters try to keep busy—or at least to give the appearance of busyness—says a lot about their tastes, values, interests and capabilities. Some seniors play bingo, hand out canned goods in a food pantry, shuffle to the table to shuffle and play cards, work crossword puzzles, watch TV, collect kazoos or recollect stale memories, take naps, over-observe grandchildren who would prefer to be overlooked, discuss in great detail their ailments (called by some an organ recital), and otherwise pass the time of day in somewhat insubstantial and non-productive pursuits. Other seniors remain hyper-active, with travel, attending performances, frenetic social activities, participating in charitable organizations and events, dining at restaurants, managing or mismanaging their investments, attending meetings and other forms of busy-body behavior. How people behave in old age tells you something about how they pursued their experiment in living in the earlier years.

What Edward de Bono called "lateral thinking" too narrowly describes the multi-dimensional perspectives required to give you a well-rounded view of situations. For a complete picture you need not only lateral thought processes but also perceptions which give you an in-depth image. To envision a set of circumstances in a complete way it's necessary to transcend recent events, immediate and highly visible evidence, known factors, consensus attitudes, obvious considerations, widely-held opinions and common assessments regarding such situations, and other easily accessible and generally available inputs. Many numerate people over-value data, models, formulas and figures, algorithms and other quantifiable information because those numeric formats which math wizards can fairly readily calculate seem to offer precise and authoritative actionable decision-making computations. But numbers in many ways represent only "faux amis" as they mislead you into thinking that by using quantified material you can reach a rational, logical conclusion. A truly informed decision depends on such intangible and less accessible factors as hints, nuances, comparisons, associations, analogies, connections, gradations, differences, instinct, intuition, subtleties, judgment, how previous choices worked out, and other practical real-world considerations derived not from numbers or constructs but from experience. Lateral thinking along with a deep dive into your treasured memory bank and valuable store of perceptional skills will best enable you to cope with challenging situations and difficult decisions.

Hope over experience, wishful thinking, magical solutions, exaggerated expectations, unrealistic aspirations, excessive ambition, fantasy beliefs, dreamy scenarios, fairy-tale endings and other such idealized visions represent many of the factors which lead to a failed experiment in living.

For Mark Twain to call German an "awful" language (as he did in *The Innocents Abroad*) seems perverse, as his own language is in many ways just as awful. As Dr. Johnson noted in his Dictionary, many phrases in English lack sense in a literal way: the words don't on their face yield any meaning. My brief encounter years ago in Tokyo with two local boys studying English exemplifies how vexing the language can be. The students offered to guide me around one afternoon in exchange for conversation in English. When they asked me for some idioms, one I mentioned was "If I return to Tokyo some day, I'll look you up." When we parted a few hours later one of the students said, "When you come back I'll look up you." My wonderful native language can indeed be "awful."

My modest house which I moved into 47 years ago this week brought me "a local habitation" as here I've lived in a comfortable little corner of the world I called my own—a soon muted call that will no longer be heard after I'm gone. My obscure plot on this dead-end lane didn't match for drama the plots in Shakespeare's plays nor will it be as permanent and as care-free as my eventual cemetery plot. But the house was fit for purpose, and served to shelter me and also offer me a haven to which I could retreat at any time during or after my wide-ranging adventure travels to far lands. Wherever I happened to be out in the great wide world I was comforted by knowing that the comfortable and pleasant little home I left behind to roam the lonely planet would soon again receive and house me in the one place on earth where I belonged.

Christmas exerts on me an effect opposite to its intended meaning. I marvel not at the marvelous miracle of the nativity (or Nativity as the devout believe) but at how in this day and age true believers continue to accept the many myths religions claim to be true. But those made-up doctrines serve the useful purpose of offering to the devout some consolation, comfort, guidance, faith and hope to help the believers endure their otherwise somewhat harsh and meaningless experiment in living, an experience the rest of us have to pursue on our own without the benefits of belief.

JANUARY 2016

The odds of my remaining alive for yet another year are by now quite long, but to my surprise I've made it into 2016. The next new year just now seems quite remote, especially as leap year will add another day which extends the time until 2017 arrives. If I fall short by one day, I'll be able to attribute the lapse to the extra February day which prolonged the duration of 2016 by twenty-four hours too long for me.

The baffling conditions on the lonely planet induce humanimals to seek some sort of help in dealing with the nature of things. Those creatures hope to come to terms with their terrestrial situation by adopting all kinds of odd beliefs, doctrines and practices which promise certainty and guidance but deliver only misguided ideas and rituals. Those constructs distort an experiment in living by making it less functional, practical and realistic than is a terrestrial experience unburdened by strange and misleading religions, cults, ceremonies, rituals and other invented formats.

Born by chance into a problematic existence in a world permeated by randomness, luck, coincidence, happenstance and other capricious forces, each humanimal is by nature a creature forced to be a chancer. Uncertainty and risk aren't simply factors in life: they represent its essence. The play of infinite forms operates as an experiment, one suffused with chance and random happenings and conditions. Existence is less a state of being than a becoming, a provisional and unstable mercurial flux shaped, or often misshaped, by chance and luck.

At an advanced age it's somewhat demoralizing to recognize and accept that your life is essentially a done deal, as by old age what has been comprises almost your entire experiment in living.

Death doesn't form part of life because no one actually experiences death—only the dying. You don't even know that you're dead. That mortal condition doesn't form part of your experiment in living, as a decedent remains forever unaware of his or her non-being.

Death is especially inconvenient for a curious person, as no longer can he find out "what's new?" or "what's next?" or "who won?" or "what happened?" or "what does that mean?" For a decedent, nothing means anything any more. Unfortunately, or perhaps fortunately, never will you learn what it's like to be dead.

Seeing familiar faces in unfamiliar places far from home offers one of life's most prized experiences. At out-of-town weddings, for example, you encounter many people you know well in a setting other than where you know them. Finding those familiars at a hotel, in local restaurants, at parties and other wedding events in a strange town gives you a warm feeling in an otherwise cold city where no one else knows you.

Being cast into existence activates a brain which switches on to plug into the flow of current sensory impressions, a confusing but fusing jumble of sensations reduced and introduced into the receptor circuits which act to transform the unwieldy inputs into organized images, thoughts and responses. Some people, like Benjy (a "loony") in Faulkner's *The Sound and the Fury*, suffer from a short circuit which prevents the connections from functioning properly. The human body below the brain which crowns the creature may exist only to support and help to animate the mind's functions. What the brain discards from sensory overload may sink into the subconscious to resurface in the form of dreams, perhaps meant as a method to rid the mind of debris. But who knows? As miraculous as the human brain is, it can't comprehend itself.

Suitors sometimes uproot themselves and accept many inconveniences for the sake of what appears to be a mediocre romantic relationship. The need for human companionship often tends to worsen rather than to improve a person's situation. The more you contort your life to adapt it to someone else, the more likely you'll regret your decision.

The expression "portfolio career" describes someone who's led a diversified professional life in various different fields and activities. Similarly, a portfolio life consist of pursuing activities and experiences in different endeavors which bring an experiment in living a wide variety of what the play of infinite forms happens to offer the experimenter.

By now thousands and thousands of tick-tocks have clicked and heart beats pulsated to bring me ever closer to the final moments of those time-keepers and destroyers. At the same time, those count-down clicks and beats also operated to enable me to exist. Time delivers life and then takes it.

In very old age time actually becomes less precious than in earlier years, as so little time for senior seniors remains they can't accomplish much, and in any case it's far too late to make any substantial changes in an experiment in living. As you approach the end, the time that's left delays that finality but otherwise offers little utility.

Now near the end I'm glad that I refrained from pursuing wealth, fame, possessions, prestige, respect, stature, acclaim, status, power, standing and all the other rewards many earthlings admire, value and seek. I have much less to lose than those who managed to attain any or all of those various accomplishments, which I probably couldn't have managed to produce anyway.

"Dunbar's Number" (named for an Oxford psychologist), which suggests how many friends an individual can effectively maintain, sets the limit at about 150. Far fewer peopled my life, but I believe that members of my much smaller social circle gave me as many satisfactions as the three times as many Dunbar sanctioned.

Over my by now long life I somehow noticed and managed to retain many details, nuances, subtleties, trivia, comparisons, gradations, differences, contrasts, obscure impressions and passing images which my rather hyperactive powers of observation happened to perceive. This grab-bag of random miscellaneous perceptions sometimes came in handy to help me understand, appreciate and deal with whatever else by chance came to my attention from the play of infinite forms.

Older people are understandably reluctant to recognize how dispensable and disposable they are. Among the world's 7.5 billion [now nearly 8 billion] earthlings only a few if any (thanks, Fido) are aware you exist and fewer will notice your disappearance, even fewer mourn your demise, and before long almost no one will think about or even remember the deceased. Such is life—and death.

The spectrum of spending presents gradations which range from miserly to stingy and then cheap and frugal. When it comes to letting go of money, some people favor avarice, others are just averse to forking out. Of the four traits, frugality represents the least unattractive. A frugal person is willing to spend but tries to avoid wasteful, inefficient or unnecessary expenses. Such careful spenders go out of their way to find a Motel 4 rather than stay at a Motel 6, and they'd opt to eat at a Burger Prince and not at a Burger King, at a Dairy Princess instead of a Dairy Queen, at a White House rather than a White Castle. Frugal money managers willingly accept some discomforts and inconveniences to save the closely-held wads of dollars, but those tight-wads also spend on valued experiences such as travel and simple inexpensive treats like M & M's (or, preferably, cheaper bags of just M's). The other types—misers, stingy or cheap—hate to spend on anything and fail to enjoy their experiment in living, as pinching pennies brings you only squeezed coins and not much in the way of experiences you can profit from to enrich your experiment. Some say that copper wire resulted from two misers who simultaneously found on the ground a penny they both grasped and then held to pull the coin away to keep. Penny-pinchers like that get both deformed coins and spend their life, but little money, in an impoverished way which results in a poor experiment in living.

Some of my extensive reading I pursued for practical purposes focused on specific topics I needed to learn about, but I undertook most word-based learning to satisfy my curiosity. Like an infinity of mirrors, the more I read the more curious I became about additional topics I happened to come across, and so my ever more expansive curiosity has to a large extent remained unsatisfied and never will be.

FEBRUARY 2016

This rare February 29th occurs only every 1460 days and adds number l461. Very inventive of mankind to create out of thin air an additional day. Maybe the same trick would work to extend the number of days in other months as well. But that manipulation of time wouldn't extend anyone's life.

MARCH 2016

Although youngsters look forward to what's yet to come, they should also cast their thoughts when still young to the more remote time near the end so they can reach that late point in ways which will reduce their regrets. Without such a long-term end-game perspective in view, time will draw you in like a magnet which inexorably pulls you toward the end until it's too late to make any changes. Beware of the magnetic field, a force that ensnares people in its grip before they can get a hold on their experiment in living.

So compelled are humanimals baffled by the conditions which prevail on the lonely planet into which earthlings are cast to seek explanations and guidance, those benighted creatures pursue such longed-for aides as predictions of what might happen and also interpretations of what has already occurred. It seems to me quite odd how people desperate for meaning and direction so readily accept forecasts by authoritative figures seldom proved correct and explanations of events after the fact by pundits who never foresaw or really understand what they so glibly purport to explain. Gullible and naive believers in experts, supposed sages, credentialed observers and other such commentators somehow continue to put credence in failed predictors and in fabricated wise-after-the-fact analyses, criticisms, opinions and second-guesses. Forecasts and post-event supposed wisdom are useful only to the purveyor, who from such mostly useless pronouncements get attention, professional advantages and a reputation for shrewd thinking. The observers, commentators, journalists, academics, advisers and other operators who tell the seekers of certainty why something will happen or has occurred are characters who only comment on events but rarely, if ever, actually foresee or participate in them. The "know-it-alls" "explain" what they know little about to an audience eager to be told why inexplicable things happen to occur.

For a senior both he (or she) and the world have become old. Whatever younger people experience for the first time represents a unique one-time completely new sensory impression. Never again can oldsters capture the delights, excitement, anticipation, marvels of such initial happenings as eating cotton candy, visiting Disneyland, encountering a dog, using a telephone, licking an ice cream cone, kissing someone (especially if they want to kiss you back), watching a puppet show, visiting Paris, reading a Shakespeare play or one of my books, riding on a train, a pony, a bicycle, a Ferris wheel, a merry-go-round, an elephant, attending a movie or a baseball game, drinking soda-pop, sucking a popsicle or popping into your mouth Popeye's chicken or munching popcorn or a popover or enjoying a sleep-over (as a child or, even more exciting, as an adult with a lover), and on and on. Such long ago initiations into some of the most delightful experiences offered by the play of infinite forms gradually lose their effect (except for ice cream and the grown-up sleep-over) as they repeat. The world ages as we do.

Just as many first-time experiences occur randomly at unpredictable times, so we never know when last times will bring to an end to each specific kind of experience. In old age we can only assume that every category of happening might well be its last. The day will inevitably come when my final sensory impressions will reach me, when the very last lines of this by now lengthy Journal will be entered into its pages, when—after many breath-taking adventures—I will take my very last breath as I expire, never again to respire.

The most important skill for a professional adviser is the ability to put himself in the client's position. These are tough shoes to fill, as fitting yourself into another person's shoes to offer well-grounded advice can cramp your style, if not your feet. No matter how experienced, astute, perceptive, wise, sophisticated, clever and creative an outside counselor might be, he can never really be aware of all the considerations or the subjective elements which influence the client's decisions. Only the principal can take into account the full range of nuances, implications and relevant matters which bear on the situation. No adviser can formulate complete and thorough recommendations which consider every relevant element, as outside advice always lacks some of the essential components the decision-maker factors in. An even more serious problem arises due to the modality that many advisers deal in a far too limited way with problems the client faces. Tunnel vision confined by the adviser's specialty often operates to narrow what he proposes. Many consultants offer only technical rather than more general and practical solutions when the client is in fact seeking a holistic perspective rather than one based only or primarily on the practitioner's field of expertise. Finally, moral hazard sometimes distorts advice both because it's often self-serving and because the adviser has no stake in the outcome and suffers none of its consequences. For those reasons I avoided most advisers, other than for highly technical science- or technology-based matters.

Shortly after I saw (but didn't converse with) Bill Gates in Omaha a few years ago I drove to Kansas City where I ate dinner at one of the well-known Gates Barbecue restaurants, a modest moderately priced local chain. Within the span of a few hours and relatively few miles I passed through the gates which divided one Gates from another. At Gates blue-collar families ate inexpensive meals in an inelegant drab setting, far from the Omaha financial monarchs Bill Gates and Warren Buffett, their seemingly regal realm briefly buffering me from the real world I found at the Kansas City Gates, a mundane place filled with commoners which represented the ordinary every-day world rather than did the exceptional magic kingdom scene I'd seen in Omaha. In Kansas City I was back where I belonged.

None of my Journal entries purports to offer any advice, opinions or suggestions to guide how other people should pursue their experiment in living. The Journal simply records my long-term and often flawed efforts at self-education as I gradually over many years tried to teach myself as an autodidact some useful principles to carry out my own experiment.

Undertaking to write a book represents a somewhat foolish and in many ways unrewarding enterprise. Such a project always takes much longer than you expected and also requires a lot more effort than you imagined. Like the first touch of a tar-baby, starting a book leaves your fingers stuck with a hands-on connection you find hard to release. The sticky nature of a book-length manuscript makes it advisable to reduce the long-term effort to a short story, to an article, or perhaps even better simply to abandon the baby before it tars you with black marks on paper you're unable to continue to produce a smooth and usable tarmac route to completion.

Even or perhaps especially in the digital age old-form written works consisting of print on paper offer great gravitas as compared to words on a screen. But in whatever format writings, no matter how vivid and descriptive, fail to capture reality. Although written works may seem authoritative, they represent only derivative versions of the world and simply present the author's subjective views and opinions. Writings distances you from life more than connecting you with it. Too many literary types, authors and readers alike, confuse and over-value the word in place of dealing with messy reality. *Caveat lector.*

Two weeks ago I saw for the very last time, although I didn't know that at the time, one of my long-time good friends who died today, not unexpectedly as he suffered from many ailments. But no matter how obvious terminal conditions and proximate death may be, it's difficult to prepare for the finality which brings the departed's eternal absence. At our last encounter we enjoyed a normal conversation, but now he's forever hard of hearing. Such a loss of an old-time friend perhaps resembles a phantom limb effect, as it seems as if a once permanent attachment has been amputated.

When someone in our circle dies we mourn the loss, but to some extent our emotions apply not to the deceased but to ourself as the power of suggestion induces us to view the friend's passing as a *memento mori*.

Of all the randomly endowed characteristics which happen by chance to benefit humanimals, a sense of humor, unique to those creatures, ranks as one of the most desirable. My definition of a good sense of humor: the kind possessed by someone who laughs at my jokes.

Early in life I decided that it would be more convenient and workable if I remained on my native turf here where I originated rather than seeking a better experiment in living elsewhere. Unlike many people, I didn't think the grass was greener in another place, and if perchance it was the new lawn might require cutting even more often than my familiar yard at home.

APRIL 2016

The greatest mind ever known to mankind went blank 400 years ago today. Faced with his own mortality rather than that of many characters he wrote about in his plays, what did that extraordinary character think about his own end? As he neared his own demise, did Shakespeare change his mind about any of the views he expressed in his writings or what he thought about the play of infinite forms which informs the content of his dramas and comedies and of the human comedy? Did the playwright suffer from any regrets, and what main satisfactions did he enjoy from his short life? To what extent did the Bard suppose that his works would remain after his remains occupied a grave? How did it happen that some 450 years ago in a small provincial English town by chance there appeared a character able to create the remarkable works Shakespeare produced from airy nothings? There was a divinity which shaped his ends, rough-hew them how Will willed.

For someone age 20 who in the end lives for 80 years, a single year represents only 1.66 percent of the total time left; a 79-year-old has by then lived nearly 99 percent of his life.

The preconditions necessary for any humanimal to exist require at least one session of intimacy by the creature's remote ancestors: copulation for population. Without the amatory activities of my grandparents x 10 and then on down through the generations of generated descendants I wouldn't have been cast into life unwillingly, as for every humanimal, as an improbable and random current incarnation of the family line. I wonder where and how my remote ancestors lived, what their lives were like, what sort of problems they faced, how they coped with the then current social, political and economic conditions. What would any of them say (in German, perhaps dialect) about their distant descendant now writing these lines hundreds of years after my forefathers and mothers existed and copulated? Reverting to those long ago times, how likely was it back then that I'd ever be engendered? And yet, here I am, the random result of an infinite number of possible outcomes which by mere chance happened to bring the specific me into being. Had one tiny variation occurred along the way I would never have existed. Would my non-being have been a better fate?

Humanimals by chance endowed with an acute sense of curiosity suffer from sensory overload as they obsessively seek, observe and process as many as possible of the play of infinite forms.

This may spread you somewhat thin, but gives you interests wider than for most people. Although it may be preferable to live a curiosity-free kind of life, no one chooses curiosity: it chooses you.

It somehow somewhat startles me to come across someone with my name. What seems to me so personal and proprietary in fact represents only an arbitrary designation with no exclusivity. Anyone could be called "Tom Weil" and a few people are. I wonder what those people who share my name are like, how their experiment in living has fared, and if the way they pursued their experiment tended to enhance or to degrade the brand name we have in common.

MAY 2016

Hail to May, hopefully hail-less in contrast to last night's hail storm the last day of April. Hail offers one of nature's most rhythmic performances, a rattling good show featuring a catchy staccato tempo, a way the system tells earthlings, "I, not you, control the elements which determine how you live."

The phrase "Beware the vividness of passing events" offers a useful reminder not to let transient and momentarily seemingly significant matters influence you. So real, compelling and immediate do current and very recent happenings seem they often exert a disproportionate influence on how people view the future. But those momentary passing forms don't necessarily affect what takes place in the very near future, and in any case it's not possible to foresee either those follow-on effects or longer term developments. Only two of time's dimension—the quickly vanishing fleeting present and the forever settled past—are knowable. It's just as well no one can perceive future events, as many of them might be very unsettling.

In old age it's a race with time before the erase of time.

What has been sown to seed into existence what matures to a ripe old age and then starts to wilt death finally reaps by harvesting your life and planting you in the earth as an annual and not a perennial.

Although the lonely planet as it somehow happens to exist represents a highly improbable place with an incredible play of infinite forms, nonetheless the world we know actually does exist. Against incalculable odds, the odd and baffling terrestrial spectacle came into being, as has each and every humanimal who was by chance incarnated into an earthly form. Both the entire system and each individual component of the play of infinite forms could have been different, in some ways better and in some worse.

Although the past before our time was and the future after our era will be as vivid to people of those times as our own brief earthly interlude is to us, we really can't imagine how other periods seemed to those who knew or will know them. Nor could earthlings from different eras ever truly comprehend how those of us presently experienced existence on the lonely planet during the years randomly assigned to us. Each generation encounters the specific play of infinite forms in its own unique way, even though being alive at any particular time comes with many common characteristics, one such commonalty being not continuing to be alive for very long.

Whoever undertakes a long-term project—attending medical school, learning nuclear physics, writing a book, mastering a foreign language, reading and understanding everything Shakespeare wrote, collecting every different Chinese fortune cookie slip, and whatever other activities require much time, energy and effort—has to believe that the pay-back justifies all the work involved. So all-consuming are many of those activities the time left for you to enjoy and benefit from your accomplishments is shortened by all the time you invested to attain them.

AUGUST 2016

Over the spring and summer an epidemic of mortality felled half a dozen or so friends, all in their early to mid-eighties. That unusually large cohort of departed contemporaries exerts on those of us who survive a strong power of suggestion of the kind we prefer to ignore.

To remain invulnerable to loss of your good friends and family you must avoid all close relationships—not much of a life; to avoid loss of your own life it's necessary never to be alive.

An experiment in living has no end in view except the one which ends the experiment.

The primacy of wealth in American society endows rich people with an authority they lack in most other countries. Americans seem to view wealth, whether earned or inherited, as a kind of monetized intelligence or as giving people who possess riches some sort of special insights, expertise or credibility. "If you're so smart why aren't you rich?" people ask of those who lack the weight of money to support their opinions, and the corollary is, "If you're so rich you must be smart." The net result suggests that one's net worth validates what's said by whoever happens to possess a fortune. Since chance and luck play such out-sized roles in who gains and keeps wealth, any belief in or pretense by the rich to speak with authority should be viewed with great skepticism.

Owning a dog will in some ways give you a companion as satisfying as a child and without such complications as having to educate the pet how to read, study, drive, deal with adolescence, understand mathematics and scientific subjects, handle money, find a mate, get into a good university, pursue a graduate degree, earn a living, raise children, avoid bill collectors and much else. A doggy's inbred natural characteristics to induce the service provider to respond to the pampered pet's needs—puppy eyes, tail-wagging, a pretense to affection for the animal's handler, highly effective begging strategies, a winning personality—require no special training.

SEPTEMBER 2016

Few labor on Labor Day, and those who do usually get double-time. Time can never be doubled, so only the pay is.

If you look like Frankenstein, behave like Dracula (his behavior sucks), sport the sharp personality of a cut-up like Jack the Ripper, feature like the Creature From the Black Lagoon, conduct yourself like King Kong, your social life will be quite limited but, unlike for most people, you'll certainly be noticed.

More striking than bodily failures are its successes, as maintaining homeostasis and a well-functioning complex organic operating system is truly amazing.

From what I've observed over many years I'd estimate that about half of desired close personal relationships—in marriage, parenting children, sibling connections—prove reasonably satisfactory while the other half or thereabouts are by any reasonable standards unsuccessful. Dog-humanimal relationships bring a much higher success rate. But in spite of the failure of an estimated half the attempts by earthlings to establish and maintain a close connection, the creatures persist in trying to create those relationships.

One function of dogs is to serve as constantly pleasing surrogates for problematical, difficult or failed relationships between humanimals.

OCTOBER 2016

One advantage of pursuing what curiosity impels you to discover is that such a compulsive trait broadens your life, but at the same time the compulsion often leads you away from concentrating on practical matters.

Apart from my innate frugality, another reason why I avoided other than the most basic and necessary consumption originated from the abject poverty and lack of possessions common in many areas around the world I visited. I saw that many people lived, even if not very well, with very few things. As a result I tried to make-do with as little as possible and for sure without any fancy, deluxe or frivolous acquisitions. If I were any more of a non-materialist I'd be a disembodied wraith.

Humanimals engage in much inhuman behavior, as unkind practices typify many of mankind's animalistic misbehavior. Devilish as they sometimes are, people are also capable of angelic acts. The split-personality creatures are the strangest animals in the menagerie of terrestrial beasts.

Rather too often ambitious people view highly successful and exceptional over-achievers as role models and as examples to emulate. This unrealistic perspective fails to take into consideration survivorship bias. Thousands of failed venturers and their ventures remain little remembered. It's misleading to ignore those mostly forgotten chancers whose undertakings don't survive. Failures— much more common than successes—should serve as cautionary examples of ill-judged and misbegotten risk-taking.

Having personally witnessed modern developments, many oldsters believe that they've lived through history's most significant and momentous era, a time which brought the most turmoil, the fastest changes, the biggest advances, the greatest and most profound developments mankind has ever known. During my time many scientific and technological innovations—such as television, the digital revolution, medical discoveries—occurred. From a geopolitical standpoint only three major changes took place: the fall of the Soviet Empire, the rise of the East, and the spread of militant Islam. My generation for the most part enjoyed especially stable, favorable and benign social, economic, political and geopolitical conditions, at least up until recent times. In any case, I've never viewed my time as unique or even as one which brought a distinctive or particularly meaningful play of forms more momentous than those of other eras. Each generation has its own congeries of forms which coalesce into the *Zeitgeist* of that era.

The usual hustle-bustle and activity animated the scene as I walked into the village yesterday: Delivery vans on the streets, pedestrians briskly moving about, traffic flowing, shoppers browsing and buying, workers working away, restaurant patrons eating and drinking, consumers consuming, and all the other hustle and bustle, motion and energy typical of the neighborhood, as if it were a kind of wind-up toy-town activated by a mechanical force which gradually unwinds as the day winds down. Overnight the springs of action would rewind to prepare for the next day's doings and comings and goings, all of which seems purposeful and meaningful but which, viewed from a cosmic perspective, is really just insubstantial motion.

I benefited greatly by avoiding the literary life, by not taking reading and writing as representative of the real world, and by not letting print interfere with the primacy of experience. Although I had my way with words I never allowed words to have their way with me.

A few days ago what may be the last presidential election of my lifetime was held. Being uninterested in politics, I make that observation by way of relief, not by way of regret.

2017

You can calculate the passage of time both by what it takes and by what it brings. In 2015 and 2016 the year brought much longer Journal sections than in 2017 and 2018. Each year took the same amount of time from my allocated life span while bringing varying amounts of noteworthy thoughts I deemed worth recording in the Journal. Toward the end, beginning in 2019, the longer sections resumed as if I were trying to cram into my rapidly dwindling time as many closing thoughts as possible.

JANUARY 2017

A time pivot on a fulcrum day like January 1st usually prompts me to reflect on yesterdays and tomorrows. This day and the eventual last day of 2017 will bookend what the year will bring. As usual on the opening day of the year I wonder if my Journal will contain an account of thoughts over the entire year or if the entries will fall short because of my absence.

The last day of the month signals that January now comes to an end. Only the final ending, the termination point which eventually brings the end of everything in the cosmos, will bring an end to endings.

FEBRUARY 2017

Anyone who lives, say, for 85 years has survived for more than 31,000 days. Of those, very few are memorable or remembered. An old person has thus for the most part spent his life in quite forgettable and mostly trivial ways.

Although a non-believer, I've probably attended as many religious services as some of my devout friends, including the practical ones who've confessed to me that they go to church only on the few Sundays when free doughnuts and coffee are served. I went to holy rituals all around the world unmotivated by eats and treats but only for cultural purposes to observe how humanimals participated in the odd and in some cases rather exotic and often other-worldly ceremonies demanded by the various religions the creatures had fabricated.

The back-story of how things happened to develop on the lonely planet and in its societies often remains little noticed. The way that people, things, events transition from the realm of possibility into existence seldom gets as much attention as the specific form which happens to result as the only and thus the definitive version of reality. The ignored processes, however, suggest how complex, unlikely and convoluted are many of the systems which produced natural phenomena and the human interventions which invented or discovered and continue to produce electricity, fuel, food, means of transportation, consumer goods and services, medical care, pharmaceuticals and much else. Even objects as simple as a pencil or pen or as common as paper depend on complicated production and distribution infrastructures. Although I have no idea how the ballpoint pen or the sheet of paper I join to write this Journal entry were manufactured, I marvel at and appreciate those two minor wonders of human ingenuity and effort.

After 48 years of keeping the Journal I now reach page 1000, which sounds like a lot but amounts to an average of less than 21 pages a year, which represents fewer than two per month. In the next 48 years the Journal will contain far fewer pages.

Incarnating a child represents an attempt by the parents to bring some meaning into their lives. As for the humanimal cast unwillingly into existence, the creature must seek for itself its own meaning.

A major perceived benefit to producing a child is that he or she brings you the opportunity to be needed. In addition, over time the little bundle of joy will presumably give you various other satisfactions: some surprises and excitement; an on-going presence in the gene pool; a chance to nurture someone who will hopefully nurture you in your old age; a way to live vicariously though the life of your child; a person over whom you can exert some authority to compensate for how you're subject to the authority of a boss, governments and other controlling powers; to engender someone who looks like you to remind you of yourself; to please your parents; to give you a person deeply embedded in your life you can talk and hopefully brag about; to furnish you with an eventual companion who can accompany you on various activities; to give you convenient access to someone you can play ping-pong, tennis or board games with; to expand your social circle by giving you something in common with other parents; and to create an eventual survivor to remember you after you're gone. Dogs can fulfill only a few of those functions, although it's sometimes claimed that over time pet owners come to resemble their doggy's appearance and so the pets serve to remind people of themselves.

Producing children and religious faith represent two of the most common, even if not universal, practices of humanimals. Another typical practice is keeping a dog as a pet. Which of the trinity is preferable—offspring, belief, canine—is a matter of taste.

APRIL 2017

By now the only major life experience remaining for me is the departure from it.

The process of being develops by a constant transition from the general to the specific. For the young the future presents an amorphous generalized prospect which over time gradually evolves into the specific content which represents an experiment in living. The most striking element of this process is that in your early years your non-being seems abstract and theoretical in a generalized way, while in old age your demise becomes all too specific, apparent and easy to visualize.

The telephone operates as a flattering device, as most calls evidence that someone somewhere is thinking about you and wants to reach you. You're wanted, needed or otherwise remembered by the caller. You're at least momentarily the center of his or her attention. But in some cases the ring may result from a wrong number, from a robocall, from a salesman, from a fund-raiser, or from another kind of nuisance caller. In those kinds of cases the phone fails to flatter: it only annoys.

A surprising number of people who enjoy and value a long, stable, close and loving relationship abuse that intimate connection by failing to prepare for the aftermath of non-being in a way that makes the postmortem transfer as easy as possible for the survivor. Such negligence forces the remaining half of the couple to deal with many otherwise avoidable problems. All too often caring and considerate companions fail to provide appropriate arrangements for handling as efficiently and as care-free as possible all the matters with which the beloved survivors must cope.

In the *teatrum mundi* perform many shady characters, actors who present a false face to the audience. Politicians number among the most deceptive players as their guile attempts to appeal to the public regardless of what those characters actually believe. They seek applause and acclaim by assuming roles disconnected from their actual behind-the-scenes personalities. Similarly, many hard-bitten businessmen feign an interest in the arts and cultural matters to show a more humanistic image by attempting to dull how people perceive the cut and thrust of the competitive edge wielded by the sharp operators. High-profile theologians may not always preach what they practice or believe, as much of their devotional gab consists only of marketing, salesmanship and promotional chatter. All those kinds of actors play their parts not to reveal character but to conceal it.

In a bountiful land with a cornucopia of products, services and endless options for consumption and ways to live people face over the years thousands of choices and decisions, most of those possible selections relatively inconsequential but a few of them momentous. Many situations force you to deal with a counter-party more informed than are you, as when you buy a car, a process for which you're at an informational disadvantage. That kind of deficit also prevails any time you interact with professionals, such as doctors, scientists, lawyers, accountants who possess technical domain knowledge. Because you confront so many diverse matters it's impossible to gain the detailed knowledge and experience to put you on the same footing as the counter-party so you can make an informed judgment. Operating equipped only with fragmentary, imperfect and uncertain information and knowledge presents many challenges. Trust in the person you deal with as much as in his or her competence represents a crucial and necessary component of the relationship. One way to compensate for your disadvantages is to leverage your own particular field of expertise in dealing with less informed people who know little or nothing about your specialty. Although at a disadvantage in most areas, in your own circle of competence you enjoy many advantages.

The nostalgic and comforting recollections of shared experiences with the friends and family who peopled your life become melancholy memories after those cherished mortals disappear. You lament that no more will you enjoy their companionship and be able to create new fond memories. If you live long enough eventually all of your close relationships will disappear and, with them, so will much of your past.

The complexity which supports intricate contemporary societies and economies also operates to bring a great vulnerability to disruption and failure. Third World countries lack both the benefits and the risks of a complicated system. Mies van der Rohe's dictum for architecture, "Less is more," might well apply to societal matters, as advanced countries are more likely to collapse from attacks or systemic failures than underdeveloped places with much simpler systems.

Although we know nothing in a specific way about strangers, we know a lot generally about our fellow humanimals as each such creature spends a good part of his or her time engaged in identical activities, including sleep, eating, drinking, eliminating, along with personal maintenance like cutting toe- and fingernails and hair, plucking nose hairs and picking one's nose, brushing teeth and brushing off dandruff, washing (self and clothes), and also day-dreaming, night dreaming, night-maring, fantasizing, looking, listening, thinking, smelling, tasting, touching and all the other processes and procedures necessary or desirable for an animal to remain comfortable, presentable and alive.

A person's claim to be "busy" denigrates those he or she interacts with as the statement implies a sense of self-importance as if indicating that the "busy" person is doing you a favor to take time out from his or her filled schedule to deal with you. You should appreciate that you're one of the favored ones chosen to get a few precious moments of your benefactor's time. Those self-described "busy" characters may suffer from low self-esteem which they try to boost by suggesting how much in demand and how important they are.

A close look at claimed busyness (as discussed on the last entry) often reveals that many of the activities which take up so much time consist of frivolous, unproductive, trivial, boring, time-wasting and rather inane busy-work or other such time-fillers which keep people occupied but not truly busy.

To some extent, people in my immediate surroundings and in circumstances similar to mine served the useful function of anti-role models. Those conventional types offered me living examples of how I didn't want to live, and suggested to me other ways in which I preferred to pursue my experiment in living.

MAY 2017

A rational humanimal is in some ways a misfit in an irrational world. To confront with a logical, cerebral, contemplative, orderly and reasoning mind the chaotic and arbitrary play of infinite forms represents the clash of a precise and controlled mentality with an insensate, mechanical and baffling cosmos. This encounter between a thoughtful and logical earthling and the unsettled and unsettling conditions on the lonely planet can never bring understanding and satisfaction to the mindful humanimal who tries to think things through.

Parents sometimes say they hope to give their children roots and wings. Seldom do doting parents realize or want to admit that many offspring can't wait to cut their roots and wing their way away to live their own lives as soon as possible.

Outlets such as a journal, a diary, a newspaper column, published books and articles—to all of which I've had access—offer the benefit that such written accounts encourage you to observe the world and its passing play of infinite forms more carefully than if you don't write about them. Aware that in one way or another I'd be recording my impressions of the passing scene, I remained alert to my experiences and concentrated more intently on what happened to reach my attention in order to recall as many details as possible. This served to enrich my experiment in living even if—unlike Henry James, who aspired to be a person on which nothing was wasted—all too much of what I experienced I failed to retain and which thus went to waste.

Only in very few rare cases do the necessary components combine for someone to enjoy sufficient free time, health, some wealth, a suitable temperament, the interest and curiosity, a sense of adventure, a willingness to ignore many conventional practices, a rejection of some societal values and various other factors which serve to enable an independent, productive, free-form kind of largely satisfying experiment in living. The extent to which any of those components are absent will diminish the experiment.

In this obscure tiny terrestrial sub-lunar corner of the cosmos earthlings remain vulnerable to all sorts of difficulties, troubles, problems, threats, risks, intrusions, suffering. Some of those afflictions nature imposes and other unpleasant behaviors and conditions mankind itself brings to the lonely planet. This leads me to believe that life on earth resulted from a cosmic experiment gone wrong.

Although most people believe that in their own era occurred the most significant and momentous events and changes known to mankind, this perspective arises mainly because what happened seems so real, vivid and immediate it creates a kind of reality bias. Although many things changed during my time, I'd say that in the first two-thirds of the twentieth century when my father was alive the world saw many more meaningful developments and happenings than in the era I've known.

Two preoccupations dominate and haunt the thoughts of the very old: first, you fear a prolonged and painful illness which eliminates your participation in life without ending it and, second, you dwell on the rather unsettling fact that before long you won't exist. Apart from those two rather minor matters, old age can be a serene and pleasant stage of life.

Although equipped by chance with a logical, rational, analytical, precise, orderly, detail-oriented and somewhat rigid Germanic type mentality, fortunately I recognized rather early that in fact irrational and capricious factors such as luck, chance, randomness, coincidence, serendipity and happenstance largely control how our experiment in living happens to fare. This realization allowed me to understand and accept that my mental processes, no matter how cultivated and refined, played a subordinate role in how the play of infinite forms affected me.

OCTOBER 2017

Indian Summer—or is it now more correctly called Native American Summer?—represents a seasonal no-man's land, neither autumn nor summer but an in-between transitional time. This ambiguity evokes many natural terrestrial phenomena—neither fish nor fowl, not this or that, neither here nor there but only gradations, slight variances, vague variations, subtle formats, imprecise alterations, minor differences, mercurial mutations, nuanced forms, gradual becomings. Many things present over the short term very slight hard- to-notice changes, but night always falls on a different world.

The number of keys a person must use evidences how simple or complicated his or her life.

Analogues to dying while still alive include: (1) the hazy twilight-like interlude between retiring for the night and going to sleep; (2) the indistinct state of a surgery patient sedated by anesthetic; (3) the dazed and barely conscious condition while lying in the post-op recovery room; (4) being in a highly medicated fog in an ICU. In each situation you exist on the edge of non-being but cling to life with some slight consciousness or awareness of still existing. Although those states mimic dying, nothing really resembles the unique actual version of the process which transitions you from being to non-being.

NOVEMBER 2017

Regression to the mean not only applies in life but also for it, as the norm is not to exist.

Life as it occurs is not a dream—*"la vida no es sueño"*—but in retrospect what appeared at the time so vivid and real indeed becomes phantasmagoric, insubstantial and dream-like.
[This reversal of Lope de Vega's—or Vega de Lope's?—play title I also noted April 2020.]

If a man's home is his castle, he's forced to abdicate and give way to a new monarch when a dog resides in the palace.

People who most often best enrich your experiment in living are friends, acquaintances and sources with views, interests and attitudes which differ from or, especially, are opposite to or contradict your own settled perspectives.

Life-tired oldsters aren't necessarily tired of life but only of how the long years have depleted the seniors' energy, their ability and willingness to deal with relatively routine matters, and the oldsters' now limited tolerance for things which don't go as hoped. Aging seems as if over time you're a wind-up toy which gradually winds down and down until finally it comes to a dead stop.

The potluck menu which happens to be served up by luck and chance to bring you a potpourri of diverse experiences might end by leaving you a pauper abandoned in a potter's field, but even if you repose and decompose in a known marked grave you'll quickly be forgotten by your survivors, few or none of whom will ever visit your final resting place.

One benefit of a consumer society is that buying entertains people and gives them a pleasurable activity they value, but the disadvantage is that acquiring lots of wanted but unneeded stuff damages the efficient allocation of resources which could be better used for other purposes.

DECEMBER 2017

Eliminating gladiatorial contact sports such as football, boxing, wrestling, ice hockey, roller derbies and other violent or contentious human activities and characteristics including war, terrorism, politics, greed, competition for resources, religious rivalries, tyrannical regimes, and also doing away with rampant consumerism, social media and other digital time-wasters, financial advisers, bureaucracies and heavy-handed regulators would deprive many people of pleasure, even if perverse, of a livelihood, of purpose and meaning, of satisfactions while at the same time greatly improving society and bringing about a more efficient and useful allocation of resources.

Perhaps many humanimals suffer from a winter of discontent as well as discontented springs, summers and falls, but a lucky few—men and women for all seasons—enjoy every phase of the annual cycle.

In old age memories far exceed anticipations. This is not a bad thing, provided that your memories have proved to conform to your hopes and aspirations.

At the advent of humanity humanimals had their chance but over the millennia the creatures carved the lonely planet into territories secured and defended by territorial imperatives; fought destructive wars; brought about the spoilation of nature's bounty and the original pristine conditions; populated the world with swarms of earthlings, many of them in miserable conditions; misused and abused many of the benefits the natural system endowed mankind with. By now it's far too late to remedy any of those damaging effects inflicted by the hand of man.

Reality fragments into very small slivers perceived in those tiny formats by the individual consciousness of anyone who ever lives. If it were somehow possible to combine into one vast pattern each and every sensory impression received by humans from the play of infinite forms the totality would represent a complete picture of how mankind viewed and experienced its collective experiment in living.

When an old friend recently asked me, "What are you doing for fun?" I started to think that perhaps I should have been somewhat more frivolous, spontaneous and devil-may-care in my experiment in living, bedeviled and diminished in many ways by my rationality and compelling curiosity. But I realize that neither the devil or any other force in the insensate cosmos knows or cares anything about what happens here on the lonely planet. Even the devil lacks interest in the place, as he (or she) has other fish to fry.

If I last until the end here in my "starter" house, acquired nearly half a century ago, the residence will be my "finisher" house.

Christmas Day, along with the impending year-end and my recent passport renewal all prompt me to wonder if I'll ever see another Christmas, reach the end of next year, and survive long enough to amortize the full $110 passport renewal fee over the new document's ten-year period of validity. For every year I miss I'll lose $11 of my investment. This gives me a great incentive to try to stay alive for another decade.

New Year's Eve: it symbolizes both an ending and a beginning, but for me now almost everything represents a closing rather than an opening.

JANUARY 2018

Much of whatever I do and what happens now in early January will be a first for 2018, and every such first might also for me be a last.

Being alive plugs you into the current play of infinite forms from which death soon disconnects you, cutting you off from the energy source which briefly brought you the lights and delights of existence, after which you're left in the dark.

It's strange to me how so many people believe in such an unbelievable human construct as religion. Since those invented theories first appeared in human society, it's a close case whether or not humankind in general has benefited or suffered from the fantasies presented by religious belief.

The hygiene hypothesis no doubt applies to mental as well as to physical resilience and well-being. A serene, secure and comfortable childhood may ill-prepare a person for many of the challenges and difficulties faced later as an adult. A difficult upbringing, however, may operate to immunize a humanimal from the mental and sentimental pathologies which inevitably afflict all such creatures.

As you age the formerly colorful and vivid kinds of experiences you once enjoyed gradually fade into black and white and then finally come to an end in a complete black-out.

The most common, mundane and ordinary things, happenings and people in existence during your time seem much more vivid and real than do long ago events and renowned past figures. More concrete to me than Abraham Lincoln is the Lincoln parked in my neighbor's driveway; the most abject rag-pickers and rickshaw-pullers I saw in Calcutta seem more like human animals than past ghosts of famous figures which haunt mankind, such as Shakespeare, Napoleon and Rin Tin Tin. A hail storm strikes us as more significant and the burial of a close friend leaves a stronger impression than Alexander the Great's famous battles and victories or the eruption of Mount Vesuvius and its burial of Pompeii. Nor can we imagine how existence on the lonely planet will be for earthlings who will occupy the place in the far future. For each generation life presents itself only in the here and now, not in the then or the will be.

FEBRUARY 2018

One definition of old age: the stage when you've lost more close friends and family than the number who remain. I may by now have reached that point.

Hefty females often sport large breasts. Are they truly big, or only so because the woman herself is over-sized?

By coincidence this February date [20th] marks the double anniversary of when someone close to me died and the day in an earlier year when another intimate member of my circle was born. Which of those two happenings represents the more desirable event?

MARCH 2018

Mortality both gives life some meaning and deprives it of meaning.

APRIL 2018

It's better to be respected than to be popular. Popularity can arise from various beguiling but undesirable traits, from emollient but insincere behavior, from poor values, from unsophisticated or easily misled admirers, and for other insubstantial and inappropriate reasons, while respect should result from admirable characteristics and exemplary behavior.

How the young and the old perceive exactly the same events and experiences varies because of the age differences. At a recent performance of "Brigadoon" the presentation struck a familiar note and brought me some notes I knew well, while for most of the young people in the audience the show represented a new experience, one never to be repeated.

Whatever "is" eventually becomes "was"; what "was" gradually fades and becomes as if it "wasn't."

Bernard Berenson's book on Lorenzo Lotto, which I recently read, presents in great detail the famous art connoisseur's descriptions of how the artist portrayed ears, feet, noses, hands and other anatomical features. The author no doubt spent hours and hours studying each little wrinkle of Lotto's portraits. It seems strange to pass your time examining and writing about such matters, but there's really no telling how or why many humanimals choose to occupy their time. Some of the odder specimens of those creatures keep a Journal.

The skills and characteristics which enable someone to gain fame, wealth, position, influence or prominence often represent traits which lack any intrinsic merit. Who you choose to admire, respect, support and believe in says as much about you as it does about the people you favor.

A biography of Elon Musk I recently read presents a picture of someone so phenomenal and exceptional he seems other-worldly, a character as rare and valuable as the coveted aromatic substance found in a male musk deer's musk bag. So daring, entrepreneurial, risk-oriented and capable is Musk he makes almost every other earthly mortal seem ordinary, unproductive and undistinguished, which in fact accurately describes them. Or I should say us.

JUNE 2018

Today marks the beginning of the end of so-called "longer" days, one of those natural phenomena which isn't universal as earthlings who live near the Equator don't experience "longer" and "shorter" days as we do in my part of the world.

When chatting with a friend a young woman with three small children I noticed pointed to her swollen stomach to indicate that yet a fourth child was in the works. She will thus before long have expelled into unsought existence a quartet (and later perhaps more) of humanimals condemned to find their way as strangers in a strange land here on lonely planet into which they've been unwillingly thrown.

JULY 2018

From my back porch I can hear but not see some July 4th fireworks sounding nearby like bombs, cannon fire, shells, bursting bullets, activated mines, sheared shrapnel, destroyed targets and other explosive and destructive weapons. Terrestrial beings also often engage in shouting, yelling, bellowing, clapping, chanting, screaming, demonstrating and other loud behavior, perhaps as if meant to take revenge on a cosmos deaf to every earthly sound, but the insensate Big Bang which exploded the entire system into its purposeless existence finds no meaningful echo from the puny voices and noises raised by mankind here on the lonely planet.

SEPTEMBER 2018

From age zero on to early old age, the seventies say, life expands, after which it contracts until finally, like a deflating balloon, it collapses. Also like a balloon, humanimals fill the globe with a lot of hot air.

Expressing age in the German way—five-and-seventy, say—seems a more benign and less demoralizing method for oldsters than in the English format which puts the bad news at the beginning.

In observing how the devout cling so tightly to their comforting superstitions I sometimes wish that I could also suspend my disbelief to benefit from the security and certainty enjoyed by believers who seek and accept what religion provides. But moments later I devoutly hope that I don't get my wish.

Albanian novelist Ismail Kadare divided humankind into two major and defining categories—those alive and those dead. As for living humanimals, I also classify them into quite different groups based on (a) the by-standers who express opinions, offer advice, second-guess what doers decide and criticize the mistakes of activists and (b) the hands-on responsible parties who act and who, unlike the observers, must live with the consequences of their views and decisions.

Summer clings with some residual warmth until, as today, the tone changes and autumn starts to take hold. No season survives: each faces a losing battle and is fated to give way to its successor.

NOVEMBER 2018

After two weeks in London to see for the last time an old and very close friend I was happy to return home and enjoy my haven's many conveniences and comforts. Back in the good old days I accepted the discomforts and enjoyed the challenges and benefits of traveling in far exotic lands. Those long-gone days of adventure travel remain good even if by now old, but if I revive my travel life it would bring me not eventual good old days but bad new ones.

Old age comforts as well as disquiets me, as now in my late years I feel somewhat relieved of my life-long compulsive sense of curiosity, an unexpected development which makes me curious as to why that long-standing compelling trait has started to atrophy.

DECEMBER 2018

As usual at year-end I reflect both on my surprise at still being around to reflect and also on the possibility that I won't survive to continue this annual personal tradition a year from now.

JANUARY 2019

I've made it into the new year, easy to say now that it's a done deal but on January 1st last year I faced an uncertain survival prognosis, as I do today for the year 2020.

FEBRUARY 2019

Following a cruise this month through the Panama Canal, then up the west coast of Central America and Mexico we stayed a few days in San Francisco. In Chinatown I observed two woman at the Golden Bakery in Ross Alley putting dough into molds to shape fortune cookies, a job which involves a lot of daily dough but which pays very little dough. The work could be described in fortune (or misfortune) cookie terms as, "You are condemned to life-long menial labor." No gold enriches the lives of the workers at the Golden Bakery.

MARCH 2019

The most simple, basic, routine and ordinary daily tasks of the kind I continue to perform no longer demand any attention from my departed friends, now forever free from any and all worldly functions and concerns.

Because luck and good fortune are stingy with their favors and represent the main factors in whether or not an earthling happens to become an over-achiever, only very few humanimals excel. If everyone over-performed, no one would excel.

Unlike most objects, books bear no relationship between their worth and their value. Infinite riches can lie buried within the covers of a treasured volume which might sell for only a dollar or two. Moreover, unlike many things which deteriorate and eventually become dysfunctional books retain their intrinsic worth and usually their physical integrity. Books are certainly more durable than are people, for it's more likely a hundred-year-old volume will remain in good condition than will a centenarian. For that reason, any earthling who wishes to repeat his earthly existence should hope to return as a book.

In old age the facial features of some women begin to resemble those of men, but the reverse isn't true. This seemingly unequal and unfair treatment by nature no doubt arises because good looks which enable women to attract men no longer matter. Senior females may in fact be relieved that they're finally free from the male gaze which even old geezers, or gazers, persist in activating. Or do the old women miss that sort of lascivious masculine attention and hope that the gazing continues?

A regression to the mean swings good fortune toward misfortune and bad luck back toward good, those capricious forces all the while passing through and sometimes remaining for a time in the neutral zone. But some especially fortunate or particularly unfortunate mortals somehow seem to enjoy long stretches of good luck or be condemned to suffer a run of bad luck. Those random effects operate in lumpy and thoroughly unpredictable, uneven and even unjust ways.

Among the billions of humanimals alive during each modern-day generation, a mere few ever manage to rise above the undifferentiated masses to prominence. To the anonymous billions those figures seem larger than life, but to the universe such celebrities end, like all humanimals, smaller than life.

The Dublin world as perceived by Leopold Bloom on a particular June day reflects not the actual reality of the city but only one man's perceptions of the place. Everyone else there that day saw the metropolis in completely different ways. Bloom's sensory impressions were his alone, without any necessary commonality with any other Dubliner.

Anyone who has never engaged in the activity of confronting an amorphous mass and mess of material and then shaping it into an orderly integrated whole can't really understand the vexations and the pleasures involved in such an endeavor.

A normal progression in life involves evolving from a know-it-all youth to a know-little older person, but less common is a transition from a wise guy to a wise man.

Writers like William Faulkner and Mark Twain offer especially impressive and admirable models of the creative life, as they persisted in their writing and produced voluminous and enduring works while suffering the complications of many distractions, interruptions, intrusions and personal problems. And think of Churchill, his life so action-packed and full of people, places and events it's a wonder how he ever found time to write even one line.

In the back of his mind a young person realizes that the end will come for him someday, while for an oldster that realization lodges in the front of your mind, remaining there never again to retreat to the back.

APRIL 2019

Recently I observed to the survivor of a long and exceptionally compatible and satisfying marriage that to have to relate day-by-day for more than 50 years to her husband in an intimate way no doubt presented a considerable challenge. She replied, "I didn't have to—I was happy to get the chance to relate to him." Her heart-felt way of describing the close relationship certainly represents a different perspective on their marriage than does my outside and largely uninformed view.

Oldsters perhaps engage in such busy-play if not busy-work activities as bridge, bingo, building model structures with toothpicks, collecting Kewpie dolls or bottle tops, buying stuff for grandchildren, reminiscing about the good old days, talking about their ailments, watching reruns of favorite old-time TV shows, and similar such pastimes and time-passers in order to avoid thinking about mortality. I'd add to that list writing in a journal, except that in my case a fair number of the entries deal with the very topic other old people seek to avoid.

To reduce the endless racket and chatter of modern-day monologues or dialogues the government should institute a regulation which assigns each person a fixed lifetime spoken-word quota. Once you utter your allotment, no longer could you speak unless on the New York Word Exchange you bought from someone else part of their unused quota. Otherwise you'd have to remain mute. The rule would not apply to written works, as authors should enjoy the right to write as many words as they can produce.

In the spirit of Easter this entry resurrects an observation previously recorded in the Journal—that one element of a successful experiment in living relates to being able to associate only with people you want to be with. This thought recurs to me today because I'll soon join for an Easter meal old friends I always enjoy being with.

MAY 2019

Taxation exerts a charge on energy, creativity, risk-taking, productivity, efficiency, ingenuity and other desirable traits and practices which contribute to the economy and to society. Those gifted with the ability to create wealth will refrain from such efforts to the degree that incentives are diminished. Animal spirits (as Keynes called them) will animate go-getters much less if the wealth the producers manage to bring forth they can't keep.

Two different marriage formats: one involves a very close relationship with continuous intensive togetherness; the other, a looser connection, often with two working professionals, who seek to gain an identity which transcends the marital connection. Both kinds of relationships seem to work well.

JUNE 2019

Because every intellectual and artistic concept and variations based on previously conceived themes have by now been imagined and used original works are no longer possible, and at almost any time in human history, except near its beginnings, were rather rare.

For some reason contemporary popular culture seems to favor fantasies, virtual realities, incredible scenarios abstracted from real life, unrealistic tales and other such invented stories detached from the real world. Perhaps those kinds of fantastic works represent what Baudelaire more than a century and a half ago called "evasion," an escape. Maybe the world as it actually is has by now become so hostile, threatening, unpleasant and difficult humanimals seek to retreat from life into make-believe alternatives.

It's somewhat strange and even disappointing that some of civilization's greatest figures—such as Shakespeare, Lincoln, Vermeer, Montaigne, Goethe, Snoopy—failed to produce any continuing line of descendants.

In recent decades the world has produced hedge funds, high frequency traders, computer games, social media, more artificial intelligence and less of the real kind, loss of privacy, ransomware, the dark web, drones, ever more lethal weapons of mass destruction, cyber insecurity, civil disorder, violence, political and geopolitical turmoil, 9/11, revolutions, corruption, military adventures, terrorist and drug gangs, social pathologies such as widespread narcotics use and a proliferation of guns, and many other such noteworthy contemporary human accomplishments: the humanimal is a clever and creative but often destructive creature. Perhaps I was born a generation too late. The previous era faced only two World Wars, the 1918 flu pandemic, the Great Depression, atomic warfare, the rise of Hitler and of the Soviet Union, the Korean War and a few other such minor problems. Or, on second thought, maybe I was born a generation too early. But the next group of humanimals may face even more fearsome problems. On third thought, I should probably stick with the hand chance and fate happened to deal to me.

Scandinavia celebrates the June 21st "Midsummer's Night" but not the June 30th mid-year day, which seemingly no society marks with a special celebration. It's not too often humanimals fail to impose their constructs on time to create supposedly meaningful artificial holidays which in reality are nothing but fantasies invented to pretend that special days exist.

JULY 2019

The unsought opportunity to pursue a brief experiment in living works best by combining a life of action with a life of thought. This sort of synthesis gives you a foothold in the real world while at the same time enabling you to contemplate some of the lonely planet's workings. Action without thought or thought without action would give you only half a life. For those without action or thought: get a life.

Some happy-go-lucky people never give a second thought, let alone a first one, to their experiment in living. Such free-spirited types may be happier than more contemplative people, but—unaware of much of life and ignorant of many of its elements—they better be lucky.

Reading addicts many people as that passive and solitary activity enables you to avoid dealing with the outside world; lets you control your imaginative life; allows you to expand your knowledge while remaining at home; permits you to retain your privacy and solitude; and gives you a means to escape unwanted and unexpected experiences you hope to evade. But the great disadvantage of reading is that it distances you from life by removing you from the world and bringing you only a vicarious and derivative version of reality which represents a pale copy of the original.

Control of appetites—whether for food, for drink, for sugar, for stimulants, for sex and also for such highly valued statuses as wealth, fame, prestige, power, possessions, success, approval—represents an essential factor in creating a satisfactory experiment in living. Unbridled appetites are likely to lead to an experiment marred by happenings, practices or events which produce unwanted consequences and, late in life, regrets.

My age group has been called "The Silent Generation," which I consider a compliment as, unlike more recent generations, we kept our mouths shut and quietly went about our business. A regression to the mean has in recent decades created a more mean and noisier society.

Artistic types greatly exaggerate the value of their works and the significance of public acclaim. Apart from a few obvious especially notable cultural offerings, most are mediocre at best. My own efforts are no different. They simply represent some modest experiments within my larger experiment in living meant to contribute a few minor value-added forms to supplement the infinite play of forms, with the hope that my offerings will serve to amuse, entertain, inform or at least to help pass the time for the few animate forms—a/k/a readers—who might happen upon my works.

Few legitimate quantifiable or verifiable standards exist to evaluate the merits of creative products. Critical praise, public acceptance, prizes, awards, publicity, academic recognition, press reports, reviews and even commercial success don't necessarily evidence quality or serve to validate a work. Out in the real world beyond the realm of ideas and wordy constructs pragmatism rules: either a product or a service is effective or not. A car has to start and go; an air conditioner, cool; an airplane, fly; a can opener, open; a lawn mower, mow; electricity, electrify; a toilet, flush; a word-processor, process. Producers in the demanding real economy must fulfill the needs or wants of customers or they'll refuse to buy. Creative products lack the same sort of discipline. Society needs plumbers more than poets; dentists, mechanics, veterinarians and other hands-on professionals more than artists; a chip (potato or digital) more than sculptors; short-order cooks rather than long-winded kooks; chicken pluckers more than idea pluckers; waiters more than writers.

AUGUST 2019

Contrary to my usual sporadic Journal entries, on 19 of this month's 31 days I wrote something as if somehow trying to make up for lost time. But even keeping a diary with daily details 365 days every year (the extra day in leap years off for good behavior) won't let you restore elapsed time, for—as Proust wrote in the last line of "Swann's Way" in *A La Recherche du Temps Perdu* ("In Search of Lost Time")—"remembrance of a particular form is but regret for a particular moment; and houses, roads, avenues are as fugitive, alas, as the years."

Although opportunity costs apply to most undertakings and situations, some people never factor those costs into deciding how to carry out their experiment in living. Time, effort, energy and attention devoted to one pursuit diverts and depletes resources available for other activities. Although it's obvious that money you spend on one thing can't be used to buy anything else, that kind of principle often escapes the attention of humanimals when applied to other contexts. Those creatures sometimes spend their time in inefficient and frivolous time-wasting ways as if those kinds of activities were cost-free and without any opportunity costs.

Not length but condition is the most important factor in surviving to an old age. More than death itself, death-in-life represents an even worse fate. In such a state you continue to exist but not really to live. Along with a wish for longevity should be included the desire to be able to function while still alive. Without functionality, there's no reason to persist in longevity.

Diaries, journals, letters, memoirs, autobiographies, biographies and other personal accounts which describe the deliberations and decisions of high level government officials and businessmen allow you to contemplate with hindsight counter-factuals. Because you already know how the actual decisions happened to work out you can more easily imagine better alternate scenarios. At the time of deciding prevail far too many uncertainties, ambiguities, confusions, contradictions, conflicting opinions and inconsistent advice for decision-makers to make truly informed choices. It's all just a guess. Only bits of fragmentary evidence and perhaps a few verifiable factors, always muddled by many different and often incompatible factors, equip the decision-maker with some possibly helpful and relevant guidance. Little is clear as the fog of war or the mist of peace always cloud the scene and what's seen, so limiting the ability to envision the consequences oi a particular decision. Ahead of a choice the results it will actually produce remain contingent and subject to the workings of luck, chance and other capricious influences. How and why operatives in a commanding position happened to formulate their choices and how any mistakes resulted can be informative for ways to make your own decisions.

For frugal types spending habits can be better described as non-spending habits. Frugals suffer more discomfort than the benefits they might gain from the pleasures offered by expensive meals, costly cars, luxury material goods (for the penurious more like bads), elegant clothes, antique-filled mansions, and other conspicuous and even some inconspicuous consumption. I was always more inquisitive than acquisitive.

One of the best ways to address challenging situations is to ask yourself, "What must I believe in order for my decision to be an effective one?" If your perceptions and assumptions bear a reasonable relationship with what seem to be the relevant operative factors, you'll have a better chance to succeed. Decision-making represents an epistemological process which involves a realistic assessment of how much we can know, what we think we know, what we do know, and what we can never know.

It's well to view with skepticism or even to avoid decisions based on the opinions of people without a stake in the outcome, who rely only on subjective or self-serving factors, who formulate their views from incomplete evidence or fragmentary considerations, or who may not be well-informed or otherwise capable of dealing with the matter at hand. Such purveyors of advice include many agents, commentators, wealth advisers, portfolio managers, academics, social "scientists, " supposed experts (either self-described or so viewed by the public or both) and in the realm of creative works gatekeepers such as publishers, editors, first readers, literary agents, critics, reviewers, humanities professors, commercial participants, parties with a self-interest, publicists, journalists and other purportedly authoritative deciders and would-be influencers and taste-makers. An experiment in living which depends largely on outside opinions, advice and judgments is likely to be a failed experiment.

To this day I marvel at and fail to understand the workings of such commonplace and ordinary everyday devices and systems as television, the telephone (fixed line or fix-less), refrigerators, plumbing, heating, air conditioning and many other seemingly simple modern-day conveniences. Even further beyond my comprehension are more complex products and processes mankind's ingenuity has created, such as cars, jet planes, ships, space exploration equipment, gas and electric production, processing and distribution, computers, the internet and world-wide web technology, the supply chains for and products in supermarkets, hardware stores and pharmacies. Vast, complex, inter-related networks, systems and infrastructure underpin the availability of many goods and services, a remarkable hinterland unknown to and little unappreciated by many people who take it all for granted.

Although nothing endowed this day with any particularly memorable or noteworthy thoughts or happenings, nonetheless I now enter into the Journal mention of this ordinary pleasant mid-summer day which will soon fade away and disappear from time and my memory if I fail to refer in writing to these brief fleeting, dreamy, insubstantial, evanescent moments fated to vanish without a trace.

Some significant societal and cultural changes which bring about a "paradigm shift" shift into high gear only over an extended period, so it sometimes takes time for the implications and effects of such developments to diffuse throughout society. Other changes bring more immediate impacts. Martin Luther's "Theses," the severing of King Charles I's head (bad career move), the Lewis and Clark Expedition, Elvis Presley's songs and gyrational moves (great career moves), and many other major happenings over the years all operated sooner or later to change perceptions, procedures and processes of how people see the world and how things work.

Back in the caveman, Marco Polo, medieval and other early-day eras disruptive developments spread much more slowly than now. In modern times inventive means of reproduction and dissemination such as the press, photography, radio and television, cell phones and, most significant, digital technology serve to spread information with few delays. Now that humanimals perceive reality through those new formats, perhaps the essential nature of those creatures' life experience has also undergone a paradigm shift.

My references to mortality discomfit the friends to whom I mention the topic, but coming to terms early in life with my eventual demise enabled me better to prepare for it.

As noted in the last entry, mortality represents a toxic topic, off-limits and almost sure to deal a death blow to a conversation. No one wants to be reminded that the Grim Reaper may scyth you down at any time. You never know when He (or is the Reaper a She?) will strike, but for sure that killer will as he or she is never on strike.

Although summer lingers, a slight touch of autumn cools the air as if hinting at the soon-to-arrive seasonal change. Time will tell, but today a preface now introduces the coming tale relating to the tail-end of summer.

Today, the last day of August, 2019, the Journal has reached 1200 pages. As I turn over a new leaf to start on number 1201 I wonder which page will be the first to remain blank after I exit and can no longer continue my Journal entries.

SEPTEMBER 2019

As the globe spins and tilts the days get shorter and cooler. The celestial cycles and the cosmic system operate completely oblivious to and ignorant of human life on the lonely planet, just as earthlings exist almost entirely ignorant of one another and of what their presence on the planet is all about.

Before recently renewing my *Economist* subscription I calculated the benefit of the lower annualized price over two years with the more expensive one-year cost. Taking into consideration my age, I renewed for just a year—an existential rather than a financial decision.

Here in the secluded Midwestern neighborhood where I live, a context where provincial suburban bourgeois values, beliefs and practices prevail, I gratefully enjoyed most of the many amenities and conveniences available in such a setting while at the same time happily avoided many of the ways people here carry out their experiment in living.

I somehow felt morally compelled not to extract from society more than what I contributed to it, but this proved a difficult aspiration to fulfill as I contributed so little.

OCTOBER 2019

Most old people remain on the sidelines as spectators, observing rather than continuing to participate in the play of infinite forms. For us, the show is largely over. We live in a kind of twilight zone as if in a theater without an audience where only a ghost light slightly illuminates the nearly empty stage.

By now nights arrive earlier in the day, and Halloween, with its grinning skull-like pumpkin forms and nocturnal activities, bring the additional feeling that the forces of darkness prevail here on the benighted lonely planet.

NOVEMBER 2019

The truly heart-warming expression, "Honey, I'm home" evokes all sorts of good feelings and kind characteristics of the kind humankind is occasionally capable of demonstrating. But the most gratifying greeting comes from the family dog, its enthusiasm for your return based on the fact that your adored pet views you as a service animal.

Whatever its genre or technique, writing represents an environmentally friendly practice as it recycles time's debris into new forms which use former passing and discarded sensory impressions that would otherwise go to waste.

Now or never represents the alternatives senior seniors face for activities during the closing phase of their experiment in living. Very old people should live as if there's no tomorrow, because for them soon there won't be.

Deceased former humanimals you personally knew seem dead in different gradations depending on how long the decedent has been missing in action. The senior generations extant during my grandparents time comprise the most dead, while the next most moribund departed are my parents' contemporaries, some of whom I knew fairly well and vaguely recall. Then there are my own defunct contemporaries, friends who peopled my life, acquaintances, others I engaged with, all of whom I remember well. Those more recent mortals seem the least dead of all. As for those of us still alive but on the brink of death, it's hard to image us being dead, although soon that state won't be imaginary but real.

The friction involved in dealing with the world grinds you down, slows you down, puts you down until finally you're down for the count, down and out forever. The way the system operates produces those downers, as every worldly interaction brings friction, wear and tear, decay, deterioration and other effects which cause depreciation. Eventually you wear out and are written off as disposable scrap without any salvage value.

DECEMBER 2019

The year now begins to end, a statement which surprises me, not because a year-end is surprising but simply because I never thought I'd be around long enough to mention that closure. I'd be surprised if I'm still able to record the same comments a year from now, but in recent years I've always thought that and have so far been proved wrong.

As for every terrestrial form, the American Experiment is indeed only an experiment, one of the temporary forms which comprise the ceaseless play of infinite forms. As the U.S. system changes shape and mutates into new and unpredictable formats, I won't be around to see how things play out. I believe my absence from the scene will be a great advantage for me.

"Wow! That was sure a fast half-century." So I began my email this month to my old London friends for whom I served as best man at their wedding there 50 years ago today. After an equal time period as from today, all memories of their wedding weekend, of our friendship, of the two of them, of me, and of almost everything else from our era will be long forgotten.

If I can remain alive for the next three hours I'll enter into yet another new year and decade, the former perhaps my last and the latter for sure my final one.

VII. 2020's Visions: January 2020–September 2022

Along with 2015, the concluding three early 2020s sections are the longest in the Journal. During the three years 2017, 2018 and 2019 when I was writing A PLAY OF INFINITE FORMS, published in June 2021, I made relatively few entries in the Journal as my attention was focused on the book. Once free of that writing project I returned to the Journal which again began to serve as an outlet for my noteworthy (so they seemed to me) passing thoughts, my late-in-life Journal entries before I pass.

JANUARY 2020

Just about the only success you hope to accomplish in old age is to be extant rather than extinct.

Those who create artistic works become completely redundant after the products take form, just as once an egg is impregnated the paternal agent is no longer needed.

People who engage with the world in irrational, illogical, confused, capricious, impulsive ways behave just as the world itself operates. That sort of behavior adds to rather mitigating the prevailing chaos and confusion and the intrinsic randomness and unpredictable nature of things.

Late in life Graham Greene said that his remaining time was so short he'd give up writing novels and produce only short stories. At my age I probably should never start reading another novel but stick with short stories or perhaps only comic strips or maybe even just Chinese fortune cookie strips.

At the end of life it reverts to square one or, more accurately, to ground zero (or square zero, ground one) as an experiment in living is a zero-sum game.

It's over-kill to over-think decisions, which anyway are best based on instinct, intuition, hunches and experience more than on pure rationality, reasoning and logic.

The phrase "No pain, no gain" correctly suggests that without effort you can rarely bring about noteworthy or praiseworthy accomplishments, but the reverse aphorism—"No gain, no pain"—also expresses a useful concept, because the less you accomplish the less you have to lose.

Public policy in developed countries often operates in a horizontal way as it cuts across many diverse classes, affinity groups and people with similar identities. In underdeveloped areas fragmented societies function in vertical ways based on clans, sects, families, tribes, religions, languages, cultural and ethnic identities and other competing groups broken into silo-separated factions.

If you stereotype people and identify them by their characteristics—such as race, gender, ethnic origins, sexual preferences, religion—eventually each affinity group you characterize will organize as its been defined and in a kind of jujitsu maneuver respond according to how that particular cohort has been singled out and identified.

The novelistic analogue to cinema's Charles Kane in *Citizen Kane* (which I recently saw again) is Willie Stark in *All the King's Men* (which I periodically reread), both characters based on larger-than-life real-life figures. Kane and King would well understand one another.

Old age offers the advantage that it brings you closer to the one certainty which life has to offer—its end.

If forced to choose which church to attend, I'd select either a Methodist congregation I know where coffee and donuts are served after some Sunday services or an Episcopalian place of worship where members of the sisterhood often offer a delicious and copious buffet which follows various religious services or events. In both cases I'd occasionally try to time my arrival after the devotional service but before the food service.

If forced to choose a religion I'd favor Buddhism, not for its food (as for churches I'd be willing to join) but because many of its doctrines seem sensible and useful. One belief encourages the suppression of "*tanha*"—desire, craving, temptation, self-gratification—which could come in handy to suppress my stated interest in free church food.

Attempts to individualize one's self, to stand out from the crowd and gain some sort of notice or distinction among the nearly eight billion humanimals now alive, characterizes how many of the creatures pursue their experiment in living. One example in my suburban neighborhood is how the condition of a resident's front yard signal various values. Impeccable grass, elaborate plantings, always neatly clipped bushes display wealth and also concern as to how your neighbors view you. You wouldn't want scruffy uncut grass, weeds or shaggy bushes to ruin your reputation. Interior decorations, furnishings, fixtures, appliances, artifacts and art works also show wealth and evidence taste (or its lack). Children (how many, how they dress, whether they attend private or public school, where they go to summer camp, and which universities accept them), pets, cars, clothes, jewelry and other stuff, hobbies, personal interests, charitable activities, church and club memberships, travel destination formats (kinds of hotels, status level with airlines, tour companies used, and similar prestige indicators), along with various other consumption characteristic, operate as signals to express individuality, importance, wealth and standing. By those standards I no doubt suffered from rather low prestige, as judged based on the superficial criteria common in my setting.

MARCH 2020

One month from my last entry, as in the meantime I flew to Buenos Aires (my third visit), then sailed up the east coast of South America with stops in Montevideo, Rio de Janeiro and a few other places in Brazil, then some Caribbean islands before luckily docking in Florida and back home a few days before things shut down because of the Covid pandemic. The time, effort and energy required for me to write that description of my travels are considerably less than for the exertions the trip itself required. No words can ever match the actual living versions of experience.

Americans usually operate with a can-do attitude. Even someone like me, who recognized at a relatively early age the strange, often ridiculous and ultimately meaningless nature of nature's experiment on the lonely planet, was willing to accept the given terms of engagement and pursue my own little experiment with a largely optimistic and pro-active mentality. Positive pessimism and realism rather than nihilism characterized my view.

As part of their national character, Americans believe in the question "Why?" They think that why things happen can be explained, that reasons exist for many events and conditions, and that if you do a sufficiently deep dive to analyze random occurrences they can be understood. Many of my countrymen suppose that problems have a solution, difficult situations can be resolved, puzzling happenings are comprehensible, baffling phenomena can be "un-baffled." Americans believe that the world largely operates in a rational, logical and orderly way so that "Why?" can be accurately answered. Because it's the kind of question I've found rather useless, I've almost always avoided the query, as do many people elsewhere in older and more mature and realistic societies and cultures. Residents of those countries realize that most often no "why?" can be explained. My non-American mentality conforms more closely to how people view the nature of things in places where more practical, skeptical and less gullible earthlings live.

Residents of developed countries like the U.S. demand and enjoy efficiencies and amenities rare in much of the rest of the world. In my homeland systems usually operate as intended: always-on electricity, a stream of clean water, efficient heating and cooling, functional transportation and communications, on-demand goods and services of all kinds, effective channels of distribution, well-stocked stores, and the effective and efficient delivery and availability of many other conveniences and necessities. By way of contrast, in many other places the daily existence of the unfortunate impoverished locals suffers from inefficiencies, dysfunctional systems, undelivered necessities, unexplained disruptions, frequent breakdowns, closures, stoppages, shortages, outages, failures, defects, delays, goods and services which fail to perform, and any number of similar intrusions, interruptions, flaws and inconveniences. Such is life out in the big wide world beyond the privileged precincts of a place like America. In those benighted lands people seldom ask "Why?" The faults and failures are simply in the nature of things.

This notebook could well be titled "A Journal of the Plague Year" as by now the Covid pandemic has plagued humanimals the world over. The pervasive and often fatal disease offers all too vivid evidence of how mankind is a plaything of nature and always subject to its capricious and destructive effects. The pathology which has so unsettled the world may finally settle me by reducing or eliminating my worldly travels, or perhaps even bringing to an end my presence in the world.

Peggy Lee's song, "Is That All There Is?" defines how oldsters view their late-in-life situation, as we face the reality that yes, this is IT—all there is. We answer "Yes" to Peggy's question as toward the end our brief nearly concluded encounter with the play of infinite forms represents all there is for us. If that's all there is, "let's keep dancing...break out the booze...have a ball," advises the singer. But by now the music has faded to a faint echo, the cup is empty, the ball is over. In his rather sober and somber novel *All That Is* (2013), James Salter tells of Philip Bowman who cavorts with a series of women not so much for conquest but in his quest to settle what a friend of mine called "the boy-girl thing." Toward the end he takes a commuter train back to New York City, the route passing by crossings crowded with "evening traffic, lines of waiting cars with their headlights on. The boulevards were jammed. Houses, trees, unknown places flowing past, embankments, mysterious ponds," the same sort of scenes "as fugitive, alas, as the years," described by Proust [also quoted in the August 2019 entry above]. All that is: the fugitive years.

Because an oldster's past greatly dwarfs his future, optionality, possibility and potential no longer offer very many choices. You face a one-way street, a dead-end with no turning back. Like unfilled empty pages in a Journal notebook, at the end your life becomes a blank.

Over the years my Journal has synthesized and reduced to a coherent and useful form many of the observations, principles, beliefs, concepts and conclusions which happened to occur to me, and in that way the document became a handy handbook to help guide me for my experiment in living.

APRIL 2020

Typical signs of old age: labeling and putting order into a chaos of old photos before you drop out of the picture; arthritis; night-time micturation; reminiscing; forgetfulness; and—oops, forgot what else I was going to add to the list.

Even if oblivious to their good fortune, my lucky deceased friends enjoy the benefits of having escaped the disadvantages of being alive during such postmortem (for the departed) destructive conditions as those brought by the current Covid pandemic. But perhaps the recent dead would nonetheless have preferred to remain alive, even with the current toxic and often fatal misplay of infinite forms.

Creative types often suffer and perhaps also benefit from substance and self-abuse, but which is cause and which is effect? Do addictions and an unstable personality typify and facilitate creativity or do those traits result from the stresses, anxieties and uncertainties of the creative life? I wouldn't know, as I never tried to escape from or to enhance reality with booze, drugs or any other addictive behavior (addiction to ice cream and M & M's doesn't count). The only "trips" I took were to foreign lands, stimulation enough for me. Mind-altering substances never attracted me as I saw no need to alter what worked well for me and which enabled me to experience and appreciate a wide range of the play of infinite forms. Writers and artists with relatively normal, settled, well-balanced and conventional lives may create less meaningful works than can tormented or demented disturbed dissolute types whose errant habits and drugged behavior bring altered states of being, fanciful artificial sights and special insights. But are those addiction-fueled works worth the trip? Was Shakespeare an alcoholic or a drug addict?

As time goes by warfare will become less weaponized with old-form heavy-metal conventional armaments and will be replaced by immaterial stealth weapons launched from afar without the traditional need for boots on the ground to fight in and occupy enemy territory. Remote attack devices include drones, rockets, hovercraft, satellites, as well as electromagnetic emanations to disrupt communications, electricity transmission and the systems needed to distribute fuel, water, and many other essential goods and services. The new weapons will also damage or eliminate digital networks and hack into and steal from them; shut down industrial production, companies, hospitals, governments and other organizations. Toxic attacks delivered from distant enemies will bring about vast morbidity and mortality: Atomic, Biological, Chemical, Digital and so on through the alphabet of disruptions and killers on down to induced Zoonotic diseases. Any or all of these fiendish bellicose devices conceived by those clever ingenious rascals, humanimals, will cause a collapse in civilization and humankind will revert to a state of nature as it existed in the pre-prehistoric area.

To get an idea how the world might look after an attack by weapons which (other than nuclear bombs) cause little or no physical damage, I need only walk around my village these days. Empty streets, shuttered restaurants and stores, an absence of traffic, dark interiors, an eerie silence, lack of a human presence all evidence not only the life-limiting effects of the current pandemic but also show how a once lively village can suddenly become a ghost town.

Anticipation and possible participation no longer animate the old in the same way that those future-oriented perspectives motivate the young. As you age your forward-looking hopes and expectations atrophy. Late in life you look back rather than ahead. No longer does your life seem an open book, but resembles more a story nearing the final page and "The End."

More than any other nationality, Americans are future-oriented. Americans characteristically face forward and imagine how things will get bigger, better, faster, how the country will grow and the economy expand, how innovative new constructions, constructs and developments will obsolete old places, procedures and practices. Optimistic can-do Americans believe in perpetual improvement, think that almost all problems have solutions, and view as heroes change-agents, entrepreneurs and risk-takers who shake up and throw out existing institutions and processes. Residents of other countries, where in a way people live behind the times, think less about tomorrow than the now and yesterdays. For those backward-looking and future-averse types, what's to come will most likely greatly resemble or hold less value than events which have already occurred, so there's no reason to favor the primacy of what will happen over the experiences and lessons of the past.

A warning "For entertainment only" should accompany such practices and professions as astrology, fortune telling, clairvoyance, crystal ball or playing card predictions as well as many pronouncements and predictions by economists, financial market commentators, social scientists, academics in non-scientific fields, newspaper columnists and editorial writers and perhaps also many or most entries in a journal.

How you view the future represents your concept of time. For Americans, today serves as a bridge to the promising promised land of a new improved version of their country. The American Dream will yield ever more wonderful dreamland wonders. In stagnant lands today is simply a dead-end bridge to nowhere as the future will only resemble the present, which resembles the past. In the United States time seems linear, as it leads on to progress, while in retarded places people see time as circular as it only repeats, without producing any forward motion. In a similar way, young people view time as stretching straight on in a direct format which leads to new and better experiences, while the old consider time as repetitious, somewhat circular and largely lacking in promise.

Eternal oblivion represents the fate of all but very few creative works. The ratio of time, energy, effort, thought and ingenuity invested in creating artistic artifacts and how long a work happens to survive is off the charts. What goes into the product rarely conforms to whether or not the creation turns out to be an enduring cultural asset. Browsing in the stacks of large libraries evidences that those collections serve mostly as tome tombs where long-buried dusty volumes repose unseen and untouched by readers, who seldom or never resurrect the defunct pages bound for oblivion. Apart from a few now decomposing composers like, say (or sing), Sondheim (or "Soundheim"), an untold and unheard number of hard-won music pages languish soundless in permanent obscurity, and most artworks are our of sight and out of mind and probably never were in mind. The cleverness, skill, creativity, and intellectual effort to produce all those forgotten works as well as the great struggle to get them accepted for distribution and presentation to the public contrasts with their eventual moribund state. Faced with this almost inevitable perverse outcome, it seems strange that creative types continue to create, an odd quirk which must represent the nature of the beast.

There's an art both to engage in and to exit from an experiment in living, but most people ignore the exit strategy in favor of concentrating on the experiment as it develops. To disregard the end diminishes how you curate and create the way you proceed from beginning to end.

Much as life seems to be an insubstantial dream-like experience, perhaps human existence isn't a dream but a dream is life. Lope de Vega might well have reversed his image and written, "*El sueño es vida.*" [This variant I also noted November 2017.] If what what humanimals know as life is such stuff as dreams are made on, then who on earth could be the dreamer? Perhaps some monstrous diabolic cosmic consciousness, amusing itself by a dreamland based on the play of infinite forms on the lonely-planet. If such a sadistic dreamer exists, then the sensory impressions from the play of forms which happen to form an earthling's experiment in living might be better described as nightmares, from which we awake at such time as our wake is held.

Shakespeare put into Prospero's mouth the notion that we are such stuff as dreams are made on. Born on this day 450 years ago (happy birthday, Bill), the playwright also claimed that "All's well that ends well," a formulation which on its face seems reasonable. But just as in the last entry I reversed Lope de Vega's dream-line, so I would revise Shakespeare's statement because judging an undertaking only by its satisfactory result ignores the process of reaching that hoped-for outcome. If a person suffers great privation to initiate, carry out and then bring to a satisfactory conclusion an extremely difficult unpleasant project, the effort can't be judged only by how the undertaking turns out. A horrendous experience to achieve a desired goal may well end well but without all of the process being all well. For the parents, a perfect pregnancy with a flawless delivery which produces a sensational baby represents an all's-well procedure and ending, but for the child, unwillingly cast by chance into a brief and problematic existence on the lonely planet, the episode may well not bring the new earthling an "all's-well" experience.

Even now as an old man for whom only a brief time remains I follow my life-long practice of casting my thoughts ahead to view how an imagined later retrospective perspective might enable me better to shape my closing experiment in living as the experience nears the end. This entails assessing how to allocate my limited remaining days or months or years (which measure will apply I don't know) for their highest and best use before time reduces my being to its lowest and worst use, namely non-being.

My shared experiences with and recollections of all the people who knew me well and no longer exist now lack half of what once comprised a full relationship and mutual memories. As the survivor, I carry in my mind the only remaining reminders and no new ones of how my now absent friends and I engaged with one another. With my demise all traces of the connection will disappear as if the relationship and the memories never even existed.

Old people think less about "What next?" than "When next?" Having by old age experienced most of the "what's" in life, we now wonder when will occur the last of each particular kind of event: When will my last trip take place, or will I for the last time see a friend, eat my last ice cream cone, read for the last time a favorite book, see my last spring or autumn, put into this notebook my last Journal entry? But the last laugh always belongs to the humorless grinning Grim Reaper.

By now I consider it likely that each kind of event I experience will be the last in that category, but even at this late stage of my life every so often an unexpected, novel and surprising event or happening occurs, either for me in particular or in general out in the wider world.

One benefit of life-long friends is that they make your life more predictable. People you know well seldom surprise you. Accustomed as you are to their beliefs, interests, habits, routines, practices, personalities, values and characteristics. those familiar presences in our lives almost always behave according to form, just as you expect. For that reason it's advisable to seek out every now and then new people who, by bringing you less certainty and predictability, endow your experiment in living with more diverse and stimulating relationships.

Although my close friends and I have enjoyed wonderful relationships, the day those who peopled my life learn about my death they'll only briefly discuss that passing event and memories of me before the momentary mourners turn their attention to their own lives: plans for the rest of the day, the dinner menu, a visit to the grandchildren, watching TV or surfing the web or both at the same time, maybe a card game, working in the garden, all the this, the that, and the other usual activities and trivialities of everyday life. Meanwhile I'll be lying stone-dead in cold storage awaiting burial, if not already interred. This I know, because that's how I behaved as one by one some of my close friends predeceased me. Life goes on, even if yours doesn't.

The world's greatest killer, far more lethal and inevitable than any pathogen, operates in a stealthy way with a toxic effect which always proves fatal. No cure exists for the fatal force, invisible under the most powerful microscope and benign for many years before it eventually kills you. The killer never touches you or enters your body. You feel nothing and never know for sure how far the pathological effects of the ailment have progressed to end your earthly existence. The present-day unseen-by-the- naked-eye silent killer, the Covid virus, seems almost harmless compared to the most ineluctable pathological force to which humanimals are exposed: Time.

Where the final moment which ends my long experiment in living will occur I cannot know. Hopefully, I'll finish the experiment here at home. Perhaps the living room will become my dying room, or maybe the dining room will serve as the dying room. My preference would be to finish close to home, if not in it, so that my deep roots here on my native ground will be severed where I began and where I'll then be planted, never to bloom again.

MAY 2020

The great cosmic experiment which at random happened to establish on earth, of all places, all the specific necessary conditions to enable humanimals to exist produced a glorious failure but succeeded in one at least one respect: the failed experiment has given earthlings a spectacular show. The play of infinite forms presents a truly remarkable performance—a bizarre, colorful, complex, unimaginable production, a spectacle which unfortunately hasn't worked out too well. Better luck next time.

Property and casualty insurance companies measure underwriting results by taking into account the combined ratio of operating expenses and the frequency and severity of losses. For the Journal my operating expenses are the efforts to think and the time to write. The frequency and length of the entries indicate how much of an investment I made in the inputs necessary to produce the outcome. Infrequent entries from under-writing results when the undertaking has long gaps between entries.

The topic of dreams, both personal and in general, is one of the most boring of all subjects, as an individual's dream is really of no interest to anyone else, nor has anyone yet explained the meaning and purpose of dreams. Nonetheless, a few dreamy matters prompt me to ask: (1) Do infants dream and, if so, what do they dream about? They know so little of the world, what kind of content fills their little minds? (2) Do the dreams of the young and of the old differ and, if so, how? Perhaps hopes activate the dreams of younger people, and memories the nighttime visions of oldsters. (3) Apart from humanimals, do other animals dream and, if so, of what, and how would we know? (4) What stimulates the neuro-chemicals, the neurons, the synapses to produce dreams? (5) What sort of selection process governs the often odd and disparate components which comprise dreams? Is there any logic or rationale for the dream contents or are they purely random and irrational? (6) Dreams perhaps represent veiled vague visions which hint that some sort of other realm of reality exists and that life as we experience it may in fact be otherwise. What is that alternate vision and can we access the other scenario post-death or, most likely, is death just an eternal dreamless sleep?

Many scientific findings over the centuries evidence that in some ways nature is orderly and predictable. First, natural intelligence and more recently artificial intelligence enable researchers to see trends, connections, relationships, cause-and-effect, a process which formats otherwise amorphous and chaotic data and information into comprehensible and useful categories. But even if every scientific principle eventually becomes known and all of the infinite forms are reduced to rules and reproducible outcomes, the development and plot of the play couldn't be accurately predicted, as what happens always remains subject to capricious forces creating random forms which lead to unforeseeable second-order (and later) effects.

If beauty lies in the eye of the beholder, how would the force which created the lonely planet view its dominant creature? Are humanimals beauty or beast?

JUNE 2020

Once cast into the world a humanimal knows just when and where that unsought random event occurred. As for the exit, a very old person stands or, if infirm, lies on the edge of an abyss into which he or she will soon tumble, but the when, how and where of the tipping point remains unknown until we're disembodied from our body and reduced to remains.

Because humanimals find talking easier than writing, speech is usually of a much lower quality than written works. Texts offer more selective content than talks because for the most part writing, less spontaneous than speaking, includes only material the author considers worth all the effort required to put words into a more time-consuming and meditated permanent form. Talking is as evanescent as breathing, while thoughts expressed in writing can last a long time.

Orphaned aspirations never adopted by realizing them remain like forsaken forlorn dogs in the pound. Abandoned hopes, dreams and wishes represent a kind of euthanasia often inflicted on homeless canines.

Americans are probably the most demanding of all nationalities as my fellow citizens expect their systems—economic, political, social, medical, cultural, distribution, continuous availability of goods and services, other commercial operations—to function perfectly in an always-on mode. This expectation borders on an entitlement mentality. In many and perhaps most countries around the world, efficient and proficient operations are neither expected nor produced. So-called "American Exceptionalism" is exceptional both by its efficiency and productivity and by a misplaced belief that it's in the nature of things for a society and an economy to function well.

All creative work, even a journal meant for a single reader, represents an escape from life because artificial constructs—whether books, paintings, sculpture, music, performances—offer only a derivative version based on but not the real world. Intellectual-cultural creations rank below actual experience, as how you encounter the play of forms when you're out and about on the lonely planet puts you in contact with things as they are, not as filtered through the often unreliable minds and the sometimes questionable sensibilities of creative types.

Because every intimate relationship requires compromises, it's wise to determine how much you're willing to contort your existing way of life in order to accommodate the needs and wants of another person. The more you need to revise your regular way of being, the higher your hopes and expectations that the relationship will last, often an unrealistic belief which may lead to eventual disappointment and resentment. A more prudent practice would be to engage with someone for whom fewer adjustments are required.

Pleasurable or useful habits come to rule many of our activities and daily routines. This seems to conform to Hebb's Rule that neurons grow more robust as they process information which reflects more effective or pleasing behavior patterns. That process suggest why it's so hard to change habits. An advantage of habitual behavior is that it reduces or eliminates the need to make decisions. Many routines bring both convenience and fewer circumstances which might lead to mistakes. The best run operations—a company, a business, a program, a project, an organization, a life—require the least number of major decisions.

Staying in the middle of the road is less exciting but also less dangerous than living on the edge.

The training, education, backgrounds, conditions, rewards, job requirements and procedures and much else all differ greatly for knowledge workers as compared with employees who deal directly with tangible hands-on jobs. Writers produce (or once did, pre-digital) words on sheets of paper printed on paper sheets, while sheet metal workers deal with a hard substance less malleable than thoughts and words: mental versus metal. Knowledge workers deal with concepts and constructs; laborers, with construction. Many professions—law, consulting, accounting, financial, politics, culture—largely involve concepts, intangible services and the manipulation of words or numbers. Labor-intensive activities require direct contact with substances and apparatuses, such as metal, materials, chemicals, agricultural products, food, buildings, machines, equipment. An Ohio union official brilliantly summarized the difference between the two categories of employment by noting that blue-collar workers shower before work, while white-collar types shower after work.

At a very advanced age there's no tomorrow. When I say to someone, "I look forward to seeing you," I can't really look very far forward as the visible future for a near-sighted senior like me is now quite limited.

Americans are conditioned to value ambition, productivity, accomplishment, wealth, success and other such characteristics the culture promotes and endorses, but the quest for standing, status, acclaim and similar no doubt contorts many experiments in living which could otherwise be more enjoyable, productive and satisfying.

Profits don't necessarily create wealth, as many activities produce goods or services without adding much to the country's assets or net worth. Gross National Product measures economic churn without any relationship to GNW—Gross National Wealth. Much of what's produced and spent is indeed gross as all too much is unneeded and wasted.

Late in life I've come to the belief that I was by chance created as a humanimal for the purpose of experiencing some of the play of infinite forms here on the lonely planet and then to record a few of those sensory impressions for the possible benefit of my fellow earthlings. As an incarnated being, my function was to serve as an intermediary between the forms my experiment in living happened to bring me and other humanimals who might happen to read about my encounter with those forms. This belief may be as far-fetched, illogical and ridiculous as the superstitions of gullible devout types I've often ridiculed who seek meaning and purpose by their faith in religion. In any case, my own belief serves to console me as much as cults comfort the religious, even if both kinds of faith are equally incredible. Every earthlings is entitled to his or her own fantasies.

While I ridicule religion, true believers would in turn no doubt disdain my apostasy and disbelief in all religions. In reply I'd observe that although the paths of glory lead to the grave, the paths from the grave lead not to the glorious promised lands of heaven, eternal life, salvation or any other such paradisical postmortem wonderlands but only to a netherland of eternal oblivion.

In its ability to disseminate all manner of opinions, criticisms, fantasies, obscenities, rants, screeds, attacks and similarly destructive comments the internet might be as lethal to society and human civilization as other such invisible toxic forces as weaponized radiation, chemicals, biological agents, damaging electromagnetic emanations, malware, ransomware, digital hacks. These days transmissions on the world-wide web can ensnare anyone and anything and destroy institutions, organizations, reputations, traditions, established beliefs and practices, cultural values, community standards, effective societal procedures, and many other existing useful economic and societal benefits. Technology often creates a two-edged sword: just as both good and bad effects resulted after science split the atom, so digital developments have brought many advantages to society while also in many ways operating to split it.

In his many letters to Ada, his mistress 30 years younger, Toscanini exhibits extreme obsession and compulsive behavior toward her. Profound love is a form of acceptable madness, a feverish state of insanity many humanimals desire and seek. The acute condition is acceptable because—except in a few truly addictive cases like the extended period when Toscanini conducted his affair— the mania soon passes.

AUGUST 2020

Anyone who writes frequently about time, as do I, obviously enjoys enough free time to ponder such an ethereal topic. Sages all through the ages have devoted much contemplation and many writings to express thoughts about the strange play of infinite forms experienced by humanimals here on the lonely planet. Philosophers, sophists, wise men, wise guys, professors, preachers, pundits, experts, observers, deep thinkers, shallow minds, theorists, know-it-alls, know-nothings, religious believers and many other supposedly authoritative types confident in the validity and merit of their own views present all sorts of opinions, beliefs, doctrines and systems about conditions here on the lonely planet. All such efforts are meaningless and of no use to readers and listeners as such fabricated philosophies and belief systems serve only as a "*passe-temps*" to occupy and amuse their author. No one really knows anything about the existential matters those busy-bodies claim to explain. The seemingly solemn and definitive thought-games heavy with gravitas represent only abstract theoretical speculations which tell us nothing about what they purport to reveal. I read some of those accounts not to help me understand the world but for entertainment purposes only. Many of the theories indeed made me laugh, not because they were humorous but because they were so ridiculous.

Perhaps centuries ago on a balmy summer day like today tribesmen camped here by the creek behind my house and as dusk fell saw fireflies, then as now blinking and glowing in the twilight, and watched shadows creep over the scene, and then to bring some brightness into the darkening day lit a campfire which before long smoldered away into ashes. In my turn on the same land, I'm as transient as the campers, as the fireflies, as the fire and whatever else happens to take place here, whether a long time ago or at any time.

A perspective even more expansive than the one I described in the last entry prompts me to wonder how this land I briefly occupy looked in prehistoric times, how it was formed over the millennia into its present configuration, and how the same land, after nature has its way with it, might look many millennia from now. I sincerely hope that occupants here in the far future won't have to pull weeds and cut the grass in their front yard as often as I do.

Although only very rarely do current events inspire a Journal entry, the tremendous and highly destructive August 4th sea-side explosion in Beirut prompts me to comment, as in many other Journal entries, on the hazards of fortune or misfortune which afflict humanimals here on the lonely planet. The explosion in Lebanon echoes the cosmic chaos engendered after the initial Big Bang exploded into existence the vast play of infinite forms. All remains subject to chance, luck and inexplicable random forces. The Beirut blast left nearly 300,000 people homeless, a portent of the eventual fate of humanimals who one day in the far future will no longer have a home here on the lonely planet which, for an instant in cosmic time, hosted those creatures. Given mankind's destructive and bellicose nature and the weapons of war now available, the end of the brief humanimal era may come sooner than earthlings expect.

Just how the benefits produced by wealth-creating "animal spirits" (as Keynes put it) should be shared with other less fortunate humanimals has inspired any number of economists, academics, politicians, bureaucrats, social scientists, journalists, observers, pundits, think-tank staffers, government functionaries, "experts," activists and other influential opinion-makers to suggest all sorts of policies to deal with the problem of equitable distribution of resources. It seems something of a paradox that the loud-mouths and wise men who formulate views on how to allocate wealth are the characters who have created so little of it.

August now half over and so, *meine Damen und Herren*, *mes semblables*, *mis hermanos y hermanas* and dear *fratelli e sorelle* time rushes on for us all, quickly taking everyone toward autumn, in its turn soon to fall away and give way to winter, and then spring can't be far behind, and before long it will all be over for us all.

The Covid pandemic has infected and affected the world. So far I've suffered no infection and few effects from the disease, as my life here at home continues on just as regular, repetitious and uneventful as before. This is why I've never kept a diary here.

Refusing to procreate represents one of the very few ways a humanimal can defeat nature, a compelling force which contrives to engender gene transfer so as to perpetuate the animal.

A creature which refrains from cooperating thwarts one of nature's purposes, and even that supposed purpose in fact lacks purpose or meaning.

Works by authors who write from the outside in based on real-life experiences differ from books with content invented from internalized self-referential sources. Word people limited to inventing rather than to the more reality-based process of imagining include such types as academics, writer workshop students and graduates, literary clique pretenders, bored suburban housewives and boring scribblers of self-oriented confessional works, would-be creative characters based in and largely confined to New York City. Because it's far easier to make up stories than to live them, writers inspired by inward-looking invented notions produce works which rarely match the quality of books imagined by more worldly and experience-rich authors.

A satisfactory experiment in living depends in part on the degree to which your perspective on life matches its reality. If you adopt beliefs, ideas and opinions unrelated to how the world actually works your experiment will suffer. The popularity of religion, superstition and fantasy suggests that too much reality makes many people uncomfortable.

In that many people are confined to rather predictable repetitious, routine work-a-day lives, unscripted spontaneous entertainments offer ways to bring some excitement into an otherwise limited experiment in living. This explains the popularity of sports, quiz shows, computer games, political campaigns, bridge and other card games, board (but in truth bored) games, bingo and similar luck-related pastimes, competitions, mystery and suspense fiction, gambling, horse races, auctions, raffles, lotteries and other pursuits with uncertain even if trivial outcomes. To this list I'd add travel, which for me represented a way to diversify my regular home life by visiting far-flung exotic lands with trips often as suspenseful and with as many unanticipated experiences as for the spontaneous entertainments enjoyed by more confined, conventional and less adventurous people.

I've made no attempt to enlarge my ever-shrinking circle of friends, acquaintances, contacts by replacing the departed with new people. For one thing, many such relationships are irreplaceable. Also, it takes a lot of time, effort and energy to establish and maintain successor connections. My lack of new friends has made the lonely planet even more lonely for me.

While science endures and accumulates, works of the imagination come and then quickly go. Unlike the sticky nature of tested theories found valid, of proved facts, of confirmed research and experiential findings, very few creative products stick around: they dissipate rather than accumulate because there's no reason for most works of the imagination to persist. Few of those evanescent, forgettable and soon forgotten creations are useful or missed. Art works face quick mortality because they depend for validation not on verifiable principles but on the capricious and subjective views of such taste-makers as critics, reviewers, museum personnel, journalists, academics, publishers and editors, galleries and on fashion, trends, mass-market appeal, public cultural (or culture-less) taste, special interests, commercial considerations and various other ethereal and often insubstantial non-scientific factors. Humanimals can live quite well without most creative works, but those creatures live longer and better with scientific knowledge and advances.

Given the reality that most creative products soon disappear and are forgotten, it seems strange that so many people engage in the unrewarding effort to produce those works. The fantasy-based faith that those products will receive popular acclaim, survive and bring their creators fame and fortune resembles the equally far-fetched notions held by religious believers, whose views are similarly disconnected from reality.

SEPTEMBER 2020

"Fall" suggests how the year is falling away; "spring, "how it springs to life; "March," how time is marching on; "May," the tentative nature what the days may bring and how they may or may not prove benign.

Failing to face mortality is like fox-hunting sporting types in a pursuit which ends badly for the pursued failing to make a connection between the animal's fate and their own. The entertainment of the hunt helps distract the hunters from thinking about how Time hunts every mortal to its death.

Associating with my friends indifferent to the arts greatly pleased me as I preferred to avoid creative types lost in abstract thought games in favor of associating with less arty folks engaged in real life. I also enjoyed knowing and dealing with truly creative and effective practical operators such as entrepreneurs, small businessmen, problem-solving professionals and similar hands-on producers remote from the realm of purely intellectual products.

Just as many academics, abstract thinkers, observers, writers, artists, theorists and similar thought-full if not thoughtful types kept their distance from the outside world, so I kept my distance from them.

Sensory overload burdens the brain with far too much to absorb. What we manage to glean from the play of infinite forms represents almost nothing compared to their quantity and variety. Far more vast than a three-ring circus, the spectacle unfolds in a performance with a huge number of rings and also with a human menagerie which includes more clowns and exotic animals than a circus. The tongue-wagging barkers in the carnival atmosphere of the "big top" are less genuine and likable than the furry little tail-wagging barkers humanimals adopt as pets.

Each book I set aside on my library shelves remains inert unless I return to the volume. What discomfits me is that very few of those books, many of them I greatly enjoyed, will I ever again read or even briefly sample. What bothers me even more is that after my time many of my familiar and treasured books will be scattered to the four winds, fated to land in the hands and, when read, in the minds of strangers.

Where you live only partly determines how you live, because wherever you happen to be your personal characteristics, beliefs, opinions, continuing influences from your background, attitudes, values and perspectives remain largely the same. Uprooting yourself to seek a new and presumably better situation and a more fertile place to replant yourself in search of possibly more favorable opportunities may bring you some of the hoped-for benefits but at the same time will for sure sever you from the existing ties tethering you to your present habitat. Of all nationalities, American are the most mobile but perhaps not the most content.

OCTOBER 2020

Even Churchill said toward the end that he was tired of it all. It's commonly thought that old people want to continue on and on, but when you've reached an advanced age and have enjoyed a satisfying range of experiences there comes a time when you no longer aspire to accumulating ever more impressions of the play of infinite forms. Most additional experiences will in any case be rather repetitious or only variations on a theme. Why bother?

At this point the Journal transitions to a new notebook, some of its 170 pages perhaps fated to remain blank. When I began the Journal more than half a century ago I never supposed that I'd be writing it for so many years, nor that I'd ever publish the material. Just as those assumptions turned out to be incorrect, a number of other early-day beliefs also proved wide of the mark and didn't survive contact with reality. But at least I attempted to formulate, when still young and enough time remained for me to shape my experiment in living, some perspectives and principles which might help guide the experiment until I reached old age, which is now. Even if some of my assumptions and perspectives turned out to be wrong I learned something from them.

Old people spend a lot of time thinking about the time when their age will no longer be of concern.

A c. 40-year-old man from an immigrant Lithuanian family I recently met told me that he earned M.D-Ph.D. degrees after arriving in the U.S. because only education, knowledge and portable professional skills can protect you from the kinds of risks common in many countries, such as the one from which he and his family came. Back in Eastern Europe, and in many other places around the world, arbitrary governments and unsettled social, political and economic conditions often operate to take assets from people who own them. Houses, possessions, businesses, investments and all other wealth remains vulnerable to to theft, confiscation, appropriation, taxation. Medical knowledge can't be taken away. But I later realized that the doctor's commonly-held belief that what you know offers immunity to appropriation doesn't really consider all the relevant factors. Apart from medicine, engineering, technology and similar specialized scientific and evidence-based professions transferable from one country to another, various other respected knowledge-based but less universal disciplines can't easily be exported. Such professions vary from country to country and use different terminology, so credentials and experience may not readily transfer. A third factor is that if someone who earns and uses intellectual capital can no longer practice his or her specialty due to disability or for other reasons the knowledge and skills the professional has so painstakingly acquired will no longer produce income or wealth. Although subject to loss, possessions such as jewelry and art works and financial rather than intellectual capital may well represent better liquidity, more desirable stores of value, and yield a more certain income stream or source of money even if the owner of the assets can't function.

Old age is when you prefer to read *The Times* rather than to participate in them.

NOVEMBER 2020

Election eve: probably my last presidential election tomorrow, but I also wrote that four years ago. How long can this keep going on?

The random sorting effect of chance, luck, happenstance and coincidence has become even more obvious to me from my late-in-life perspective. I now see quite clearly how those capricious elements played such a major role in the way the play of infinite forms happened to affect my experiment in living.

Observing my friends gradually disappear is less a spectator sport than a spectral one. These days obituaries not only sadden me when I read about the demise of a friend but also console me that my name doesn't appear in the list of decedents, even if the obit page for someone my age is mighty suggestive.

A system without the often negative random effects of luck and chance would be deterministic, a change of the prevailing format so extreme the world and each individual life would develop, for better or worse, in completely different ways than as formatted with the present nature of things.

An experiment in living converts the possible into the actual. The elapse of time mutates what might be into what is and then, immediately, into what was. Without time, nothing would take place; with time, nothing retains its place.

DECEMBER 2020

When published, letters, a diary or a journal written as a private document becomes an open book. Strangers read what you originally wrote as a conversation with yourself or with the person who received the letter. The content remains the same, but when outsiders read the text it somehow assumes a new form, as if releasing a domesticated animal into the wild.

Humanimals disturbed by what appears to be their tendency for inhuman or sinful behavior invented the myth of the Fall to explain how those creatures happened to become such flawed beasts. But no "Fall" is needed to understand why mankind behaves in such animalistic ways. That perverse way of being seems to be the nature of the beast. Perhaps the lonely planet could have been a more Edenic place inhabited by gentle, compassionate, caring, peaceful, cooperative, emollient creatures, but that's not how things happened to turn out.

The literary life—an oxymoron, because the nature of life isn't literary—never attracted me. An experiment in living based on words will be a failed experiment. I wasted no time associating with academics, writers and other wordsters, many of whom favor style over content, invented works over imagined ones, self-referential accounts rather than worldly ones. Bookish types seem to consider the great play of infinite forms simply as a spectacle to provide material for word works, not as a play to participate in. Only direct contact with the world and with experience will endow writing with sufficient granular content to validate the text, or give the experiment in living the real-life components necessary to make the experience satisfactory. It's a lively experience, not one to be embalmed in words.

On this day, a day which lives in infamy, is the anniversary of the day which began my familiarity with world events. I well remember hearing when I was a little boy—"Wuxtra, Pearl Harbor bombed, read all about it," shouted the newsboys—news of the attack, book-ended 60 years later by the 9/11 attacks. What next?

As with DNA, the presence of a single letter can change the entire word or expression. A missing "r" can change "friend" to "fiend." This has been the case with countries like Germany and Japan, which when I was a boy were America's mortal enemies while Russia was an ally. As the geopolitical wheel of fortune or misfortune turns and returns, those kinds of changes which turn friends into foes and vice versa are not uncommon.

As a non-believer, Xmas has always been for me something of an X-rated holiday. As someone indifferent to religion and uninterested in consumerism, those two main elements of the Christmas season leave me out. However, I enjoy being dealt in to the annual holiday meal with old friends.

At the Christmas dinner I attend on December 25th the guests are invited to help themselves to seconds. I wish that it would be as easy to help myself not just to seconds but also to more minutes, hours, days, weeks, months, years.

Examples of maddening (for students learning English as a second language) words spelled the same but pronounced differently depending on context: (1) "I'm content with the content of the gift box." [I also mentioned this example July 2014.] (2) "I finally read the book and it's a good read." (3) "I estimate that your estimate will exceed my budget." (4) "I use a car because its use is helpful."

With my compulsive curiosity I was more interested in the world than the world was in me. But such is the case for every earthling, whether curious or not. Apart from one form of extraterrestrial intelligence, no heavenly consciousness knows or cares about what happens on the lonely planet. The only exception: astronauts. Otherwise, the universe and the cosmos are completely unaware that you exist and indifferent to what happens to you, as is the world and, with very few exceptions, every one of the nearly eight billion earthlings you share the planet with.

In an attempt to comfort the old, we're told that 90 is the "new" 80, 80 the "new" 70, and on down the line in a progression to a younger year. With this format, the age of a 10-year-old would be zero. For people old before their time, the "new" 70 would be 80, the "new" 80 increased to 90. Such tricks with time can work both ways. Perhaps it's better to abandon new measurements and stick with the old actual chronological ones.

It would be quite out of character for me to refrain from commenting on the hinge of time represented by this December 31st. At this late date of the year and in my life nothing particularly noteworthy occurs to me to add to my many previous annual thoughts about this pivot point. I can only turn the page—of the Journal notebook and the calendar—to close 2020 while, as usual, wondering if I'll survive long enough to turn the page from 2021 to 2022.

2021

Freed from writing A PLAY OF INFINITE FORMS, published in June this year, I turned my attention to the Journal, longer in 2021 than in any other year except 2016. As the years grew longer and my time shorter, perhaps I wanted to rush to wrap things up with additional entries before I ended up wrapped in a shroud and placed in a box for recycling.

JANUARY 2021

Today everything is the year's first: the date; a cup of coffee; lunch; lines read, lines written; morning, noon and night; the first this, the first that, the first whatever, all sorts of otherwise disparate what-evers united on a January 1st not by a coherent category but by time. As from today some of the days will repeat their 24-hour cycle and include many of its standard generic contents but never in exactly the same way. One particularly notable and significant day never to be repeated awaits me: my last terrestrial day, a unique event which may occur in another year. For that occurrence no recurrence is desirable, as once is enough, both for death and for life.

For the young, life presents a question mark; for the old, soon to reach a full stop, existence suggests an exclamation point, as with the observation, "So that's how my experiment in living happened to turn out!" Few question marks needed any more, as almost all the questions have been answered.

When you know toward the end how time formatted your life, any perceived patterns, themes or coherent constructs you might formulate represent only after-the-fact imaginings artificially imposed on what in fact developed in a mostly random way. Presumed patterns may become obvious in retrospect, but never when they're in the process of being formed.

"My mother isn't ready to lose" her perhaps mortally ill c. 70-year-old husband, father of the young woman I here quote. But tell me, then, when will the wife be ready for her husband's demise? Probably never.

Modern technology both draws people together and keeps them apart. The telephone, television, Zoom videos, email, texts, blogs, tweets and all the other digital techniques connect humanimals but also distance them. With these instant and cheap means of communication and dissemination you participate while remaining removed. The technology joins people while at the same time allowing widely scattered participants to remain isolated. This may create a kind of virtual reality which tends to replace actual reality.

One of the many benefits of travel includes enhancing your ability to view your own country, culture and society as well as your own life more objectively. Like your deeply embedded native language, so familiar to you are the beliefs, customs, practices, procedures, processes and traditions at home those deeply embedded elements seem natural and normal. But other cultures often offer more effective and efficient ways of doing things. A friend originally from Shanghai recently asked me why Westerners consider it impolite to cut up an entire steak before eating it, as in China food is usually served already pre-cut into bite-sized pieces, a more sensible practice and one I never thought about until she posed the question.

The economic equation which applies to admission to top universities reverses the usual dynamics between the service provider and the person served. Contrary to most transactional monetary relationships, aspirants seeking a place at an Ivy League school are salespeople, not customers. The admissions office functions as the buyer of what the applicants are trying to sell. Conversely, for less selective colleges the relationship follows the normal format, with the school marketing its services to prospects who in this case are customers with many choices.

Contemplating alternate scenarios to imagine how your life might have been better often suffers from the common flaw of assuming an idealized rather than a more likely outcome. When realized, the actual situation often deviates from the more desirable theoretical scenario you rather unrealistically envisioned. Wishing that you had a sibling, a child, a different child, another sort of spouse, another kind of career, more success, a better job, a better house, residence in different city, another appearance, or any number of other desired "others" might well bring undesirable rather than favorable results. To long for and get what you don't have may bring you what you don't want. Just as "the sleep of reason produces monsters" (as Goya titled one of his works), so fulfilled dreams of better ways of being may produce disappointments.

FEBRUARY 2021

Just about all of economics can be reduced to two principles: scarcity and incentives, two immutable universal real-world factors based on human nature. It's common for politicians, governments, bureaucrats, NGOs (Non-govermental Organizations), charities, do-good non-profits and other such organizations and funders to ignore those two laws of economics because some of those activists operate with perverse incentives and face few if any scarcity restraints. Problems solved attract no further funding, and unlimited taxing and spending power doesn't suffer from resource scarcity.

Comic strips represent the most delightful, insightful, creative, original and informative modern-day art form. The profound and often serious funny pages offer more thought-provoking and humorous content than any other contemporary format, the cartoons' wit and illustrations all condensed into extremely concise presentations. Day after day the funnies manage to come up with original observations and perspectives pictued in highly artful ways drawn by the strip writers and cartoonists—the Shakespeare and Vermeer of our time—from their truly creative imaginations.

While the nitty-gritty (or gritty-nitty [see December 2021 entry]) details and trivia of day-to-day life are significant to the individual, to no one else do those trifles hold any interest. Even a devoted spouse doesn't want to hear that you brushed your teeth, cut your toenails, plucked out nose hair, squeezed a pimple, ate an egg sandwich for lunch, won a $5 bet at the office on a sports event. Your dog, however, is highly interested in your activities because they interfere with the pet's well-being by taking up your time and diverting you from noticing, talking to, walking, feeding, petting, grooming, playing with and offering treats to Fido (or Fida).

Fanatical beliefs, strongly-held opinions, true believers in matters pertaining to economics, society, public policy, politics, identity resemble the unshakable devotion of a religious person who against all reason suffers from illogical brain-washed beliefs and practices. There's no way to reason with someone possessed by such a fanatical mind-set, which remains firmly set and resistant to change no matter what you say or how much contrary evidence you present

The consonants B-G and B-T are the only ones which come to mind—after my rather mindless search for other such pairs—that will form a word with the insertion of any of the five vowels: bag, beg, big, bog, bug, and bat, bet, bit, bot, but. This shows not my skill in word games but ilustrates that some folks with too much time on their hands and too little to think about or do engage in rather ridiculous and useless time-wasting thought experiments. To such idlers I'd say: get a life. (G-T misses by one, as gat, get, got and gut qualify but not git, unless as in "Git along, little doggie.")

Because governments and many non-profit and non-governmental organizations lack the discipline, outside pressure and constraints faced by groups which operate in the real economy, waste, inefficiency, a failure to solve problems, an indifference to expenses, lack of cost-benefit analyses and a bottomless bottom line typify how those tax- or charitable-supported non-profit groups function. Operations which don't themselves produce the resources they use often abuse the funding such market-immune groups get by other means, such as taxation, license fees, gifts, grants and contributions. Lax practices in handling OPM (Other People's Money) usually doesn't carry over to how you deal with YOM (Your Own Money).

An ad I noticed the other day claimed, "We treat every customer like they were family," an idealized version of family life which fails to recognize that often people don't like some of their family members and treat those relatives badly. If this applies to the owner of the firm which ran the ad, customers would be poorly treated at the establishment.

Junk mail addressed to "Current occupant" reminds me how transient I am here in the house where I've lived for more than half a century. I'll soon be replaced by the next "current occupant."

The ceaseless streams of social media and the many other flows of digital transmissions which inundate the world these days resemble James Joyce's confused, chaotic, disjointed stream of consciousness which passed through Leopold Bloom's mind in Dublin on this date more than a century ago.

Many present-day dialogues are in fact only monologues as people talk past one another. Opinions, beliefs, allegations, claims, exaggerations, fake "facts," falsehoods, fantasies have in many cases replaced provable propositions as the basis for discussion. Those kinds of shrill fact-free presentations represent only arguments and speculations, as no longer do proof, logic, verifiable outcomes, evidence or empirical factors matter.

Old age operates in an accumulative way which ends only when in the fullness of time you become decumulated and finally ageless.

At times when time seems to disappear, as when we sleep, faint, are knocked out, are under anesthetic, day-dreaming, or engaged in an all-consuming activity which make us oblivious to the passage of time, we exist out of time. Fairness would decree that to replace those absent times we'd get an equivalent amount of time to restore what we lost during the interludes we weren't conscious of time. But how things on the lonely planet operate isn't always fair.

The ins and outs of world history as the past developed over the centuries can be summarized as the story of the outs trying to get in and the ins attempting to resist the outs. The fortunate few who happen to enjoy a privileged place in the scheme of things maneuver to remain in their superior position. Those below struggle to rearrange the existing economic, social, political, cultural orders with revolutionary changes to revolve the ins out and rotate the outs in, a turn of the wheel which brings new perspectives and preoccupations and substantial reformatting to all concerned.

MARCH 2021

To manage a business, a project, a problem, a life you can proceed with a holistic overview or with only a more limited situational and transactional perspective which fails to consider more general implications and matters. An analytical approach focuses on the business at hand, while the creative format takes into consideration a much wider range of factors, many of them not obvious or directly connected with the matter at hand. This less intensive and more extensive perspective enables you to transcend the specifics of a situation so as to integrate into your considerations many other relevant factors. Because it's more difficult to operate with a generalized perspective, most people avoid that challenge and confine their process to the easier analytical method rather than to the more encompassing but challenging creative way of proceeding.

Far too many intelligent people are educated beyond their wisdom. Book-leaning replaces and limits common sense. Scholarly types over-educated with an abundance of formal learning, much of it from classes, research and reading, may be smart but they often lack street-smarts. Words, constructs, theories, algorithms, models often rely on perspectives derived from unrealistic and uninformed sources which suffer from an absence of real-life experiences. Unlike the sciences, the social sciences in many respects lack credibility; such disciplines may be somewhat useful as far as they go, but they don't go very far.

What people name their dogs says a lot about their owners. Although dogs can't speak for themselves, what they're called reveals something about the humanimals who name the animals.

Old folks read the local obituaries not only for their news but also for other reasons, such as: (1) to make sure you're not included among the deceased; (2) to see if anyone you know is included; (3) to compare the decedent's birth year with your own to assess the mortality rate for your age group; (4) to read mini-biographies of your contemporaries; (5) to learn about ways of life different than your own; (6) to get something of a preview how your survivors might read your obituary; (7) to get some ideas on what to include in your own obituary; (8) to learn about the arrangements for your late friends' funeral service, a gathering at which food may be served and where you can socialize.

Of the reasons listed in the last entry for reading obituaries, the biographical (#4) is among the most compelling. It's correctly said that oldsters enjoy biographies, autobiographies, memoirs, diaries, journals, collections of letters as these formats all present an account of another person's life. The revelations in those people-oriented genres allow you to see how your fellow earthlings, past and present, carried out their experiments in living. Because an obituary contains only a limited amount of information which presents a selected and flattering version of the deceased's life story, the death notice reflects how the departed wishes to be remembered, even if some of the selected material includes statements which don't conform to how the decedent actually lived. Although I've mandated that there be no service, announcement, write-up or public notice following my death, perhaps this Journal will serve as an extended obituary which, like those published in newspapers, represents how I wish to be remembered—a wish sure to be unfulfilled, as before long no one will be around to remember me, and in any case my writings are not me but only by me.

The very old live on borrowed time as if subject to a mortgage on which the lender can at any time foreclose. The capricious creditor, Mother Nature, might let the debt continue uncollected for a time or perhaps close out the account and evict you soon to end your day-to-day tenancy, which expires when you do. By way of contrast, the young enjoy a rather long temporal loan for which the balance isn't due until the balloon note is paid off at the end.

My house, the contents, my surroundings all seem so organic and intrinsic to my existence it's hard to imagine that the day will come before long when strangers and completely new possessions will occupy what are for now my very familiar premises.

My many wide-ranging bird-of-passage travels to the far corners of the world brought me a disorganized chaos of transactional experiences which contrasted with the settled relational connections I enjoyed back in my native habitat.

A change of advisers brings you new perspectives, experience and knowledge but also removes you from the former provider's institutional memory and familiarity with your needs, wants and personality.

A very weird brief experience happened to come to me not long ago: I was incarnated as a humanimal to live here on the lonely planet, an odd existence in a strange place.

Hosts of an at-home dinner party tell guests when inviting them, "We're going all-out for you." A foreigner learning English could take that expression to mean, "We're all going out." At the buffet dinner one of the foreigners present asks if the meal is self-serving, to which the host replies, "It's self-service." English is not a self-service language.

At Kinko's recently the customer ahead of me on the copy machine apologized for making me wait, explaining that he was "on deadline." Don't I know it—aren't we all? For me at this advanced age a dead-line looms: belonging to the human race puts you into a race toward a finish line, a dead-line with no victory laps as at the end you lapse from the race.

During the current Covid pandemic people often express a wish to resume a normal way of life "next year." Covid or not, for those of us of a certain age "next year" represents a remote future far beyond the time when we might remain alive to live in a normal or any other way.

If humanimals had been formatted to be more angelic than devilish the cosmic experiment represented by life on the lonely plant might have turned out in a much more favorable but perhaps less interesting way.

A sold-house moving sale on my street was moving in the sense that the event seemed more like an estate sale, as the dissolution of the household scattered into strangers' hands all the personal belongings which once formed an integrated whole for the departed couple. Bargain-hunting buyers pawing through the possessions invaded the formerly private space to adopt the orphaned objects. The sale served as a metaphor for the end of a life as well as the end of a way of life.

Attaching the word "science" to social science subjects is an effort to establish prestige by association.

APRIL 2021

Breaking—or braking— a long-standing habit presents a challenge, but thanks (or no thanks) to the year-long Covid shut-downs I've abandoned travel and adopted a comfortable and convenient stay-at-home way of life which, to my surprise, I've in many ways found more liberating than confining.

Adult children entertain their parents and grandparents in ways different than when the offspring were young. The senior generations enjoy observing the grown kids as they deal with their adult problems, opportunities and challenges of a kind familiar to the older family members who've already coped with such matters. The elders watch how the children pursue their education and careers, establish their independence, find companions and then mate to produce yet another generation, so starting the cycle all over again.

To see situations from a perspective other than how your own views seem to support and confirm your self-interest requires an ability to put yourself in other people's shoes or on their shores. This restructuring of your perceptions gives you a chance to see things as other parties perceive them.

An insular example which may serve to expand an insular view of a current geopolitical problem: CUBA: a smallish island off the coast of America. The U.S. resents and opposes Cuba's system and has tried to bring about regime change by invasion, boycott and other means. The U.S. considers the Caribbean an American pond and won't tolerate any foreign presence or interference in that region. TAIWAN: a smallish island off the coast of China, which resents the independence of a Chinese enclave with a system which violates the principles used to govern the mainland. Hoping to bring about regime change, China has threatened to invade the island. China considers the China Sea and nearby its own domain and resists any foreign presence and interference in that region, an area where the U.S. maintains a military presence in contrast to the Caribbean where no Chinese forces threaten.

A lad's most gratifying real-world learning curve to gain a well-rounded truly touching type of experience is to explore the contours of a curvaceous female, an activity with diverse effects as it tends to make a fellow stiff and hard and then softer.

A veritable United Nations of visitors and guests moved through my house as an away way-station. Some traveled here to see me, others to visit local family, still others for professional or other reasons not connected with me. Here today and most of them gone today, they passed through as the years passed by. Some of those friends who arrived and then departed have by now departed forever. The visitors transited as transient presences now absent, a great ghostly parade from the past like vanished phantom figures who, once upon a time in the years of yore, momentarily animated my little corner of the world here at home.

As publishers know, a sure-fire best-seller based on the title alone would be "Hemingway's Hounds" or "Churchill's Canines" or "Disney's Dogs." My own suggestion would reverse the emphasis by writing a book called "Snoopy's Humans."

A modern-day liberated feminist would ask at a restaurant not for a menu but for a womenu.

As noted in the entry for June 2006 to comment on the first poem in my Journal, very rarely do I think in verse rather than prose. Other examples of poems included appear below and in entries for October 2021, and January, February, and May 2022.

The Battersea Power Station

Back in the thirties, a lifetime ago, it was built for power,
But then times changed and finally came the hour
When keeping current no longer meant
Sparking the live-wires with juice.
Then the revolting end, no more volts produced.

The Battersea, about my age, a dis-empowered powerhouse, I think about a lot:
How energy, power, a sea—and life itself—are there until battered into oblivion, and are not.

So many human activities involve such useless and often damaging pursuits, even if innovative and noteworthy, that only a deeply flawed creature would undertake those perverse enterprises. Some exploits and novelties are truly impressive: Reaching the top of Mount Everest represents a peak performance by earthlings atop the earth; space exploration is thrilling; Alexander's conquests were daring and impressive; digital technology is truly remarkable; modern-day weapons quite creative and ingenious; board games for bored gamers clever; high frequency security trading, bit coins, artificial intelligence and virtual reality triumphs of technology. But are any of those accomplishments really necessary or desirable? It all started to go wrong on the lonely planet when earthlings appeared on the scene.

Extremists, fanatics, alarmists, activists, agitators, radicals, demonstrators, revolutionaries, terrorists, progressive politicians and other such radical figures favor the flawed but highly effective technique of treating situations as structures. The activists claim that passing incidents represent examples of an entire category of structural flaws such that deeply embedded systemic defects must be remedied by abolishing the offending system. Although most often specific negative outliers evidence only rare exceptions, critics of an existing format use the failures to demand sweeping change, an effort to convert infrequent events into entirely new regulatory regimes. Innocent mistakes, human error, commissions of improper and omissions of proper procedures, unknowable defects, technical crashes and other such unavoidable breakdowns in complex economies, societies and systems serve to bring many opportunities for radicals to apply pressure to alter the entire format when solutions far short of that kind of structural change could effectively address the problem. So it is that activists claim that occasional infrequent failures justify the solution to discard satisfactory existing procedures, processes and arrangements which for the most part function efficiently and effectively. The new modalities usually bring increased governmental participation and result in far less efficiency, productivity and effective operational performance than what's been replaced.

MAY 2021

It seems to me odd that anyone but the most important figures involved in major activities and events would keep a diary, a format which would most likely bore even the writer. Everyday trivia holds no interest for anyone, even for the person involved in such mundane activities, and not even for readers of diaries kept by famous figures otherwise of interest.

Sometimes a higher education elevates scholarly types too far, escalating them to an ivory tower so high above the well-grounded riffraff below the book-worm loses contact with the dirt down in the real world beneath his or her notice. Other than academic observers, few mortals enjoy the luxury of contemplating of the world from a place above it all. Little is too far-fetched, incredible or eccentric for many ivory tower pundits to believe, propose or profess. They lack the highly educational lessons derived from the friction which arises in dealing with real-life experiences. The more removed a scholar becomes from the world as it is the less the pedant understands the place. A prolonged education often disconnects students from lively experiential learning of the kind obtained by well-grounded people connected with *terra firma* rather than what's observed by top-down views from a perch up in the clouds.

The word for "sickness" in English and in the romance languages describes the condition in different ways. "Disease" well captures the essence of poor health. With good health you live at ease. but when something goes wrong with the body your ease becomes dis-ease. In the romance languages sickness is a "mal," a malevolent and perhaps malignant malady. "Mal," which implies something evil, seems more sinister and deeply embedded than "dis-ease," an expression that refers to a passing episodic situation. When cured, a patient's disease ends and he or she reverts to ease. "Mal" evokes bad karma, an existential flaw, rather than simply a passing lack of ease which can be dis-diseased.

The strangest thing about human life on earth is not its existence but that all the random infinite forms needed to create humanimals happened to coalesce into the precise conditions necessary to create those creatures. If even just one or perhaps a few of the required components were lacking, mankind wouldn't exist here on the lonely planet suspended in space in an obscure corner of the cosmos. That probably would have been a better outcome for all concerned.

The time, effort, energy and expense devoted to space exploration and the search for extraterrestrial life would be better spent for purposes closer to home here on the lonely planet. There's no there out there in the heavens with other earth-like cosmic bodies housing organic life as that odd phenomenon by chance happened to develop here on earth. The spectacular play of infinite forms known to mankind is a one-of-a-kind performance which doesn't travel.

A world whose inhabitants engage in so many frivolous time-wasting and unproductive activities can't be a serious place. Religion, mass-market entertainments, cards (credit, playing, baseball), fashion and fads, consumerism, chronic warfare, Hobe Sound and torture chamber and rock music sounds, Robben Island and Robin and Batman fantasies, Ascot and archaic regal rituals, greyhound racing, mindless hobbies (toenail collections, toothpick albums, carving potatoes into forms, various other pastimes), bar-hopping, addictive internet sites, narcotics and other addictions, and many other human pursuits and constructs (how many? perhaps as many as half, maybe more) seem to suggest that humanimals resulted from a misbegotten cosmic experiment gone awry.

Junior generations see mortality in an abstract generalized way, while seniors view their end as so real and imminent that perspective crowds out much of the rest of reality. The two age groups also perceive time in different ways. When you're young time is a friend as it furthers your education and maturity and brings you closer to independence and adult life. For old-timers time is an enemy which adds to your aging, brings about deterioration, and moves you closer to the end.

JUNE 2021

It's very easy to predict the future. The problem is that you can't predict it accurately. It's nonetheless possible to foresee "white swan"-type events, but never a rare and completely unanticipated "black swan" surprise which comes out of the blue and usually brings bruising black and blue damage. Although you can be sure that very infrequent "black" happenings of that kind will occur, you never know just when they'll strike. Both natural and man-made disasters regularly bring a swan-song refrain to the lips of afflicted humanimals. Pandemics, drought, floods, earthquakes, landslides, avalanches, pestilence, typhoons, global warming, global cooling, tsunamis, cyclones, tornadoes, hurricanes, volcanic eruptions, infestations and other such extreme events brought to us courtesy of nature will always intrude, but just where or when those white swans will bite is unknown. Similarly, not so kind mankind habitually engages in dark kinds of white swan activities, such as chronic war, oppression, torture, terrorism, vandalism, exploitation, greed, falsehoods, conflict, pollution, crime, all well-known common pernicious forms of behavior favored by humanimals, although the specific timing, forms and location of those behaviors remain unpredictable. Whether by the hand of man or by nature, white swans causing disasters and disorder will always strike the lonely planet, an accurate prediction just as is the statement that unforeseeable and often even more damaging black swans will continue to plague mankind as long as both of those odd creatures, the humans and the swans, exist.

Swans both black and white will no doubt eventually bring an end to civilization. The necessities to sustain human life and modern society—water distribution, electricity transmission, communication, transportation, food and fuel supplies, industrial production, distribution networks, data bases, cloud computing, financial operations, ready availability of everyday goods and services, and all the rest—will be disrupted or destroyed, rendering essential modalities dysfunctional as institutions, culture, governments, entire countries and systems cease to exist and no longer operate. Society will collapse and disorder reign. Without civilization civil behavior will end, leaving earthlings as those creatures existed in primitive prehistoric times. Finally, at last, no more social media, robocalls, junk mail, advertisements, consumerism, root canals, enemas, pick-pockets, politicians, modern-version warfare, tax collectors, financial advisers. Many annoyances will thankfully be eliminated as the lonely planet reverts to a state of nature in which humanimals, true to their essential nature, behave as animals.

Random thoughts: (1) Late in life your financial goal aims not to maximize wealth but to minimize poverty. (2) Rather than thinking outside the box it's more comfortable to enjoy the security of staying in the box and to think at its edge. (3) A scientist who invented a sleep-reducing pill would be greatly rewarded for the researcher's miraculous discovery of a way to add usable hours to an experiment in living which otherwise loses a third of its allotted time to sleep.

A search for meaning entertains the searcher and occupies his time as if he's engaged in a profoundly meaningful and useful activity, but although his conclusions probably console the thinker and induce the sage to believe he's happened upon some truly actionable principles, they're in fact meaningless.

Artificial beliefs, doctrines and theories imposed on reality by humanimals distort how the creatures see the world. Those constructs include religion, much received wisdom, many prevailing societal practices, rituals and values, assertions made by social scientists, academic views professed by professors, claims by politicians and bureaucrats, financial market opinion-makers, decisions by cultural gate-keepers, and many other presumed authoritative functionaries and opinions. Those often didactic, doctrinaire and assertive but by no means conclusive or persuasive sources suggest that it's possible to bring some order, certainty and meaning to the play of infinite forms on the lonely planet, a belief which completely contradicts the actual nature of things.

JULY 2021

Although death is certain when, where and how the end will occur are among the few remaining unknowns for a life near its end.

The annual July 4th fireworks displays represent an attempt by earthlings to create their own localized little Big Bangs as if to signal the presence of those inhabitants on the lonely planet. The poor creatures perhaps suppose that making some loud noises and streaking the nighttime sky with a few evanescent bursts of color will serve to signal that here we are, humanimals exist and that those beasts can signal how clever and meaningful they are by casting some signs of life into the heavens. Those inventive earthlings also create other bangs, explosions, bursts, such as with bombs and shells, exploding chemical factories and gas lines, atomic weapon blasts, machine gun and cannon fire, and the creatures know how to produce such noisy and noisome commotions like high decibel rock concerts, loud demonstrations and political rallies, the roar of crowds attending sports events, blaring radio and TV, screaming pop culture fans, agitators shouting through loud-speakers and megaphones. The poor insignificant creatures stranded here on the lonely planet lost in the firmament and desperate for attention give a shout-out to an inattentive cosmos. No one and nothing out there listens to or notices any of the terrestrial displays.

Although all but a handful, or a mindful, of the earth's by now nearly eight billion mortals remain complete strangers to us, we know exactly how each of them spends some 40 percent of his or her time. Each humanimal devotes about one-third of its time to sleep, an hour more or less to eat and for personal hygiene, plus some additional time to perform other necessary or highly useful chores. Apart from that, we know nothing about any of them, except for the very few who happen to people our lives.

Although Donne claimed that no man is an island, as noted in the last entry each such creature exists for some 40 percent of its day in an insular and isolated personal way, with only the remaining 60 percent available to connect with the outside world. But since each person connects with only a very few of the eight billion earthly mortals, most everyone remains isolated from each other as if islands.

When Right Is Wrong

To my surprise and satisfaction I've occasionally managed to correctly perceive future trends, conditions and developments, but at the same time I've often failed to accurately assess the actual effects of those correct predictions. From the right premises I draw the wrong conclusions. Similarly, my wrong predictions sometimes lead me to correctly evaluate how things turn out. There seems to be a tenuous relationship between foresight, correct or incorrect, and what eventually occurs, a disconnect which suggests the futility of trying to predict.

Because cyber-warfare by stealth and from afar now represents the major threat to developed countries, legacy military systems with earth-bound weapons and boots on the ground forces won't be able to defend the "homeland" as such old-form equipment and out-dated battle procedures are largely ineffective for modern-day ways of fighting. Without invading, operating in or occupying a foreign territory an enemy can bring any adversary to its knees by disrupting its highly complex and vulnerable interconnected networks, infrastructure and systems. Warfare will be virtual rather than visible and no longer waged with firepower and the other direct means used in the past.

What already exists in society and civilization resists change. Both man-made and natural conditions continue on mostly impervious to attempts to alter them. It takes an enormous effort to rearrange even just a few elements of the prevailing systems. Earthlings thrown unwillingly into existence find it far easier simply to accept the existing formats rather than to try to amend them. But a few bold souls, adventurous dissidents and activists dissatisfied with what already happens to exist are somehow motivated to bring about change against long odds. To those other odds, the rare innovative earthlings who manage to bring about substantial changes, we owe in some cases appreciation for beneficial contributions to society and in other instances blame for imposing on mankind undesirable new and oppressive formats.

A subset of pondering where, when and how you'll exit your experiment in living is to wonder what your final terrestrial vision will be—your very last glimpse of the play of infinite forms which over many years comprised the overloaded and confusing content of your brief baffling experiment.

Although there's no reason for me or for anyone or anything to exist, prenatal and postmortem non-existence do mean something, as those states show that meaningless and eternal oblivion represent the norm.

The many weird and odd beliefs, creeds, doctrines, dogmas, religions, cults, rituals, faiths, ceremonies adopted by humanimals to pursue meaning on the lonely planet seem just as strange as does the place itself. Those far-fetched, incredible and often ridiculous human constructs which attempt to explain inexplicable matters may help to keep earthlings occupied, entertained and hopeful that some transcendent reasons endow human existence with purpose. But the beliefs which serve to console the creatures won't survive contact with reality. Those comforting notions divert true-believers from a more realistic view of how things on the planet actually work. To view the situation in an objective and realistic way represents for most earthlings a far too unsettling and disturbing perspective.

The way you reach the upper class influences how you participate in and are viewed by the upper crust. The fortunate few who manage to achieve a top-dog position by attaining that status as a self-made success, rising from blue collar to new blue blood, usually fail to gain prestige of the kind which attaches to less meritorious and accomplished high class members who descend from patrician ancestors. This prejudice diminishes the accomplishments of productive and effective performers who succeed by their own efforts and ingenuity, success of a kind more praise-worthy than admiring privileged types who inherit their place in high society. Although genteel old families may claim more class than the *nouveaux arrivistes*, inheritors all too often rely on their good fortune rather than on their good works and on creating their own fortune, and as such those born into the top strata often seem effete, ineffective and meretricious.

Being thrown as a humanimal unwillingly into terrestrial existence doesn't bring those stray and random creatures a favorable value proposition. It's not all bad: existing briefly as an earthling endows you with some benefits. You get a consciousness which lets you receive and process sensory impressions from the play of infinite forms, and at times the forms bring you some pleasures and delights. While alive you're able to appreciate the wonders of nature, establish heart-warming close relationships, enjoy memorable experiences which create fond memories. But all those benefits come with a price, which includes the many obvious disadvantages of existence, especially its termination which eliminates your awareness of all the experiences you treasured. Because the experiment in living you never bargained for is such a poor bargain, remaining unborn offers a much more advantageous state than being thrown into existence on the baffling and lonely planet.

AUGUST 2021

Where I happen to live, here in the place where I've spent just about all of my life, celebrates today a noteworthy anniversary, as August 10th marks 200 years since Missouri became a state. It's both comforting and rather unsettling to realize that by now, at this late date in my life, my tenure here in Missouri has spanned more than 40 percent of the state's existence. Although my coming non-existence is all to easy to imagine, it's hard to believe that one day Missouri, like each and every terrestrial form, will also cease to exist. Centuries from now no one will have ever heard of a place called "Missouri," nor of many other forms familiar to the present generation.

While the performing arts and the static arts both entail creative activities they operate in different ways. Theater, music, dance, TV, video, internet presentations and other productions and performances take place not only in place but also in time. These all present themselves by motion, which requires duration. Static arts such as writing and reading what's been written, painting, design, sculpture, architecture, still photography exist as time-less (even if not timeless) creations rather than as works dependent on forward motion. Of course, it takes time to create and to experience static formats, but in and of themselves such passive cultural products don't produce a dynamic scenario as with the performing arts. The creative instincts of producers who mount active presentations probably differ from how creative types who deal with static forms think and create. Works which move through time provide an audience with a collective experience and the live performances allow observable responses from the on-lookers. Passive works are accessed on an individual basis with no audience present. While presentations unfold in time, books, paintings, sculpture and other static formats attempt to capture and hold time. Print on paper, words read but not spoken, paint stuck to a canvas, stone statues, architectural constructs all hold in place their content and don't develop as time goes by. They stand apart from time, unlike duration-dependent works which move in time.

Revision of common phrases to suit individual circumstances often yield enlightening insights: (1) In a long-term relationship without the formality of marriage the companion should be introduced as "My better quarter" or, in less secure relationships, " My insignificant other." (2) Billionaire Nelson Rockefeller hoped to divert attention from his enormous wealth by expressing appreciation with the comment, "Thanks a thousand."

To live as a hermit, recluse or stylite protects you from establishing relationships which at any time might be lost but also converts your experiment in living into a non-living version.

Completely unimaginable were the world and its play of infinite forms before they existed and just as unimaginable, now that those oddities actually do exist, is that they'll all eventually cease to exist.

An English language oddity: "Overlook" denotes to ignore a mistake or fail to notice something. "Oversee" means to supervise or monitor so that you can keep track of a situation.

For oldsters, time not only marches on but it————(dashes) in a straight line on to the end period.

Although we owe Nature a death, we don't owe Her a life. The debt arises only for the very few who, among all the potential beings, happen by chance to became unwillingly incarnated into an earthly form, one of the countless number of terrestrial infinite forms. There's no way to escape the balance due other than for an indebted creature to pay off the death debt by extinguishing the obligation with personal extinction.

Once you become aware of your own existence your terrestrial being somehow seems to be inevitable, but in fact it was entirely "evitable." No obligation to Nature compels anyone to be born, and if given a choice perhaps most earthlings would have preferred to be "nothlings."

Predicting the Past

Predicting the past presents in some ways a challenge equally as difficult as foreseeing the future. So complex, convoluted and entangled seem the unchangeable elements of what's already transpired over the ages, it's often impossible to comprehend some of the implications, influences, nuances and meaning of accumulated past events and how they

> may happen to affect subsequent developments. Even the most diligent and studious historian finds it challenging to grasp the past and understand how bygone times might operate to enable or to limit future events. Although the past obviously influences what's yet to come, just how remains obscure. So confusing are the residues of time which resulted from passing events cast into the past, no one can really make sense out of the baffling accumulation. It seems to be a paradox that although the immutable past remains forever set in time and firmly fixed in history, predicting how those unchangeable once-passing and now past events might bear on future happenings lies beyond the scope of human understanding.

The search for a "Mister or Miss Right" represents a misbegotten enterprise as no such animal exists. For this unrealistic quest searchers invest a lot of time, effort and energy in hope of finding the "right" partner, but that idealistic and far-fetched aspiration is far too ambitious. Lower expectations which limit your search to finding an appropriate rather than an ideal ("right") companion will increase your chances. Too often a desire to meet the "right" person ends up with a wrong candidate for both parties, and two wrongs don't make a right. In romance, as for everything else in life, moderate ambitions are more likely to lead to fewer disappointments. But overly modest aspirations may induce you to settle for an inferior outcome. The most workable format is to look for a "Mister or Miss Right Enough" fit for purpose even if not flawlessly right.

OCTOBER 2021

Dreams contain unreal combinations and juxtapositions derived but alienated from reality. Dreams include many situations and episodes which you never could or did experience in real life. The process which suppresses your waking sensory impressions and then relegates them to your unconscious before retrieving them in a scrambled way to give dreams their content I will explain in the next entry.

Oops—I started to daydream and forgot what I was going to say about night dreams.

Almost every encounter between humans takes place as a transactional exchange for a specific purpose, and once the deal is concluded you move on. The usually unknown and anonymous service providers occupy a fungible position in your life, as we don't individualize and rarely notice or seldom remember the particular person who served us. To counter the transitory transactional nature of those interactions out in the world we seek and value a few stable continuing connections as provided by family and friends. Those close relationships offer an emotional anchor with caring and continuity unavailable in the indifferent and amorphous public realm populated by strangers, few of whom we ever see again.

"Very" and "quite" often mean about the same: "This is a very good Journal" and "This is quite a good Journal." But "very few" means not many, while "quite a few" denotes many. Learning English as a foreign language presents quite a few challenges with very few rules.

Very few—not *quite* a few—people enjoy favorable circumstances, as chance and luck seldom operate to bring about especially fortunate situations, while effort and will don't always produce desired outcomes, always dependent to a large extent on random factors. "Lottery," which defines how an experiment in living mostly operates, includes the misnomer "lot" as not a lot of earthlings win in the lottery of life. "Lottery" would better be described as a "fewtery." The wheel of fortune's spin most often turns favorable luck into misfortune. Capricious influences somehow appear out of the ether or the firmament, with chance and luck often producing an "infirmament."

Much of what's newsworthy consists not of what the media report but what they ignore. Good news which remains unreported arises from the efficient, effective and productive workings of the remarkably complicated but usually unremarked everyday economy, a functional part of society often taken for granted. Even the most complicated operations almost always proceed in routine expected ways which seem normal and un-newsworthy. Instead of reporting the competent and functional procedures typical of most commercial operations the media feature the rare mistakes, failures, break-downs, accidents, damaging incidents, and other infrequent mishaps. Those exceptions usually receive plenty of press coverage—"If it bleeds it leads"—but excluded are reports about the on-going smooth operation of such highly complex processes and products as nuclear energy trains; chemical plants; the petroleum industry; transportation, including planes, trains, ships, vehicles, space capsules; digital products and services; manufacturing lines with a maze of machines and lines whirring, grinding, spinning, rattling away; pharmaceutical experiments and production; medicine; utilities which obtain and distribute energy, gas, water; communication systems; the world -wide web and internet connections; distribution systems to supply food, pharmaceuticals, after-market auto parts, hardware and other wares to retail outlets and consumers; and much else. "Read all about it" or "All the news that's fit to print" represent fake news claims.

Just as the media rarely runs stories of the economy's efficient workings, so consumers usually ignore all the hidden background operations and efforts necessary to support the efficient delivery of many goods and services. Few customers ever give a passing thought to how the inventories of hardware, drug, grocery, auto part or department stores are produced, transported and put into place or how gasoline happens to find its way into service-station pumps. Flip a switch and electricity flows; turn a faucet and clean drinkable water spurts; pick up or click on a phone and you can communicate. Similarly, in a personal way trouble-free health, an on-going satisfying personal relationship, a good well-paying job and other such benefits and blessings are sometimes little noticed or appreciated. Only when defects, failures or other systemic deficiencies occur do previously smoothly-running operations attract attention.

What happens to have come into existence presents the illusion that the form has to exist. But everything was uncertain, contingent and random before chance happened to create the particular forms which comprise the play of infinite forms. If all of civilization and mankind were wiped out and the lonely plant reverted to square one and ground zero, what nature then developed over the millennia would most likely create some entirely new forms which would seem quite odd to present-day earthlings, who themselves are rather odd creatures.

What does death look like? It looks like life—like you, like me, like all living animals as every living being is ultimately a dead thing. Existence is death delayed, a postponed death-in-waiting state which shows what death looks like before it finally occurs.

The Journal includes two previous poems, the first June 2006, the second April 2021; the third one appears below. The fourth, fifth, and sixth are in January, February, and May 2022 entries. For some unknown reason, these poems happened to come to mind, four of the six recently, and stuck there until I released them into writings.

Summer's Defeat

And then suddenly came the cold as summer retreated like a defeated army,
The trees raining down leaves which browned the ground as the branches grew bare
And as the chill of fall cooled the autumn air.

The death of green brought a change of scene, the landscape now a blandscape
In a colorless world ever darker in that pre-winter chill.
Outdoor life began to disappear
And the shortened shadowy days soon would kill
The dying year.

Of all the "hard" sciences—hard to learn, difficult to apply—astrophysics may represent the least useful. Just about all the other scientific disciplines yield practical information which helps mankind cope with many of the lonely planet's harsh and difficult natural conditions, but it's puzzling to understand how extra-terrestrial explorations can serve any useful purpose. Space probes seem irrelevant for how to improve conditions here on earth, and in any case a cost-benefit analysis would most likely show that the money might be better spent in sub-lunar and sub-solar research. Curiosity may motivate astrophysicists, but much of their work seems rather spacey. To study the heavens may represent a heaven-sent opportunity for those highly trained specialists to exercise their profession, but other-worldly research and speculations come at the expense of focusing less on understanding more down-to-earth matters here on the lonely planet, so called because the place is lost in the stars and also because only on this lonely little spin-ball in the heavens do creatures like humanimals exist. After observing conditions here, the cosmic creative force which happened to establish life on the planet probably decided not to risk trying again.

Immigrants who arrive as adults in a new country face many problems to adjust to the different ways of doing things. Apart from language, the challenges include understanding the nuances, subtleties, customs, culture, common practices and procedures, habits, beliefs, attitudes, assumptions—many of them tacit and not always apparent—in the adopted society. Although every humanimal is a stranger in a strange land here on the lonely planet, newcomers are thrown into a land which seems very strange and in many ways incomprehensible. Those immigrants are thus doubly challenged, as they must cope with two strange lands, the terrestrial and the specific one they moved to.

The creative mind views with dissatisfaction the way the world is and how most earthlings perceive the strange place. The alternative perspectives which typify creative types, in a way misfits, inspires them to revise the images and interpretations of reality as portrayed in existing art works. But no creative work presents the last word or offers a definitive picture of the play of infinite forms. Any new form which re-imagines how things appear serves simply—and in a tentative, provisional, and inconclusive way, which lacks authority and a definitive or conclusive interpretation—as one version of looking at what people have for centuries also observed and tried to interpret.

The common characteristic of a creative person which enables him or her to imagine alternative scenarios and new ways of expressing old forms might explain why so many artistic types find it so difficult to establish and maintain a single long-term personal relationship, for the artist's imaginative skill also enables him or her to easily visualize many other possibilities and opportunities to create close connections with other people. A creative eye is often also a roving one.

The vivid passing moment of the "now" distracts many people from awareness of the "before" and the "after." A successful experiment in living requires being aware of not only the evanescent present but also of the past and of the future.

NOVEMBER 2021

Many people make a life and a living studying, analyzing and writing about the lives of famous creative figures. Professors, academic types, critics, scholars, tenure-seeking underlings, and other researchers examine and interpret how renowned artists lived and what their acclaimed and lasting works mean. But rarely do any of the avalanche of books, articles, essays, monographs, studies, dissertations and other dissections of creative celebrities reveal just how or why the masters managed to bring into existence their masterworks. The reason is that the mysteries of creation remain inexplicable, even to those who by chance create the material. Chance randomly happens to endow a few earthlings with the blessing (or is it a curse?) of a mind adept at creating lasting works, but no one can explain why or how those geniuses happened to conceive of and then create such wonders of the human imagination. Of course, lack of extraordinary creative powers doesn't make the rest of us idiots; we only look like idiots when measured against the "greats."

The deep secret underlying any serious creative effort, a secret understood by few if any consumers of culture, is that the creator produces the work not for the outside world but for himself. It's not worth going to all the trouble to write a book, compose a symphony, color a painting, chip away a stone block based on any pretentious belief that you're creating high culture, or even low culture, or for the sake of pleasing an indifferent public, or for fame or fortune. Such strenuous creative efforts arise from a need to please yourself by responding to a deeply embedded compulsion which by temperament or by inspiration somehow happens to motivate you to produce the work. So few cultural products find favor with the public or survive very long it's unrealistic to suppose that those hard-won products will attain acclaim and widespread acceptance. An inner-directed impulse motives the creative enterprise. A serious writer writes for himself. He'll suffer less disappointment and enjoy more contentment if he realizes that most books remain unappreciated and little (or not at all) noticed and are quickly forgotten, their fate being to rest in peace on obscure dusty library shelves.

Humanimals devote much attention and a vast amount of time to many unproductive, brief, mindless and largely forgettable activities. Mass-market lowest-common-denominator amusements, entertainments and events, most of them with passive rather than active participants, characterizes contemporary pop culture. People seek an escape from the day-to-day work-a-day world with such play-a-day diversions as TV, videos, audios, social media, computer games, blogs, tweets and other internet time-wasters, spectating professional (including college) sports, reading dumbed-down publications, using narcotics, alcohol and other addictive substances, engaging with virtual reality by withdrawing from actual reality, frolicking at raves and fiery Burning Man-type happenings, bar- hopping, and many other pursuits of no lasting, or even momentary, value. I don't know where people get the time to engage in these kinds of activities, which don't use time but simply kills it, a time-crime murder never prosecuted. My comments aren't meant to criticize or to denigrate the vast number of people who enjoy such attractions and distractions, but only to lament the great waste of human resources, energy and potential. Many more enriching ways to spend your days offer options which would produce a more lively and satisfying experiment in living and probably be better for all concerned.

Feminists apparently haven't yet complained that many female names derive from those used for the patriarchy. Males would most likely refuse to accept without protest a system in which their names originated with those used by women. Feminized names adopted from the masculine versions include: Alberta, from Albert; Alexandra, Alexander; Andrea, Andrew; Augusta, Augustus; Claudia, Claude; Colette, diminutive of Nicolas; Cornelia, Cornelius; Edwina, Edwin; Emily, Emil; Ernestine, Ernest; Frederica, Frederic; Gabriela, Gabriel; Harriet, Harry; Henrietta, Henry; Joan and Joanne, John; Josephine, Joseph; Juliana, Julian; Justina, Justin; Louisa, Louis; Lucia, Lucius; Maxine, Max; Patricia, Patrick; Paula, Pauline and Paulette, from Paul; Philippa, Philip; Roberta, Robert; Simone, Simon; Stephanie, Stephan; Vida, diminutive of David. In French: Charlotte from Charlot, diminutive of Charles; Jacqueline, Jacques. In Italian: Giuseppina, from Giuseppe. An oddity in English (as noted August 1981) makes "Joe" masculine even though a terminal "e" usually denotes the feminine version, which is the "e-less" Jo. Somehow the matriarchy hasn't objected to all these male-derived female names. But perhaps those men's names originated from the designations for women, in which case it's the patriarchy which has failed to complain.

Various Journal entries discuss sleep and its dreams, but not the topic of daydreams, less dreamy and completely different from those of the night. The main difference between a night dream or nightmare and a daydream is that the participant can choose the day versions, while at night the visions come to you in a random spontaneous way, unsummoned, uncontrolled and unedited. Another difference is that because you can select and edit the daytime scenarios, which usually involve fantasies you desire, daymares are rare as you really don't want to bring into the daylight dark thoughts of the kind which shadow your nighttime dreams

The nature of dreams—unwilled and unrequested strange baffling nocturnal visions—resembles how a humanimal, incarnated by capricious forces for no known reason, happens to be cast into and lives life. The odd phantasmagoric night images are perhaps meant to show earthlings that the essential nature of their lives is like a dream, an insubstantial, evanescent and random experience.

Each sub-unit in the cosmos occupies only an obscure minuscule place in the entirety. A person is to humankind as people are to the planet, as the earth is to the solar system, as that relatively small system is to the universe, and as the universe is to the cosmos. Ever in violent motion, the chaotic cosmos churns, seethes, spins, explodes, agitates with destructive energy to no end and with no end. Celestial bodies—comets, meteors, shooting stars, planets, galaxies, all the rest—spin and flash in random kinetic insubstantial motions. Among those hellish heavenly bodies is the swirling world, a swirld lost in the stars. Earthlings respond to their benighted presence on the lonely planet in the void by holding many pretend beliefs and by engaging in a wide range of seemingly purposeful but essentially meaningless activities, as well as by the hopefully redemptive power of love which in a small way can mitigate the dizzy reeling feeling of the vertiginous experience of brief existence as a lonely humanimal on the lonely planet.

It's rather perverse to look a gift horse in the mouth, but the ability to talk which endows humanimals with the means to communicate has produced all too many loud-mouths who mouth off with endless unformed and uninformed banal and trivial chatter. It would be far better if those chatter-boxes would hold their tongue rather than saying, "Behold my tongue." They seem tone-deaf to their largely worthless chit-chat, much of which represents a shout-out to the world in a kind of Kilroy was "hear"effort to attract attention and show that the talkers exist, although many who listen would prefer they didn't.

Some writers apparently believe that they've discovered death. For sure death will eventually discover them, but meanwhile those authors suppose that they can say something new about mortality. You can address the topic of death, but it never replies—it just happens, in silence as a one-off once-in-a-lifetime deathtime. Otherwise, death stays to itself. From the very beginning humanimals have contemplated their end, so that by now nothing new remains to be said about mortality. Although my Journal contains many passages on the topic, my thoughts make no pretense at novelty, for my contemplations serve only to help me come terms with my own mortality.

Occasionally I imagine a ghost party attended by all my departed close—but now, oh so far—friends, each distanced from me by his or her death. This bittersweet thought experiment brings me both pleasure and melancholy. Although I'd be the only living person at the party, the brief final get-together of the phantom ghost guests would be a lively event. This valedictory session would offer me the last opportunity to mingle with my friends and to bid the spectral guests an appreciative and definitive farewell. Few of those present would know the others. As the convening party I'd represent the nexus which connects strangers who have nothing in common except knowing me. The final gathering would allow me to supplement and conclude my accumulated memories of the friends who peopled my life. After the party they'd all fade away and revert to phantoms, never again to revive, a second disappearance which would remind me in a melancholy way of their first. Of course, there's not a ghost of a chance for such a festive gathering to materialize, and my invitations to the party would end up in the dead-letter office.

In enlightened and developed lands dogs are treated like people; in more primitive and repressive countries the people are treated like dogs.

Does empty-nest syndrome affect any animals other than human kind? Do birds suffer an empty-nest feeling when their birdlets finally fly away? Do dogs have an empty kennel or empty doghouse feeling after the puppies grow up and leave? Horses, from empty stable syndrome; cows, from empty barn; pigs, from empty sty; cats, from empty litter-box syndrome? Do monkeys suffer from phantom limb effect when chimps leave their home leaves and trees? Will readers of my Journal suffer withdrawal pains and empty page syndrome after they finish this book? I hope so.

What would a student learning English as a foreign language make of an expression like, "At my new job I really hit it off with my boss." On its face the phrase seems baffling. "Hit" implies some sort of conflict, maybe even a blow. The "off" suggests that something's not right or not present. Better phrased, the colloquialism would say, "I really fit in with my boss." Fitting rather than hitting and in rather than off seems a more fitting way to convey the thought.

DECEMBER 2021

When someone said to me just after Thanksgiving that she was tired of eating leftovers I responded by stating that she should give some thanks for the extra Thanksgiving food, as in many lands the unfortunate locals enjoy neither a meal's leftovers or the meal itself. Those impoverished humanimals start with almost nothing and are left with nothing—no leftovers from the all too few preovers.

Edward de Bono endorsed lateral thinking, but thinking backwards can be just as useful. It's no drawback—or backdraw—to reverse expressions to convert them to a back-to-front format, one which retains the same meaning but which can bring new insights and which also suggest how arbitrary language is. Examples include pocus-hocus, podge-hodge, less-or-more, take-and-give, turvy-topsy, around-turn, skelter-helter, every then and now, later or sooner, wow-bow, tails or heads, raff-riff, mash-mish puffing and huffing, duddy-fuddy, knack nicks, gritty-nitty, toe-to-head, downside up rather than upside down, bear and bull, lose or win, out and in, washy-wishy, and on so. Although an "off day" can denote a day off, it usually refers to a period when you don't function well. In 1913 the *New York World* published the first "word-cross" puzzle, as it was then called, a designation as descriptive as "cross-word," so why the cross-over from one phrase to the other? Some expressions can't be reversed, such as back-to-back, goody-goody, pack-rat and rat pack, while others need to retain the same order to make sense, such as first to last. One irreversible combination is here today and gone tomorrow, as gone today and here tomorrow applies to very few mortals (welcome back J.C., Lazarus, Tabitha, etc.) in the entire history of the (under-)world. All the rest of us, here today and irrevocably gone tomorrow, never get a second chance. Forth and back would be more logical than the common reverse format, as something or someone must go forth before they or it can come back. A pow-wow would have been better formatted as wow!-pow. Such is the gritty-nitty of my thought experiment.

The reversal experiment described in the last entry raises the larger question why forms created both by nature and by mankind exist in their present configurations rather than in other versions. Almost any form could have been different, and many of them seem largely arbitrary. Examples of alternate forms for colloquial expressions noted in the previous entry suggest how common practices could be different and still function as intended. Random influences shape how whatever exists happened to develop. Although the existing forms as they now appear seem natural and perhaps even inevitable, they're all odd constructs and quite "evitable." Pope's claim that whatever is is right is wrong, as things just happen to exist, right or wrong, in a particular form. No Pope's pronouncements represent definitive or authoritative opinions.

Just as the more Pascal saw of people the more he liked dogs, the more I saw of the world the more I viewed the place as a very strange, unusual, abnormal, arbitrary meaningless play of infinite forms. The seething spectacle which plays on and on here on the lonely planet serves to entertain but not to inform earthlings, who live and then don't without the slightest idea of what it's all about. What chanced to come into being originated with no presiding force but only as a chaotic play of forms. Although most people never give a second thought to how things might have been different, I gave not only a second but many more thoughts to other possible formats, most of which would no doubt be as odd, but in some cases more desirable, as the existing ones. The infinite forms which by chance happened to furnish the prevailing system with its content resulted from a spin of the cosmic roulette wheel ruled by the capricious operation of luck.

Familiarity breeds content. To interact with your familiar family members, with good friends, with known colleagues, and to engage in regular habitual routines brings a comforting sense of order and well-being. In a world of constant change on a lonely planet lost in a cosmos seething with ceaseless motion, stable settings offer some welcome reference points. It's pleasant to see a familiar face, someone who knows your back-story and you theirs, to be surrounded by long-standing furniture and objects in your home base, to pass through well-known cityscapes. to revisit cities and museums whose turns and twists you remember from many previous visits, to reread favorite books. To all our familiars we cling, even if only briefly, to continue connections which offer a temporary fixed base-point in a universe in endless flux.

The romance languages offer more appropriate ways to express passing states which the English description wrongly implies are permanent. To say "I'm thirsty," "I'm hungry," "I'm cold" suggests that a temporary condition endures as a part of one's being. The romance languages more accurately recognize that thirst, hunger, chill are only passing phases and not intrinsic characteristics. Those languages say "I have thirst...hunger...cold." If you say, "*Je suis froid*" (I am cold) in French the expression means that you're a cold person, an embedded trait.

Somehow I was by chance born with a strong death gene, not the universal one which kills everybody off, but a personal type which prompted me from a young age and on to the present day to contemplate my mortality. This helpful perception allowed me to carry out my experiment in living in light (or dark) of the grave reality that before long the experience would be over and that only a few lines engraved on a grave marker would in the end mark my brief earthly presence, soon to be an absence. Thanks to that rather dominant gene, I now approach the end serene with the belief that I made of the experiment the best I could, given the particular circumstances which chance, luck and fate happened to endow me with.

By now, my "yesters" far outnumber my morrows. The long accumulation of yesterminutes, yesterdays, yesterweeks and months and years have depleted the remaining tomorrows. As time goes by, the "yesters" become "nosters." for the distant past fades away leaving no traces.

As from today, December 21st, the days will start to lengthen, but only as measured by their light, not be any increased number of minutes and hours.

A certain symmetry defines a humanimal's passage through life: from womb to room to roam to tomb. Inception at conception starts you off in a fleshy, cozy and comfortable chamber from which you're suddenly and unwillingly expelled, forced to leave your private little hidden comfort zone and thrown out into the discomfort of the inhospitable outside world. You eventually roam beyond home as your horizons widen, only to find them narrowing as time closes in on you. Then comes the end, after which you again occupy a hidden container, this one not a nurturing life-giving space but a lifeless box where you decay away, confined forever to eternal non-being.

JANUARY 2022

The year-end transition to the new year always provokes me to think about endings, less so to contemplate beginnings as by now ending dominates my thoughts.

As the new year dawns I advance into a year many of my contemporaries failed to reach. Some never even survived long enough to see the twenty-first century. As I've observed in recent year-end or new year comments, at my age it seems unlikely I'll cross over into the next year, an observation so far proved wrong every time I've expressed it—among the most gratifying incorrect comments I can make.

If a notebook page, mute until an entry puts words onto its lines, could talk: "odd," said the odd page to the even, "that we were given lines to speak," to which the even replies, "I was bound to be of service to the Journal-ist who th-inks on us." The odd: "True, even me."

A good friend of mine in his mid-seventies who recently suffered a potentially life-threatening illness was cured, and after brushing off this brush with death the recovered patient continued on without any apparent change in his awareness of or concern about his mortality. Maybe an ability to ignore existential matters and shrug-off death represents a more sensible attitude than how some of us perhaps all too frequently ponder mortality.

Missed opportunities far outnumber the few you seize, but many of those possibles you opt to reject would most likely have led to poor consequences. Unfortunately, so do some you accept.

Three seemingly new products for the widely diversified 3M company: (1) Butterscotch tape, which emits an aromatic butterscotchy scent when you unwind the roll. (2) M & M & M's. (3) A new soup promoted by the advertising jingle, "Mmm, mmm good." Do these ideas offer worthy commercial opportunities for 3M, or are they just mmmisbegotten proposals?

Presentational skills, product positioning and trade dress can endow ordinary offerings with an aura which helps to justify premium prices. If, *par example*, a service or a product bears a French name you can most likely charge more than for the same offering designated in English. French-labeled dishes in restaurants cost more than identical items listed in English. A "*croque monsieur*" is more expensive than a simple toasted ham and cheese sandwich; "*petits pois*," more than plain old peas; "*pâtisserie*," more than common varieties of pastry. A *garçon* seems more upscale—and deserving of higher tips—than a mere "waiter." If the ultra-elegant and expensive Pierre Hotel on Fifth Avenue in New York City were renamed the Peter Hotel, the top dollar prices charged there would no doubt peter out and be much lower. Similarly, if South Dakota's capital changed its name from Pierre to Peter the city would lose a certain "*je ne sais quoi*." White Castle renamed "*Le Chateau Blanc*" could slide up the price of the chain's legendary sliders. This book would better have been titled "*Un Journal*" ("*merci*" to my publisher for the suggestion) and its price accordingly increased.

Below is the fourth poem I included in "Le Journal." The others appear in the entries for June 2006, April 2021, and October 2021. The last two appear in the February and May 2022 entries.

Love's Labor Lost

And when she turned 50 soon she said,
"Wouldn't it be nifty if now we wed?"
After a long affair a fair question, that—
One to inspire a friendly chat.
A reasonable response expected—
But even if the questioned request rejected?

We held that friendly chat, in fact more than one,
But with none was won the hoped-for "yes"—only always "no,"
And so no longer am I her beau
As she failed a happy ending to complete,
Just a defeat.

At times I can't recall her name,
A lapse I do regret with shame
And for which I accept the blame.
But no regrets for my "no,"
As with this verse I clearly show.

Salespeople in many stores stand around with vacant bored expressions as the zombie-like attendants wait and wait for something to happen as if waiting for a Godot, a no-go who never appears. Godot never was much of a shopper. Every so often a browser shows up, and once in a great while after a long wait a buying customer may appear. The minutes and hours must hang heavy for the mostly idle vendors. But such a quiet life is no doubt more satisfactory than being shot out of a cannon, working in a meat packing factory, editing one of my books or searching for the elusive Monsieur Godot.

The definition of a serious writer: one who prefers to excel rather than to sell.

In that a terminal "e" in English denotes that the previous vowel is pronounced long, it's odd that exceptions like "relative" and " tentative" exist. But it's clear that "live" (like "alive" and "survive") has a long "i" to distinguish it from "live," which rhymes with "give," but why isn't that word pronounced like "alive"? Nor does "determine" come with a long "i" like "mine." The terminal "e" doesn't always determine the pronunciation.

The word "play" in "the play of infinite forms" (my description of the ceaseless cosmic chaos) functions both as a verb and a noun. The forms play as they present the play, the longest running play in history, a production any producer would greatly value. It's a spectacular presentation—boffo box office—beats Broadway—a sell-out with a huge captive audience. Unlike stage plays the terrestrial pageant lacks a plot, a theme, any meaning. The "Playbill" for the show offers only blank pages, with the only bill the one rendered at the end paid by the players when they permanently exit with no encore or revival. With that morbid ending the production can't be described as a comedy, nor can it be called a tragedy as nothing and no one in the terrestrial spectacle is truly tragic. The strange play is obviously a farce—a ridiculous empty show. How on earth any producer could green-light and stage such an odd production rather than red-lighting the absurd farce is mystifying. Viewing the show with a selective perspective to see the play as a farce offers a sportive supportive way to help the participants understand the largely baffling spectacle. Some players, programmed to believe that the show follows a religious script (or scripture), put credence in the program notes which say that the plot was formulated by some sort of "deus ex machina." If so, a madman (or woman)—or a sullen creator for some reason mad at the lonely planet—must be the author. More realistic non-believers think that the play develops almost entirely in an ad lib way with no rhyme or reason, just blank verse empty of meaning.

Truly, the only way to respond to the farcical nature of the terrestrial play of infinite forms (as described in the last entry) is to laugh at the show, and also to help other earthlings see the humor of the performance and join in the laughter. Some participants may say it's no laughing matter, but for the few of us who are in on the joke the play is really a hoot, a funny (if not fun) laff-filled riot with the joke on you, on me, on everyone.

By referring to the departed as "the dead, " English fails to respect the deceased, as the collective noun lumps all the no longer living together into an indistinguishable group. More humane and descriptive would be to call them "the deads," which implies some individuality, the form used unwittingly by Simone de Beauvoir with her charming slightly incorrect English she wrote in a letter to Nelson Algren using a language not her own. The plural version shows that many specific deads—rather than just an amorphous mass of the dead—have passed away.

For the sake of equity, equality, fairness and inclusion the Caribbean island of Trinidad should be renamed Trinimom. In India some residents of Hyderabad claim that because the name has given the city a bum rap the place should be renamed Hyderagood.

When asked years ago what workers wanted, labor leader Samuel Gompers replied, "More." I tried to carry out my experiment in living with less, in accordance with the aphorism of Mies van der Rohe: "Less is more."

Sleep: the curse of mankind as it reduces the life of each humanimal by one-third, but also a blessing because the nocturnal interlude allows the benighted creatures briefly to escape existence and enjoy some welcome temporary relief from the world without leaving it.

Each survivor of a deceased person remembers the departed in his or her own limited way. For a full picture in the round all the fragmentary memories would have to be combined into one complete image as if assembling a jigsaw puzzle. But even that integrated view would remain incomplete as pieces from friends who predeceased the decedent can no longer be added. No life can be viewed in much breadth or depth by anyone other than the person who lived it, and even for the principal the self-image is usually incomplete, fragmentary, vague, sketchy.

The time, effort and energy devoted by earthlings to establish and impose on the natural order of things constructs such as culture, religion, governments and much else which comprise the elements of civilization seem way out of proportion to their value. Although "nothing ventured, nothing gained" might have inspired many of those artificial creations, they mostly seem to show that "much ventured, nothing gained."

FEBRUARY 2022

Dreams may enter our consciousness in order to bring to our attention images inaccessible to us during our waking hours—but why?

How an organization measures itself reflects its self-image. Institutions which function (or, most often, mis-function) without concern for efficiency, productivity and the market discipline of customer satisfaction typically rely on inputs to assess performance. Governments, bureaucrats, non-profits, think tanks, foundations, non-governmental organizations, international agencies and similar tax or grant supported operatives favor featuring as supposedly meaningful factors metrics which measure activities based on number of meetings, adding employees, issuing new reports and regulations, bigger budgets, establishing more programs and projects, none of which evidence effectiveness. By way of contrast, commercial enterprises forced by the marketplace to produce goods or services wanted or needed by customers at prices they'll pay assess effectiveness by outputs and results. Without such specific measurable data, those businesses—unlike organizations which focus on inputs rather than outcomes—won't survive.

A terrestrial steroid and an extraterrestrial asteroid represent two extremes between which exists as an outlier (or inlier) a strange form of earthly life known as mankind. Lost between the microscopic components of life and the vast cosmic system, earthlings seem out of place and ill-suited to fit into the nature of things. Made of stardust and stranded here on the lonely planet, the earth-bound creature is lost in the stars.

Once again a poem somehow came to mind, inspired by the discarded face masks which litter lawns and sidewalks where I walk. This is the fifth poem in the Journal. The others appear in entries for June 2006, April and October 2021 and January 2022. The sixth and last is in May

2022 below. Their infrequency evidences that for some unknown reason it happens that a poetic rather than, as usual, a prose version of what I perceive somehow surfaces in my mind. I have never by design tried to create a poem; they just suddenly and mysteriously occur to me without my permission or any premeditation.

Retreads

Like soft-cloth angle-shaped shards sheared from shrouds,
masks pave the pavement to bring a new angle on things of nature and the nature of things.
Inert they lie, masks which don't lie as they can't mask the truth of the matter
that in the end we don't much matter as our fate is to become "the late."
Before long all will be cast away like the flimsy gauzy rectangles
which once covered a face but now, as is our fate,
Lie inert in their lowly place as discarded waste and useful no more.
Underfoot they repose where the living tread
and which the dead, faceless forevermore, must ignore.

To the slogan "the land of the free and the home of the brave" might be added, as a further definition of America, "the land of the me and the home of the I," as individualism rules in the U.S.A. Here a person ranks above "the people," a collective communal mass favored in many other countries. Extreme individualism both sparks effort, energy, creativity, enterprise and venturesome undertakings and produces much disorder, unrest, self-oriented behavior, activism, complaints and grievances, an entitlement mentality and other forms of dissent and self-expression. The American free-for-all system contrasts with the free-for-none highly controlled and regulated imposed systems where authoritarian regimes suppress individuality and claim to favor "the people."

Why Tyrants Are Beneficial

Although dictators are viewed as undesirable humanimals, those tyrants in fact perform a useful service for mankind. Strong-men, corrupt officials, oppressive governments, mafia-like regimes, authoritarian rulers, tyrants, autocrats and dictators treat their subjects so poorly that many finally emigrate, so benefiting the countries they move to. Like Gresham's Law in economics, bad governments drive out good people. The most ambitious, adventurous, energetic, resourceful, educated and productive citizens seek the freedom and opportunities to pursue success elsewhere. This reallocates human resources from areas where those desirable characteristics represent disadvantages to more welcoming places which can benefit from the infusion of new talent. Tyrants unwittingly benefit society as their oppression motivates or forces the most venturesome and ambitious people to leave for greener pastures. This serves to rationalize human capital by allowing that asset to seek its highest and best use in a new and more hospitable country.

Embedded in all being is eventual non-being, but this concerns and preoccupies only humanimals as no other creature realizes that it's fated to disappear. Only earthlings know that, like *The Times*, they're discarded after their time as casually as a briefly read newspaper. Mortals never get another edition or a follow-up story. No use hoping for any sort of life-raft to cling to life, as we exist on a death-raft. The backstory tells that humanity and every specific humanimal appeared on the lonely planet by chance out of nothing. The front-story reports that all such creatures who ever exist dematerialize and disappear back into nothing. That's the end of the story.

Although identity now features as an identifying personal characteristic, a lack of identity represents a preferable format as by avoiding a niche, a special category or a narrow way to present yourself you can view and experience the world in broader and more diverse and interesting ways.

Every language presents ambiguities of one kind or another. In French *"la mer," "la mère"* and *"l'amer"* all sound the same but mean "mother," "sea" and "bitterness" The fearsome French *lycée* (high school) *"dictée"* challenges students to distinguish between words pronounced in the same way but with different meanings. In English "read" can mean reading in the present ("I now read the book") or the past ("Yesterday I read the book"). A recent newspaper headline said, "U.S. Lifts Tariffs on Japanese Steel," a truly ambiguous statement as it can mean two quite opposite things. You have to read the article to learn if the tariffs were removed or increased.

After my time at the Sorbonne native French speakers occasionally complimented me by observing, "You speak good French," to which I'd reply, "So do you." This always elicited a laugh, except in Paris where life is no laughing matter.

Schopenhauer (always a good source to quote, as his name lends gravitas to a text) said life is "an unprofitable episode disturbing the blessed calm of non-existence." Given the nature of things on the lonely planet, surely prenatal and postmortem non-existence offer a better way of life or, more precisely, non-life. The once-in-a-lifetime experience of being unwillingly incarnated into a humanimal form seems less desirable than remaining forever disincarnated as a nothing. Being alive is an experience I could have lived without.

When I recently asked an avid but now Covid-grounded world traveler if he planned to resume his travels he replied, "My bags are packed," to which I responded by saying, "My bags are unpacked."

If the earth didn't revolve, half of the lonely planet would remain in permanent darkness. If the globe didn't tilt, seasons would be unknown. A science fiction writer could no doubt vividly imagine how those revised natural elements might affect life on earth and how humanimals might behave differently with those kinds of alternate formats.

A classic inside-the-Beltway D.C. dish: a thick slice of baloney with nuts on the extreme left and right. The middle is empty.

A stellar perspective of the lonely planet would show how ridiculous much of mankind's behavior is. So would a worm's-eye view.

Because the outcome of an election is often uncertain and the result a binary win or lose conclusion politics resembles sports. Both offer unscripted entertainment, but with the difference that most athletes are competent.

Why no female versions of "mastermind" or "masterpiece"? Would feminists be content with "mistressmind" and "mistresspiece"?

To absorb too much culture can be deadening; too little, also deadening.

What preoccupies the old—when, where and how they'll exit—will after the departure no longer post-occupy them.

At time goes by, eventually nobody will remember anybody.

Which represents the least desirable missing character trait—mental or sentimental deprivation?

MARCH 2022

A devil-may-care devil-take-the-hindmost dare-devil way of life may offer excitement but is likely to turn you into an angel sooner than you'd hoped.

The cosmic experiment which happened to create the lonely plant didn't work out too well. Better luck next time, with the best luck being no additional such experiment.

The other day when I couldn't put my hands on a Marcel Proust volume in my library I told myself that I was engaged in a "*recherche du Proust perdu*."

If science operated in the same way as the cultural world evaluates creative works—opinion, taste, personal preferences, social or political agendas, vested interests, commercial considerations, favoritism, connections, networking and other subjective factors—people would still be suffering from smallpox, from surgery without anesthetic, be subject to blood-letting and probably believe that babies are brought by storks.

It's hard to understand how students of English as a foreign language can stand to learn such a maddening tongue. If you stand up for someone you support them, or if you simply stand up you get up and stand, but if you stand down you give up a position (your resolution gives out). If you stand out you excel, but a stand-in replaces someone else. To sit down means to become seated, but if you sit up you don't get up but only assume a more vertical position. These impossibly eccentric expressions might cause students to give out, give up or give in and then to be put down by teachers put out by dimwitted students put off by trying to learn the fiendish language.

It may be that existence as people know it represents a state completely different than what they believe they perceive. Perhaps humanimals aren't really alive in the way they appear to be and suppose, as their life experience may represent a degraded version of a former more complete and comprehensible existence. People as now constituted may only be mere ghost-like forms created in a flawed way as successors to much more developed predecessors. In that kind of phantom-like state humans don't become postmortem specters as in their present life the insubstantial earthlings are already mere fragmentary phantasmagoric figures like shadows cast by previous living beings who existed in a higher and more complete form. Our evanescent spectral existence would in that way consist of residues which serve to dispose of some leavings from earlier beings. If true, our lives have purpose and meaning, even if not the kind we'd hoped for.

Time is money as financial resources can give you a wealth of experiences by enabling you to convert riches into discretionary time, so allowing whoever happens to possess financial resources to buy free time, which isn't free but costs. But time and money, while synergistic, aren't equivalent as money is finite and wealth owned by one person can't belong to another, while time is infinite and spread equally among all living humanimals. and what each possesses of time doesn't limit the amount others have.

For a male with an infection, "sepsis" should be called "sepbro."

A recent obituary mentioned the family name "Sorgenfrei," passed down from a bold and optimistic ancestor who called himself "Worryfree." He must have lived a truly charmed life, or else was a complete dreamer.

Just as risk doesn't represent simply a characteristic of capital allocation but is its very essence, so for a humanimal luck, chance, happenstance, coincidence, randomness aren't just a few of various miscellaneous factors which influence how the creatures fare but comprise the basic existential nature of what defines the fundamental conditions of an experiment in living

While a cat may have nine lives, a canine includes the number in its very name.

Self-referential confessional writings suffer from three main defects: such accounts are repetitious as most follow the same formula and relate similar events, situations and story lines; most of the sob-stories pertain to rich-world matters and show no awareness of the truly acute and often life-threatening conditions and problems common in impoverished countries; a "poor me" account based on personal circumstances and self-oriented perspectives focuses on self-pitying laments while failing to recognize that many people who suffer similar difficulties manage to deal with and overcome such problems without complaining or telling the world about them. Given what all humanimals face during their time on the lonely planet, every earthling is a "poor me."

My inventory of "Home Depot" and "Away Depot" memories remind me of the highs and "Lowe's" of my home-based and my world-wide travel experiences.

As I lay abed the other night in a deep sleep, the nightmarish thought during my slumbers that my life would soon end awoke me with a start.

A willing even if make-believe suspension of belief that human existence lacks any purpose or meaning is necessary for any mortal who wishes to pursue a successful experiment in living.

APRIL 2022

Three categories of success and failure: (1) Someone richly endowed with the conditions, circumstances and traits which often facilitate success makes something out of something. (2) A similarly endowed person who fails makes nothing out of something. (3) A disadvantaged person with few or no beneficial circumstances who manages to succeed makes something out of nothing.

Fresh water is so scarce in the cosmos it's strange how that substance, without which life on earth can't exist, happened to be created here on the lonely planet.

Cupidity=stupidity.

Two signs I recently noticed in front of restaurants: (1) "Today's special is you." (2) "If you don't eat here we'll both starve."

As an old man hurry-hobbles fro and to and there and here his wife cautions the oldster, "Take your time," to which he replies, "Time's taking me, there's no way I can take it."

Writer's block never damed my stream of thoughts, which always flowed fairly freely and occasionally brimmed over with writer's flood. This free-flowing rivulet of words I attribute not to any creative powers intrinsic to me but because of one specific element which enabled me to write fairly fluidly, if not fluently: preparation.

By temperament, force of circumstances and other factors most people carry out their experiment in living as reactors rather than as actors. Only a fortunate few enjoy the freedom, independence, creativity, initiative, grit, spirit of adventure, risk-taking mentality and other such can-do self-starting elements which enable acting and not just reacting. In a more general way, the nature of things here on the lonely planet forces every earthling to react to the prevailing fundamental conditions, unchangeable by human agency. For all mortals he terms of engagement with life are non-negotiable.

A Very Short Story

Although beautiful, charming, sweet, personable and lovable, Jennifer remained a virgin as she was allergic to nuts.

Once a creative person establishes his frame of reference, seldom does that perspective change. The genre, format, ways of expression may over time vary but not the essential viewpoint, which in most cases seems impervious to revision. The content of each particular work-product represents only a variation on themes based on a continuity of thought and imagination. Once you've settled on a world-view it takes an earth-shaking experience to change the way you see things.

A few social institutions combine both public service and commercial considerations in a somewhat contradictory hybrid undertaking based on the seemingly opposite missions of doing good and doing well. Publishing and medicine represent two such enterprises as both operate with a bottom-line profit in mind while at the same time offering, respectively, valuable cultural and needed health services to mankind. Without financial viability neither medicine nor publishing could continue their public service offerings, but with a focus only on profit the societal benefits would be greatly diminished. How to calibrate the two quite different elements—money and service—presents a difficult balancing act.

Poussin in paint and Powell in print depicted "a dance to the music of time," whose rhythm each earthling follows to a different beat. Given its corrosive nature, time seems to pass less as a soothing musical lullaby and more like a murderous "good-by."

"Omicron" (the new Covid variant) means in Greek "little O" and "omega" means "big O," very obvious and logical when you think about it which, until now, I never did.

Petroleum tycoon: an oiligarch.

Although birth and death occur once and only once for each humanimals, many other experiences follow a kind of repetitive pattern. Audience members at the performance of a play they've seen before perceive the presentation in a different way than do people for whom the show is new. If you revisit a place, reread a book, hear again a symphony, return to the same vacation spot or repeat various other kinds of experiences they all strike you differently than for someone who comes to them for the first time. Similar or nearly identical sensory impressions of the play of forms people perceive can affect each observer—in part depending on how new the experience is— in different ways.

MAY 2022

Of the two kinds of minds and their formation—one formal, educated, credentialed and based on intelligence and domain knowledge, the other more general and enabled not by special training but by common sense, a wide variety of experiences, and smartness rather than intelligence—the primacy of the mentality shaped by informal practical real-world experiences offers a better chance to benefit from an effective experiment in living. Dealing with technical matters and with the specifics of a problem requires knowledge and learning acquired in an academic or purpose-focused course of study as contrasted with the more diversified eclectic catch-as-catch-can improvised skills possessed by people with street-smarts informed by the school of hard knocks.

A busy-body interferes with other people, while a busy body aims to keep itself active, connected, involved, productive, energetic and engaged in its own experiment in living rather than focusing on someone else's experiment.

Where people live influences how they view time and history. If you're surrounded by antiquities (other than in a retirement home) and evidences of the past, as in Egypt or Rome, your perspective on the passing scene will differ from how people in more go-go can-do future-oriented societies like the U.S.A. perceive present and bygone time. A Disney "Magic Kingdom" attraction suggests a different sense of regimes and realms than does living in a country with age-old vanished kingdoms such as the one King Tut ruled. In their attitude toward time, residents of the New World and new-found-lands differ from earthlings in the Old World and in Very Old Worlds aware of "the tragic sense of life" ignored by the more happy-go-lucky innocents in younger countries.

A "new" mentality typifies the American national character, as reflected in part by the nomenclature of such places as New Amsterdam/New York, New Rochelle, New Jersey, New Hampshire, New Mexico, New England towns like New Bedford, Newburyport, New Britain, New London, New Haven, New Milford, New Canaan, Newport and such others "news" (but not Newport News) as New Orleans, New Trier, New Bern, New Braunfels, Newberry, Newburgh, New Castle, New Harmony, New Ulm and other neo-name places scattered all across the New World. Forward-looking optimistic Americans believe in the power of the new to bring about beneficial changes. In the U.S. the future is a friend, and unlike in ancient lands the past remains only a distant acquaintance. The American can-do attitude contrasts with a "cannot-do" mentality common in countries which have by now seen it all.

The events of 9/11 represent the most extreme example of the need to call 911.

Habits serve as a short-cut to enable you to avoid rethinking routine matters and activities, but at the same time repetitions keep you in a rut. Both good and bad habits exert a strong grip on your behavior for both its cadence and its content. It's easy and comforting to keep the good habits, much more difficult to end the bad ones.

Words beginning with a silent "k" are usually pronounced in the same way as the twin word without the "k": knight-night, knot-not, knap-nap, knit-nit, but for some reason "know" and "now" differ in their pronunciation.

Like all humanimals, brats end up as their German palindrome says—"*starb*" (died).

"Zenteen" could be usefully added to numerical measures to designate a vast but indeterminate quantity as based on the "zen" association which suggests a kind of boundless immersion in contemplation and eternity unbound by the apparent reality of the world humans perceive. Thus "zenteen" billion would describe tens of billions without giving the specific amount.

Below is the last of the six poems included in the Journal. The others appear in the entries for June 2006, April and October 2021, January and February 2022. These few poems represent the only ones I entered in the entire Journal. Their infrequency evidences that during the 53 years I've maintained the Journal, only rarely did a poem occur to me.

The Deadly Storm

Thunder boomed like the roar of cannons, bursting from afar but striking near here
Where safe at home I heard the distant sounds blasting in my ear.
Into every rain some life must fall, and soon the storm attacked the ground,
Watery tracer bullets like tiny shooting stars firing with a machine-gun sound.
The heavens seemed at war with the world, thunder and rain blitzing lightning fast
As mortals sheltered from the storm troops, hiding from each warring blast.

It's in the nature of things for nature to war against all it made,
Just as unkind mankind is, as known, prone to kill its own
With inhumane human thundering from an attacking cannonade.

JUNE 2022

Opposites detract, as their meaning in words can be confusing. In England "to table" signifies to bring a matter under consideration, while in the U.S. the expression means to remove the topic from discussion. A "cool" person can be reserved, emotionless, unfeeling or someone admired as a trendy and with-it hot personality. The theater world good luck wish "break a leg" given to performers would be considered an unfriendly insult to anyone else. "In action" denotes the opposite of "inaction." Perhaps "grown up" could be heard as "groan up," as becoming an adult brings many groans, gripes and grimaces. In French "terrible" can mean both "awful" and "wonderful."

Extreme solipsism is the enemy of functionality. The degree to which you can manage to see situations from a perspective other than your own will play a large part in how effective your encounters with the play of infinite forms will work out. To perceive situations in a diverse way lets you adapt yourself to factors which don't conform to your own views, a useful exercise in objectivity which helps you transcend the pull of the magnetic field operating to draw you into seeing the world only in your own iron-clad way, a comforting but often misleading perspective.

I recently picked up a newspaper to read and inadvertently held the pages upside down, an angle which reminded me how arbitrary most human constructs and conventions are. Words and how they happen to be formatted might have developed in quite different ways, such that what now appears as upside down would be right-side up, and thus that up-side right.

JULY 2022

Perhaps an overlooked reason why humanimals want to engender offspring is that the children remind the parents of their own childhood, an innocent and care-free pre-adult time of life. In a somewhat similar way, pet dogs allow their owners to project onto the animal many pleasing traits and behaviors all too often lacking with fellow humanimals. Few if any people offer such winning canine characteristics as being obedient, cuddly, trainable, loyal, faithful, friendly, responsive, companionable, non-judgmental, quickly house-broken, all with tail-wagging enthusiasm.

Like most people who invest in security markets, entrepreneurs are usually unsuccessful as investors but for reasons different than for other people who chance to win in the markets. Accomplishments in one field seldom correlate with success in other undertakings. Many entrepreneurial winners who have against the odds managed to excel often suffer from overconfidence in their ability to invest in the financial markets. The very traits which bring success to businessmen work against how they approach investing: proactive and at times hyperactive; opinionated views impervious to alternate perspectives; an ability to sell, not only to customers but to themselves; certainty; enthusiasm; excitability; comfort with taking risks; impatient and impulsive behavior; ignoring the influence of chance and luck—all factors which represent the opposite of how effective investors function.

Freud's delusion that his wacky psychology system served to explain human behavior seems a case appropriate for psychiatric treatment.

A life of quiet inspiration rather than of quiet desperation, as Thoreau phrased it, characterizes how many writers produce their work.

Mortality offers many benefits, as without death civilization would be deprived of many culturally and socially enriching human constructs, such as colorful rituals and ceremonies, ecclesiastic art and architecture, philosophical speculations, books and paintings and music dealing with existential matters here on the lonely planet, and various other fanciful and entertaining practices and pursuits mankind believes will help explain the inexplicable and give a meaningless experience some meaning. Mourners would also lack the chance to enjoy some delicious buffets served after the funeral service.

In an alternate universe many things could have been better, among them: dogs adopt people; double the number of Dairy Queen locations; M & M & M's with triple chocolate; Shakespeare's brief life prolonged so that he could write more masterpieces; more frequent haircuts for Einstein and a face-lift for W.H. Auden; happy hour replaced by happy day; *lassi* widely available not only in India but also in the U.S.A, and Lassie finding her way home easily and quickly; readers of my books multiplied by a factor of 100, and buyers of it by twice that.

Englishisms: (1) "To rest my case" is to conclude your presentation; "To rest my case on..." refers to what you base your arguments on. (2) "Wrong" refers to a mistake; "wrongful" connotes an act or event with negative moral or legal implications.

A distinction without a difference: "This is like tweedle-de-dee and tweedle-de-dee."

Uncomfortable muggy summer heat in a big city is preferable to being mugged there.

Know-it-alls like academics, observers, commentators, journalists, "experts," second-guessers, critics and others who engage in such spectator sport aren't faced with making the decisions those opinionated characters babble about and judge, nor do those characters suffer the consequences faced by the do-ers and activists who actually make and execute their decisions and know from experience how difficult they are.

Very close families which operate in a largely closed and cohesive unit can be heart-warming in their tightly-knit walled garden-like space which encloses the participants in a familiar and comfortable setting. But at the same time members of such groups who confine themselves to a very narrow range of participants suffer lack of exposure to a wider range of experiences based on stimulating encounters with a more diverse and varied guest list.

The compelling opening lines of a story which recently occurred to me:

> Long after I was dead they exhumed my body to perform an autopsy on my remains. My coffin was disinterred and delivered to the cadaver lab, my body removed and then the probing slices and cuts gradually minced my innards and outtards until I was beyond recognition as a humanimal, or at least as a late one, and reduced to a messy mass of organic matter for disposal like garbage after my body was eviscerated and disembodied.

The story continues with references to Harry Lime in *The Third Man* and the title character in *A Coffin for Dimitrios,* books whose plots hint at the plot of the story: resurrection of someone presumed dead but isn't, a trick only a few humanimals supposedly accomplished.

The art establishment—critics, museums, galleries, journalists, agents, publicity shops, academics and all the rest—somehow manage to convince gullible buyers and other interested but unsophisticated parties that various artists produce highly valuable, cultivated, cultured collectible works of lasting value. Those favored painters include such color-full but artless characters as Kline, de Kooning, Louis, Twombly, Rauschenberg, Hofmann, Newman and a wrap-artist like Christo. This illustrates the folly of accepting the supposed taste and believing the opinions of "experts," taste-makers, market-makers, hustlers on the make and other influencers in fields which lack objective standards and evidence-based data and depend on subjective perspectives and personal views of no provable general value.

AUGUST 2022

Thank God I don't believe in god, a belief which would have greatly limited my experiment in living.

To help relieve some of the practices which now inflict addictive digital behavior on much of mankind the internet should be re-designated the "winternet" with access to it restricted to the winter months, so eliminating entanglements with the world-wide web during the rest of the year.

Any body can be born; every body will be borne away.

An extremely well-kept suburban lawn represents a two-edged sward: one cutting edge (the side used to keep the grass down) evidences the values and the reputational aspirations of the land-owner who hopes to sharpen his standing in the neighborhood, while the other side reflects the superficial image which typifies how bourgeois conformists hope to present themselves.

The common characteristic of: patients under treatment for a condition which is being managed and may be cured; for the creator of a cultural product whose work is in the hands of a gate-keeper who can decide whether or not to open the gate and admit the submission into the public realm; for an entrepreneur on the brink of getting financed or about to introduce his beloved product or service to the marketplace; for engaged couples soon to marry: HOPE. Unfortunately, the all too frequent outcomes include: continued suffering; rejection; failure; an unsatisfactory relationship.

Years ago I knew a girl who pronounced the name of the famed Wall Street firm, "Goldman Socks." She knew nothing about investing, finance, the stock (or the sock) market as her familiarity with Goldman Sachs arose only because she was dating someone who worked at the firm. Aware that Goldman was one of the most gilt-edged names in the industry, the girl enjoyed through her boyfriend prestige by association. She undertook a determined campaign to win the heart (and perhaps also the wallet) of her companion, and over the months the time value of patience and persistence finally concluded with a done-deal: marriage. The moral of the story: however pronounced and whatever you say, words don't carry the day as actions speak louder than words.

The more I saw of the world the less interested I became in many of its problems. I turned into something of a sterotypical Midwestern isolationist, the main difference from my fellow America-First, World-Last types being that I'd actually seen the world before deciding to ignore most of its conditions. Over time I came to lack interest in all the oppressive sociopolitical situations, the poverty, misery, suffering, economic disorder, dysfunctional systems and all the other problems all too common all around the world. In the course of my travels I saw so many of those unfortunate situations I lost empathy for the difficult circumstances faced by disadvantaged earthlings caught inescapably in hell-holes much more extreme and hopeless than the heck-holes in less inhumane countries. Nothing I could do would improve the lives of people stuck in places with such sub-human conditions. I couldn't solve any of the problems, and I grew weary of observing all the misery as I passingly visited and then left behind those unfortunate places while I was on the road, a road which soon took me away from such oppressive scenes and situations.

After a few days in Calcutta, my introduction to India on my first (of three) visits to that country, I realized that a person could spend his life in a purposeful humanitarian way trying to alleviate some of the pervasive misery, or simply ignore it. I knew I was no Father Tereso who would work hand-in-hand with Mother Teresa there in Calcutta. I was a hands-off fly-by-night or by-day passing stranger content to hand the problems on to more compassionate humanists while I retreated to my cozy little house back in the isolated and isolationist U.S. Midwest.

A literary classic is a work you never have to read yourself but can pretend you did simply by paging through the Cliff Notes summary.

Almost anyone who enjoys some success should to some extent suffer from imposter syndrome, as all accomplishment depends in large part on chance, luck and random factors which more than personal agency happen to bring good fortune.

What would a student of English as a foreign language make of these sentences: (1) "We put grandpa in a care facility because he was out of it." (2) "I'm glad you're present to present me with the present, so I really appreciate your presence."

Recently I saw a reference to the 1989 book *Panzer Commander* by World War II German tank officer Hans von Luck, a truly evocative family name which in colloquial English can be translated as "Johnny Lucky," although "Luck" in German doesn't quite mean what the word says in English (Germans say "*Glück*"). The commander's last name ranks with Goodluck Jonathan, president of Nigeria, as a proper name which best describes the single most determinative element which affects a humanimal's experiment in living. Goodluck indeed enjoyed good luck when, as vice president elected in 2007, he succeeded president Umaru Musa Yar'Adua when he died May 5, 2010, and then served until 2015. After his good luck in becoming president Jonathan might have adopted as his middle name the politically appealing first name of the Zulu king Goodwill Zwelithini, who died March 2021 after a 50-year reign. Goodluck Goodwill Jonathan is a great name for a politician.

Luck brings humanimals both great challenges and great opportunities. You can't know which without the modifier "bad" or "good." Luck in and of itself denotes only an abstract force with no implications attached. To say you want to attract luck represents a dangerous wish without specifying "good luck," but perhaps that's implicit in the wish as you'd only hope for bad luck to afflict an enemy or someone you greatly dislike. Although good luck is ever very elusive, coy and capricious it's perhaps possible to nudge, flex or bend favorable opportunities your way. Left uncoaxed, luck is more likely to be bad and challenge you with troubles and problems. Based on my own nearly concluded experiment in living, I believe that the chances to attract good luck can be improved, although never assured, in two ways. First, by establishing and maintaining as wide a range of friends, relationships, contacts and connections as possible. Such a variety offers the possibility of accessing a diverse talent pool of people with many experiences and skills which gives you many networking possibilities and also improves the chances that members of your extended group will at times call your attention to opportunities you'd otherwise miss. All those potential benefits from a wide circle might somehow facilitate some good luck. Second, as an intellectual analogue to being able to access an extensive number of contacts, a wide-range of reading, experiences and knowledge will broaden your view of the world to enable you to better understand how things work here on the lonely planet. This expansive perspective should bring to your attention possible good luck situations you might not otherwise notice. The great play of infinite forms seldom delivers good luck, but your chances for favorable chances might be enhanced if you expand and nurture relationships and can activate a broad comprehension of the nature of things and the way of the world. To my innate compulsive curiosity I attribute some of my good luck.

One sure way a lifetime habit is broken: when a humanimal so familiar with and addicted to the habit of being alive finally no longer is.

The U.S. economy has been increasingly Federalized but not nationalized, as the Federal government doesn't want to take over and be burdened with managing the private sector, a remarkable economic machine which produces resources accessible to politicians and bureaucrats without the need for those bystanders and observers of the wealth-creating process to create the assets. The operatives who control laws, regulations and taxation can appropriate the riches the politicians didn't produce and allocate the money based on political rather than on market-oriented factors. To the question, "Are we working for the politicians and the government or are they working for us?" the answer is ever more that those who produce wealth toil for the intruders who take and spend it.

I would have liked to learn a few more languages to add to the four tongues I took pains to acquire. But on second, or fifth, thought why bother? Once you know a word for, say, "dog"—whether such arbitrary form happens to be "*chien*," "*perro*," "*cane*" or "*Hund*"—there's really no need to learn any other ways to describe an animal which everywhere possess the same characteristics, and makes the same demands on their service provider, no matter what the creature is called.

In the contemporary algorithmic world quantitative skills can take you a long way toward success—to and through medical school, to six-figure starting salaries (plus free lunches and dry-cleaning) with digital companies, and to many other advantageous well-paying positions and opportunities. These days numbers pave the path to a garden of delights, but it's a walled garden. Exceptional computational skills in some ways represent a negative positive, as the ability to deal with numbers isn't always accompanied by an ability to deal with people. Of the two skills, the people factor numbers among the most useful of all personal characteristic and represents by far the more important, as you can count on the multiplier effect of knowing how to deal effectively with people to add to the ways you use to calculate a satisfactory experiment in living.

La Rochefoucauld said, "Neither the sun nor death can be looked at steadily." Nor can you without great discomfort look straight on at life, an equally overwhelming sight. But both life and death must be stared at without flinching in order to deal with those two oddities. That's really the only way to respond to and cope with that inconvenient pair of existential nuisances. Many people refuse to look life and death in the eye—understandably, as such views are unsettling. By gazing at those twin realities at a young age I was able to try to shape my experiment in living in the dazzling light of death and the shadowy insubstantial fleeting nature of life. It seems that many humanimals prefer to avoid confrontation with the harsh realities perceived by staring at life and death, the two terrestrial terms of engagement intrinsic to earthlings. I quite understand why so many of the creatures prefer to turn away from staring at those two oppressive basic factors of terrestrial existence which, looked at too closely, cause discomfort and bring unpleasant perceptions. Apparently many humans thrown randomly and unwillingly into existence and stranded in life, time and space prefer to lose themselves in alternative versions of being rather than confronting reality as it is. Those variations include fantasy, other-world sensations, false perceptions substituted for those sourced from the real world, mind-altering substances, virtual reality and varied visions and various other diversions and evasions from the mundane world as it actually appears. Harry Potter-like invented tales, space-trek stories, incredible scenarios, professional sports, sensational crowd-appealing events, much pop culture, make-believe Disney-like Magic Kingdoms and real royal kingdoms with majestic actors and rituals to distract the monarch's subjects from less pleasant subjects, many mass-market entertainments, consumerism, extreme social activism and fanaticism, spectacular spectacles, digital media, addictive pastimes and hobbies and other such common activities and attractions serve to distract people from perceiving too closely matters of life and death. I sympathize with this sort of escapism, which no doubt makes it somewhat easier for earthlings to suffer the extreme disadvantages of existence.

For the very old sleep doesn't interfere with your day; it's the day which interferes with your sleep.

Difficulties are a blessing for the people who don't suffer from the problems but who are hired to try to resolve them. What troubles the victims benefits those engaged to deal with a worrisome situation. The enemy of the afflicted serves as a friend to the service provider. Lawyers say, "God bless those who sue our clients." Perhaps doctors think, "Blessed are the bacteria and viruses which cause disease," and maybe plumbers pray, "Thank the Lord for clogged toilets and leaky faucets." Only a truly malign deity would clog toilets and inflict on humanimals diseases which profit physicians, technicians, hospitals, pharmaceutical companies and other medical operators. Those who gain from the sufferings of their fellow creatures can count their blessings. Without trouble the world would be a poorer place.

Following the recommendations of a financial adviser represents the triumph of hope over experience; earning a living as a financial adviser allows you to profit from experience rather than from hope.

Oxford academics spell the word "beadle" as "bedel," while Cambridge uses the form "bedell." If learned scholars high above it all in the secluded ivory towers at those two universities can't agree on how to spell "beadle," what hope is there for mankind to resolve its many more vexing and intractable conflicts, controversies, arguments and all the other contentious matters which plague earthlings?

Could a foreigner learning English make sense of the following dialogue? "Only about a week left." "Right." "Six days, right?" "No, seven left."

Because a scarcity of positional goods makes them very difficult to acquire, those rarities are more desirable than ordinary wealth or even the most exclusive and valuable possessions. Although the specific shares of General Motors you own belong only to you, many other stockholders own identical shares. A specially designed house on land no other structure can occupy or a one-of-a-kind antique represent distinctive assets, but other people own similar sorts of possessions. What the late economist Fred Hirsch called positional goods refers to a truly unique particular success or status no one else can claim. A Nobel Prize for excellence in a specific undertaking, discovering penicillin, finding a new planet, winning at Wimbledon, running the first four-minute mile all represent accomplishments which belong to you and to you alone. Although a few other people may achieve similar positional goods, each is one of a kind and belongs only to its owner. In an existential way, a humanimal is a hybrid of the common and the positional, as every such creature exists as a unique particular form unlike any other while also participating in general as a member of the same homo sapiens category billions of earthlings also belong to.

Second-tier but not second-rate excellent achievements short of exceptional top-level positional goods represent what might be called sub-positional goods. A very high ratio of aspirants to the very few who manage to succeed measures how highly society views their accomplishments. Examples include medical doctors, chief executive officers, state governors and U.S. Senators, star athletes and actors, renowned successful entrepreneurs, professors who hold endowed chairs, and other such performers who aren't singular and unique, like true positional good achievers, but who manage to accomplish uncommon kinds of success. Then there are various categories of noteworthy but not admirable positional goods which damage rather than benefit civilization, such as commanding predatory and destructive armies like those managed by Alexander the Great and Napoleon, running highly profitable but exploitative businesses, regimes imposed by world-class hard-edged iron-fisted tyrants. In a cosmic context the mysterious all-powerful force which happened to create the lonely planet no doubt enjoys top status for imagining and bringing into existence that unique positional good, even if bad for the unfortunate terrestrial creatures victimized by the fantastic and original creation where they suffer their brief lives.

The politics industry competes with other entertainment businesses for attention, enthusiasm, publicity, revenue and profits, mass-audience addiction to the show, cross-selling opportunities, marketing to customers (voters), for exploitable fanatics and fan clubs, and for other money-making possibilities. The not very classy political class relies in large part on its primary enabler, the media, which facilitates sales and marketing to attract and hold the interest, participation and support of mass-market audiences entertained by politics. Various brand-name characters parade, or stumble, across the stage: the heavies and the light-weights, heroes and villains, winners and losers, stars and bit players. Although we can dam streaming entertainments, cut cable's cord, cancel newspaper and magazine subscriptions, it's unfortunately nearly impossible to tune out from pervasive and invasive politics which infests society rather like how roaches, termites and other such creepy and annoying intruders swarm into our lives and bug us. For some irritants, politicians included, no pest control is possible.

If an animal could somehow change into another species what form would a man or beast (redundant) choose? It's unlikely any humanimal would want to give up its position as king of the animal kingdom (or queen of the queendom), and dogs would certainly be foolish to abandon their highly privileged status as pampered pets catered to by their two-legged service animals. But creatures and critters such as sloths, anteaters, aardwolves, bongos, bonitos, boobies, bonobos, bookworms (insect variety), hyenas, vultures, possums, porcupines might want to exchange their forms into that of a humanimal, even if that would represent a downgrade in status.

Less than a month from today the season will change, so bringing summer 2022 to an end, a fast finish which has already started to occupy a place in my consciousness. How can summer leave us so soon when it seems to have begun such a short time ago?

Few humanimals see themselves as they really are—simply momentarily walking, talking, briefly alive pre-dead creatures, phantoms in waiting.

I hate to sound like a pessimist so I'll try to express myself as a realist. I fear that it's all over. For once I'm not meditating on mortality, either mine or more generally eventual human extinction due to the nature of things. I'm referring to my concern (but not all that concerning to me, as I won't be around) that civilization and the world as earthlings know it will soon come to an end because of the inability of those creatures to control their seemingly innate destructive instincts. The greatly weaponized modern-day world seems vulnerable to serious damage and maybe even disappearance from the many ingenious innovative ways clever mankind has devised to destroy and kill. It's seems inevitable that some, many or all of those weapons—atomic, biological, chemical, firepower, stealth attacks disrupting infrastructure and critical digital systems—will be mustered, so wiping out much of civilization and killing millions of humanimals. This isn't an apocalyptic view, as my comments don't imply any sort of religious or transcendental ending based on a malevolent or angry deity or punishment for a sinful world. My attitude arises from the belief that sometime in the not too distant future someone somewhere will somehow decide to unleash the fearsome modern weapons of war now in the hands of man to bring toxic and fatal consequences. It will then be all over.

The doom-laden heavy thoughts written in the last entry raise the question: if the ending of civilization is nigh, why bother to describe the process? This the same question, rephrased in general terms and in a different context, as the puzzle posed for each individual: since your life will inevitably soon end why bother in the meantime, during the meaningless and often mean-spirited experience, to do anything at all? Extinction, whether of civilization or all of its discontents, provides a poor incentive to motivate and to encourage earthlings to continue to live and function. The answer could be that as long as you happen to be here on the lonely planet, cast unwillingly into existence to play a part as a cast member in the play of infinite forms, you might as well try to make the best of the strange and baffling experience.

Apart from a very few extraordinary earthlings—obvious examples being Shakespeare, Vermeer, Beethoven, Charles Schulz—no one's creative work-product includes more than just a small amount, if any, of high quality noteworthy and memorable material. Out of the millions of published words an author may produce over a lifetime of writing, only a handful (or page-full) offer sufficient merit to justify preservation for more than just a short passing interlude. In truth, few creative efforts manage to achieve anything of lasting value. Same for most other efforts humanimals happen to undertake.

Young-at-heart seniors grow old after their time; old-at-heart young people age before their time. Then there are those ageless, timeless types, the kind of folks who seem as if they'll go on forever. The cemeteries are filled with those poor souls.

Three digital comments applicable to apps: (1) Digital activity and crashes bring many apps and downs. (2) An app-etite ranks among the best of all apps as it gives you good taste. (3) Regular exercise is the killer app to retain good health—but maybe that's not an apt name for the app.

Although 12 represents by far the most common number of eggs sold in cartons at retail in the United States, a friend in Holland recently told me that in her country 10 and six rather than a dozen are the standard quantities. This somewhat surprised me, as I'd assumed that the American practice applied elsewhere as well. This rather naive and provincial misconception shows both the strong hold on humanimals of their familiar customs, beliefs and assumptions and also the foolishness of supposing that the normal and common formats where you live also apply to societies other than your own.

It's possible to imagine Abbott without Costello, Mutt without Jeff, Amos without Andy, Bristol without Myers, Johnson without Johnson and Olson without Johnson and Johnson without Boswell, Kinder without Morgan and Morgan without Stanley and Goldman without Sachs, Jones without Loughlin and Dow without Jones, Gilbert without Sullivan and Sullivan without Cromwell, Lewis without Clark and Clark Kent without Superman, Smith without Wesson, Rogers without Trigger and Rodgers without Hammerstein, Chase without Sanborn and Chase without Manhattan, Procter without Gamble, Simon without Schuster, Young without Rubicam, Anheuser without Busch, Abercrombie without Fitch, Standard without Poor, even Victoria without her secret, but never can you validly imagine Tinker and Evers without Chance or any other humanimal without luck, coincidence, serendipty, randomness and chance as the creature's permanent partners.

Tomorrowlands with belief in boundless potential, a horizon-less future, and an all-systems-go go-go go-ahead attitude are more likely to fail than are simpler under-developed societies and economies with fewer complicated support systems vulnerable to disruption and destruction.

At my age every night at bedtime I wonder if the morn will find me awake or at a wake where my survivors mourn as I sleep soundly and soundlessly never again to wake.

Because people typically don't like to admit to mediocrity they over-estimate their value to society, to the economy, to their professions, to employers and bosses, to family, friends and acquaintances, and to their status in other relationships and situations. It's a common human failing to exaggerate how much you're needed, wanted, admired and the degree to which you deserve notice, standing, prestige, praise, promotions, pay and other rewards, tangible or reputational. Rather often the world's judgment of a person's value falls short of his or her own self-assessment. Your presence is less significant and noticed than you might suspect and then, after you're gone, your absence less regretted than you might believe. The only exception is the extreme regret your dog feels when you, as the pet's service provider, no longer provide. Otherwise, your presence or absence is neither here nor there. Mediocrity is nothing to be ashamed about because that's normal, although most humanimals seem to believe that they're above average creatures, a view which violates the law of averages.

Earlier this week my very first visit to an IKEA store. When it comes to a soulless cathedral of consumption like Saint IKEA, for sure I won't be a regular parishioner. As for shopping I'm not a leading edge first-adopter or even a fast-follower but more like a very slow or no-show laggard. I've still never set foot in a Costco store (but may soon, out of curiosity). Although rather cheerless, the IKEA arrangement, assortment and presentation evidence in a charmless but functional setting a marvel of sourcing, manufacturing, supply, logistics, distribution and retail skills. I greatly admired the creativity, ingenuity, time, effort and energy invested to establish and maintain such an imprssive and useful establishment, one of the commercial wonders of our age. IKEA offers members of the vast and non-exclusive consumer society a shopping, buying, entertainment and activity center based in a retail monument to mediocre taste, where the Swedish meatballs on sale represent one of the few tasteful store products.

How To Cheat Death

Before revealing the secret of how to cheat death out of its due, it's worth considering if an escape from mortality represents a desirable way of life. After all, humanimals spend their entire life in the process of dying. Eliminating death would operate to deprive life of its meaning. A deathless life may be less advisable than a lifeless death. Without death, existing as an earthling would lack purpose. Eliminating life's natural outcome, or outgo, would tamper with the nature of things and bring unpredictable and perhaps undesirable consequences. Letting death have its way to take us away might be preferable to upsetting the present age-old old age arrangement. But for those who insist on cheating death, this can be accomplished simply by not being born. For anyone reading these lines and for the old gentleman now writing them, it's unfortunately too late to escape the fate of soon becoming "the late."

Although nature endowed humanimals with reason, it's insufficient to enable the creatures to find the reason why they happen to exist. Human existence is unreasonable.

Now at the end of August the patterns of light and shadow hint at the coming darkening. These waning days of summer daylight now arrive later and leave earlier than before. Before long shorter days will bring longer evenings and earlier nights. When the summer saving of an hour's daylight is reset in November and then spent day-by-day over the winter, the world where I live will grow even darker.

A recent obituary I read quoted the decedent, "I was born, blinked, and then it was all over." That's the story of every humanimal, a brief transient creature who only glancingly exists.

Galax: a plant "whose leaves are widely used for funeral decorations" (dictionary definition). Funerals merit festive decorations to set the mood for the revelry at the lively receptions which follow the service. Those animated gatherings offer an opportunity for chit-chat and gossip, good fellowship, good food, plentiful drinks, networking, social activity, lots of laughs, perhaps some flirting, and a good time to be had by all, all except the decedent whose estate pays for the galax and the gala gathering.

When most of the pre-teen kids now alive grow up they'll begin to search for spouses, companions, a significant other, a partner, a boy or girlfriend, a live-in or a can't-live-without, and other variations for a close relationship. The effort to establish a close personal connection represents one of the wildest of the wild cards in the deck whose jokers include luck, chance, coincidence, serendipity and fate. The ways people sometime manage to meet a companion depend on many uncertain and often quirky circumstances and happenings. The person (or people) all those young kids will eventually pair-up with is now most likely alive. It's strange to realize that a present-day toddler, tot or kid will one day, when grown, become your beloved, or at least your beliked. But who and where is that special him or her, and how do you find that one and only stranger who will be your intimate and very familiar day-in and day-out companion? Somewhere out there in the vast mass of humanity hides those embryonic unknowns, mates in the making. They contrast with the soon departed elderly who no longer look for partners and often have lost them. The pre-teens and the pre-ghosts are at quite different stages, one beginning an experiment in living and the other nearing their experiment in dying.

As Shakespeare wrote, "time must have a stop," by which he meant not Time, which is time-less, but every mortal's presence in time, both a life-giving and death-producing interlude you use and then lose, after which you become time-less. For me the days and the years have run and now I approach my state of time-lessness and reach the moment when I must bring to an end the fragments of being included in this book adapted from the Journal I've kept for 53 years. Although the book here ends, I intend to continue with the Journal entries until the time when I and they must have a stop. On Labor Day, September 5, 2022, I ended my labors for this book and my writing life with the entry—better described as an exit—below.

SEPTEMBER 2022

Some years ago when in the process of dying my very good friend, age near 100, shouted out impatiently to his son there with his father at the end [his death also referred to in an April 2009 entry], "Why is this taking so long?" Although much younger even at my present late stage of life than my late friend of some 60 years I sometimes wonder, "Why is this taking so long?" I've lived far longer than I expected, longer than did my parents, and longer than have many of my contemporaries. How much longer do I have? Whatever my remaining time, I sometimes think of an epitaph I saw on a New Year's Day now old from a land far away and a time long ago on an ancient Greek Elgin marble tombstone at the British Museum in London: "After many pleasant sports with my companions I, who sprang from the earth, am earth once more. I am Aristokles of Piraeus, son of Menon." With this, reader, I draw my Journal to a close and as I prepare to be earth once more I bid you good luck and farewell.

www.ingramcontent.com/pod-product-compliance
Lightning Source LLC
LaVergne TN
LVHW050627100826
845148LV00011B/1756

* 9 7 8 0 7 8 1 8 1 4 4 6 1 *